READING THE TRAIL
....
ENVIRONMENTAL ARTS AND
HUMANITIES SERIES

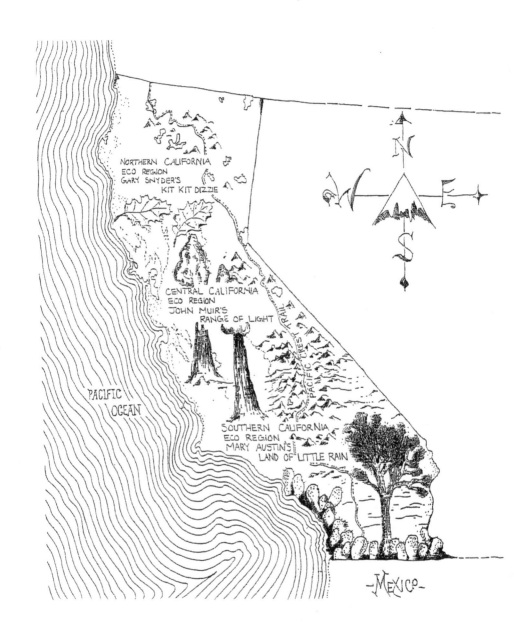

NORTHERN CALIFORNIA
ECO REGION
GARY SNYDER'S
KIT KIT DIZZIE

CENTRAL CALIFORNIA
ECO REGION
JOHN MUIR'S
RANGE OF LIGHT

PACIFIC
OCEAN

SOUTHERN CALIFORNIA
ECO REGION
MARY AUSTIN'S
LAND OF LITTLE RAIN

PACIFIC CREST TRAIL

-MEXICO-

N
E
W
S

READING THE TRAIL

Exploring the Literature and Natural History of the California Crest

Corey Lee Lewis ▲▲ University of Nevada Press : Reno & Las Vegas

ENVIRONMENTAL ARTS AND HUMANITIES SERIES

Series Editors: Scott Slovic and Michael Cohen

University of Nevada Press, Reno, Nevada 89557 USA

Manufactured in the United States of America

Design by Carrie House

Library of Congress Cataloging-in-Publication Data

Lewis, Corey Lee, 1972–

Reading the trail : exploring the literature and natural history of

the California crest / Corey Lee Lewis.

p. cm. — (Environmental arts and humanities series)

Includes bibliographical references and index.

ISBN 0-87417-606-9 (pbk. : alk. paper)

1. American literature—California—History and criticism.

2. Austin, Mary Hunter, 1868–1934—Knowledge—California.

3. Authors, American—Homes and haunts—California. 4. Muir,

John, 1838–1914—Knowledge—California. 5. Snyder, Gary, 1930–

—Knowledge—California. 6. Natural history—Pacific Crest

Trail. 7. Environmental protection in literature. 8. Pacific Crest

Trail—In literature. 9. California—Intellectual life. 10. Natural

history—California. 11. California—In literature. 12. Ecology in

literature. 13. Nature in literature. I. Title. II. Series.

PS283.C2L49 2005

810.9'32794—dc22   2004023019

The paper used in this book meets the requirements of American

National Standard for Information Sciences—Permanence of

Paper for Printed Library Materials, ANSI z.48-1984. Binding

materials were selected for strength and durability.

FIRST PRINTING

14 13 12 11 10 09 08 07 06 05

5 4 3 2 1

Frontispiece: Map of the California Crest

Illustrations used by permission of Tim Pyles.

This book is dedicated to my sons, Hunter and Bodie.
May your paths be filled with joy and wild wonder!

CONTENTS

Turning the first page of a book is much like taking that first eager step onto the trail: Although you may have some idea of the territory that will be covered, you don't know exactly where either one is going and hope for a few exciting surprises along the way. Each trail or book may lead to others, joining them as a tributary, and then leading on to yet other books and trails. Or your path may lead into uncharted territory, where the trails of others peter out and you are left to explore and navigate on your own. It is my sincerest hope that this book will do both: that it will lead you to the trails of other explorers as well as inspire you to follow your own path, that it will guide you to the words and ideas of other writers as well as encourage you to develop and share your own.

This book discusses the writings of Mary Austin, John Muir, and Gary Snyder in relation to the California landscapes in which they were composed. Thus, it synthesizes two relatively distinct fields and approaches. On the one hand, this book is concerned with adding methods of experiential education to the study of environmental literature. On the other hand, this book focuses on incorporating works of environmental literature into the primarily scientific emphasis of environmental education curricula. For those not formally involved in literary studies or environmental education, I hope that this book will offer a few interesting ideas for adding literary experiences to your recreational activities and outdoor experiences to your favorite fireside readers.

Chapter 1 provides readers with a general overview of Austin's, Muir's, and Snyder's work, as well as the history of the Pacific Crest Trail and the development of ecocriticism and ecology. Chapter 2 examines the root causes of current environmental problems and poses one partial solution through education. The next six chapters (two for each author) explore Austin's, Muir's, and Snyder's work from a variety of perspectives. For each author, the first chapter analyzes their work from a field-based, ecocritical perspective, demonstrating how field studies can be used to aid in literary interpretation, whereas the second chapter demonstrates the value of adding that author's work to environmental education curricula. Chapter 9 discusses the political activism of each author, and chapter 10 demonstrates how we can incorporate these practices into any curriculum. Each chapter incorporates narratives from my experiences with these three authors and the California crest, as well as with students on the trail and in the classroom. These narratives are designed to contextualize the sections of literary analysis and argument, while also sharing some of the richness and joy that can be found on the crest itself.

Originally, this book was written as a dissertation in order to fulfill the requirements of my doctoral studies in the University of Nevada at Reno's Literature and Environment Program. However, the impetus for this work lies much deeper, in my experiences as a youth and younger scholar. During my graduate studies, I perceived three related needs that must be addressed if we are to successfully respond to the current environmental crisis. First, I recognized that, as a general rule, Americans are largely ignorant of ecological issues and values, and that no positive political actions will be taken until the public becomes aware and active enough to demand them. Second, I saw quite clearly that although ecocritics had succeeded in reintroducing environmental values into environmental debates, we were often failing to achieve the results we wanted with our students, and even ourselves, because we were relying too heavily on the textually based methodologies of classical literary criticism. And third, I became aware of the common failure of ecologists and environmental educators to incorporate explorations of environmental values in educational curricula and political controversy. In short, I came to believe that with some innovative changes the educational system could become part of the solution, reforming how we perceive, conceive, and behave toward the natural environment, rather than part of the problem.

Although there have been many people who have helped to shape this book and bring it to you, the reader, I would like to offer my sincerest gratitude to the following. To my mother and father, Nancy and Lon, and my brother, Bart, I would like to say thank you for teaching me to love literature and the land. To Lavetta Rolfs, who first introduced me to experiential education and environmental activism, I offer my deepest "Ho!" And to the dedicated members of Friends of Nevada Wilderness I offer both gratitude and admiration for being, and teaching me to be, effective environmental activists. Greg Eiselein, Linda Brigham, Elizabeth Dodd, and Nate Cairney offered me both generous support and demanding intellectual rigor that helped to sharpen my mind and solidify my interests. My doctoral committee—Scott Slovic, Mike Branch, Michael Cohen, Cheryll Glotfelty, Glenn Miller, and Nancy Markee—also provided me with much appreciated mentorship and guidance, without which this book would not have been written, nor would it have seen print. Thank you all. In addition, I would like to thank Jerry Keir, founder of the Great Basin Institute and Nevada Conservation Corps (NCC), for his inspiration and example, as well as our students and NCC members. It has been a pleasure working with and learning from you all. Tim Pyles, my old trail companion, supplied both artwork and campfire conversations that have been integral to this project. Gary Snyder's generosity was also inspirational and much appreciated. Finally, I would like to thank my wife, Micki, for her support during the completion of this project, as well as for trekking the backcountry and byways of the California crest with me. Each of these individuals has contributed in his or her own way to this project.

Like the full-bodied rivers that roar down from the California crest each spring, this book joins the varied voices of a hundred individual streams into a full-throated song, a symphony of spirit united in a common cause. All I can say to you, the reader, is "Jump in and join us. The water is fine!"

ACKNOWLEDGMENTS

For permission to reprint all works in this volume, grateful acknowledgment is made to the holders of copyright, publishers, or representatives named below, which constitutes an extension of the copyright page.

"The low road," from The Moon Is Always Female by Marge Piercy, copyright © 1980 by Marge Piercy. Used by permission of Alfred A. Knopf, a division of Random House, Inc.

"Kusiwoggobi," "On Climbing the Sierra Matterhorn Again After Thirty-One Years," from *No Nature* by Gary Snyder. Used by permission of Pantheon Books, a division of Random House, Inc.

"Mid-August at Sourdough Lookout," "Piute Creek," and "Riprap," from *Riprap and Cold Mountain Poems* by Gary Snyder. Used by permission of Shoemaker & Hoard, Publishers.

"Front Lines" (excerpt), "Control Burn" (excerpt), "The Call of the Wild" (excerpt), "Tomorrow's Song" (excerpt), "Two Logging Songs" (excerpt), "Toward Climax" (excerpt), "Manzanita," "Ethnobotany," and "For the Children" (excerpt) By Gary Snyder, from *Turtle Island*, copyright © 1974 by Gary Snyder. Used by permission of New Directions Publishing Corporation.

"Foxtail Pine" (excerpt) By Gary Snyder, from *The Backcountry*, copyright © 1968 by Gary Snyder. Used by permission of New Directions Publishing Corporation.

CHAPTER ONE

....

Readers and Writers of
the California Crest Trail

If the public will not follow a poet's personal example they will never completely comprehend his art.

LAURENCE GOLDSTEIN,
"Wordsworth and Snyder: The Primitivist and His Problem of Self-Definition"

Dry snow whips and rolls off cornices above us, exploding into the clear blue sky in sparkling ribbons and billowing white clouds. The glare and warmth of the bright Sierra sun radiates up from the snowpack under our feet with a fierce intensity that echoes my own thoughts as we climb: "I am here! I am alive!" Our snowshoes crunch over the jumbled remains of an old avalanche, but the snowpack is set—safe and hard—after weeks of warm days and cold nights with no new snow. After cresting the barren, windswept ridge, we forge on, toward the cover of red fir and lodgepole pine. I scan the trees ahead for the familiar Pacific Crest Trail (PCT) emblem, a small metal disk in blue and white, telling us that we are still on, or in this case above, the trail. Somewhere, several feet below our snowshoes, lies a section of the Pacific Crest Trail as it winds its way from Mexico to Canada. My wife and I are snowshoeing for the day on one small portion of the 2,650-mile-long PCT, following a high ridge in the Sierra Nevada toward the Five Lakes Wilderness Area. Our two-year-old son, Hunter, rides contentedly in a pack on my back, intermittently shouting excitedly, "Tree!" and "Snow, Daddy, snow!" Occasionally, his attention turns from simple observations to urgent commands, exclaiming, "Go higher,

Live Alone Two Months" (Nash 1967, 141). Knowles kept up his notoriety through a series of dispatches written on birch bark, detailing how he was surviving in the wilderness. Although Knowles's account later proved to be primarily fictitious, when he emerged from the Maine woods in October 1913 he was swept up in a wave of enthusiasm for the values of wilderness experience and primitive living.

At this same time, the proper use of the West's public lands received national attention as preservationists led by John Muir and conservationists led by Gifford Pinchot joined the battle over the fate of California's Hetch Hetchy Valley. The split between these two camps, best summarized by the men themselves, exemplified a larger philosophical division in the country. In 1912, Muir wrote, "These temple destroyers, devotees of ravaging commercialism, seem to have a perfect contempt for Nature, and instead of lifting their eyes to the God of the Mountains, lift them to the Almighty Dollar" (1962, 202). A year later, Pinchot argued in response: "As to my attitude regarding the proposed use of Hetch Hetchy by the city of San Francisco . . . I am fully persuaded that . . . the injury . . . by substituting a lake for the present swampy floor of the valley . . . is altogether unimportant compared with the benefits to be derived from its use as a reservoir" (Nash 1967, 161). The question about Hetch Hetchy, and by extension the rest of our public lands, was whether they should be managed solely as storehouses of natural resources designed to give the greatest economic good to the greatest number of people or whether they had an inherent ecological, spiritual, and recreational value that transcended their immediate economic worth. That question would come to be answered in a number of different ways over the years; however, a shift from the former attitude toward the latter was slowly beginning to occur within the American environmental imagination.

In 1921, Benton McKaye began his successful campaign to establish the Appalachian Trail along the crest of the eastern mountains from Maine to Georgia. McKaye, like Seton and Baden-Powell, recognized the value of primitive outdoor recreation and sought to make recreational opportunities available to all Americans as a counterforce to the increasing urbanization and industrialization of the time. McKaye was not alone in his insistence that Americans needed opportunities for recreating in unspoiled primitive areas. During the 1920s and 1930s, a number of influential environmental thinkers surfaced within the U.S. Forest Service, helping to shape both public perception and federal policy toward recognizing the values of wilderness. At the same time that Fred Cleator was working on the Oregon and Washington sections of the PCT, Arthur C. Carhart, Aldo Leopold, and Robert Marshall were persuasively shifting public lands policy from resource extraction toward landscape protection.

Finally, in 1932, Clinton C. Clarke of Pasadena, California, proposed, in *The Pacific Crest Trailway*, "to the United States Forest Service and National Park Services the project of a continuous wilderness trail across the United States from Canada to Mexico." The plan, according to Clarke, was "to build a trail along the summit divides of the mountain ranges of these states, traversing the best scenic areas and maintaining an absolute wilderness character" (Schaffer et al. 2000, 1). Thanks to McKaye's work with the Appalachian Trail and already shifting attitudes toward the environment, the stage was set for the completion of Clarke's dream. It would take another sixty-one years to come to fruition, but finally, just before the century turned again, in 1993, California would complete its own section of the grand Mexico-to-Canada Pacific Crest Trail.

THREE CALIFORNIA ICONS

Throughout this long history of cultural change, the works of western writers reflected and directed the development of Americans' dawning environmental consciousness. As urbanization and outdoor recreation grew, so too did the number of works of western environmental literature, as well as Americans' appetite for consuming them.

Of the many authors who aided in this cultural transformation, writing about and in the California landscapes the PCT passes through, three stand out as veritable icons of environmental literature: Mary Austin, John Muir, and Gary Snyder. Much like the trail itself, the body of their work stands as a symbol par excellence of the American environmental movement and our cultural imagination as it has been played out within our literature and upon our land. Each of these authors lived in, and wrote about, a different ecological region, corresponding directly to the three distinct ecoregions the PCT passes through as it bisects California lengthwise. In addition, both the literary work and the activist efforts of these three writers have been responsible for engendering a greater environmental sensitivity in the American public and protecting a number of the now preserved wilderness areas and national parks through which the PCT passes.

Mary Austin (1868–1934)

The harsh beauty and vast stillness of southern California's arid lands were most memorably brought to America's attention through the work of a tough pioneering woman named Mary Hunter Austin. As a single mother and self-supporting woman in the frontier regions of the American Southwest during the end of the nineteenth century and the beginning of the twentieth, Austin was anything but conventional. An inveterate traveler, she roamed a rugged and unsettled country when the only means of transportation was by stagecoach, horseback, or on foot. Austin's travels and interests brought her in close contact with the Paiute and Shoshone who still lived in the area, the Basque and Mexican sheepherders who ran flocks in the high country, and the many luckless pocket hunters who roamed the borderless lands of California and Nevada in search of valuable ore. In addition, traveling through and camping in the wild regions of the Southwest taught her much about the desert's nonhuman inhabitants, the "wild creatures," "hill folk," and "little people," as she called them, who still populate southern California's wildlands.

James Ruppert notes that the early 1900s enjoyed "a revitalization of the arts through a return to American materials, the American landscape, and aboriginal American arts"; leading this revolution, he argues, was Mary Hunter Austin (1983, 376). Austin's contribution to western environmental literature and the southwestern landscape has indeed been great. In her sixty-six years of life, she published thirty-four books and plays and an extensive assortment of articles, gained the ear of a number of important literary and political figures, and opposed the diversion of life-sustaining waters from the Owens Valley to the city of Los Angeles.

Mary Hunter was married, at the age of twenty-two, to Stafford Wallace Austin, a young man who soon proved incapable of supporting his new bride. By the early 1890s Mary and Stafford had settled in the Owens Valley, on the eastern face of the Sierra Nevada and the western edge of the Mojave Desert, and she had begun publishing stories in the *Overland Monthly* about her beloved Southwest and those who inhabited it.

Austin's first and most widely read book, *The Land of Little Rain*, was published in 1903 and is among one of her most comprehensive and insightful explorations of the arid lands, diverse wildlife, and unique cultures of the southern California region. The next three years saw her publish in succession *The Basket Woman: A Book of Fanciful Tales for Children, Isidro*, and *The Flock*. In these works she displays her anthropological interest in native cultures and her love of the southern California coastal region. *Lost Borders*, published in 1909, returned Austin and her readers to the arid deserts of her heart, and *California: The Land of the Sun*, published in 1914, continued to explore the region in print for what had become a sizable American audience. Along with her autobiography, *Earth Horizon* (1932), which oscillates interestingly between first- and third-person prose, Austin's work represents one of the first, and most comprehensive, studies in literary natural history of the American Southwest.

Austin's rhythmic prose introduces readers to many of the species, geographical features, and ecological processes one encounters when hiking the sandy southern portion of the PCT. Both Austin's work and the PCT explore a vast, sparsely populated land of desert dwellers who have learned to live with a lot of space and little water. From dry lake playas and barren ocher-colored hills to creosote, shade-scale, and sagebrush scrub communities, up to Joshua-tree and pinyon-juniper woodlands, Austin's books and the southern PCT carry readers and hikers through a diverse landscape with the power to inspire awe or exact death. In her books, and along the trail, one may encounter such unique creatures as the kangaroo rat, which goes its whole life without drinking a sip of water, or the pinyon jay, whose evolution is so closely tied with the pinyon pine forest that its beak, unlike that of other jays, is specially designed to extract the nutrient-rich seeds from the pinyon cones. Or the solitary traveler might lie quietly on the sand, staring at the innumerable stars and listening in awe to the high-pitched yelps and howls of coyotes in the night.

John Muir (1838–1914)

As one travels northward on the trail, the pinyon and juniper give way to ponderosa and Jeffrey pine, the southern Sierra Nevada rise still higher, and the red, brown, and gold of ore-laced andesitic rocks give way to the grays and whites of high Sierra snow and granite. Manzanita and squaw carpet dot the forest floor, as sugar pine and sequoia soar overhead in grand cathedral-like grace. In the distance, the hulking shapes of glacially cut granite domes shrug off the skirting trees growing around their bases and stand naked and solid under the everlasting sky. From the high Sierra Nevada to the Yosemite Valley floor, this is John Muir's country. And running right through the middle of it, following a granite-blasted, switchbacking, and carefully constructed route, lies the central portion of California's Pacific Crest Trail.

As with Austin, the central importance of the western landscape in Muir's life and work has been widely acknowledged. The two contemporaries have often been compared as defenders of wild nature and pioneers in the field of literary natural history. Ann Zwinger argues:

> Both Muir and Austin are the first truly *western* nature writers. They delineate the personality of pine and spruce, describe the delicious sibilance of sand, portray the palatial grandeur of glaciers, divine the cut of the wind and the shocking immensity of the sky that it swirls out of. . . . Their writing, their point of view, their dedication to the mountains and deserts of the West, has sustained western nature writers from their day forward. (1994, x)

In addition to sustaining future writers, it should also be noted that Austin's and Muir's work has inspired millions of readers to explore, enjoy, and protect California's wildlands and natural areas.

John Muir first saw the Sierra in 1868, after completing a thousand-mile botanical expedition from Indiana to Florida on foot. He came to California to convalesce from a bout of malaria contracted during that trip. Muir spent the summers of 1868 and 1869 in the high Sierra Nevada country above Yosemite Valley, herding sheep, botanizing, and developing his theories of glaciation. These experiences were later collapsed into a single season and published in 1911 as *My First Summer in the Sierra*.

In 1871, at the urging of fellow botanist and friend Jeanne Carr, Muir published his first essay about the Sierra Nevada, a piece in which he first argued his theory that the Sierra were carved by glaciers and in which he announced his discovery of a living glacier in the high Sierra. Initially scoffed at by professional geologists, Muir's theories were later corroborated by the scientific community.

In 1892, Muir founded the Sierra Club and two years later published his first collection of essays, *The Mountains of California*. Recognized by many as the "father" of our national park system and of the modern American environmental movement, Muir and his writings and ramblings in the Sierra Nevada have left an indelible mark on our history and our public lands. In 1901 he published *Our National Parks*, a collection of sketches first printed in the *Atlantic Monthly*. In the preface of that book Muir states: "I have done the best I could to show for the beauty, grandeur, and all-embracing usefulness of our wild mountain forest reservations and parks, with a view to inciting the people to come and enjoy them, and get them into their hearts, so that at length their preservation and right use might be made sure" (1916d, vii). In 1912, Muir published another book focusing on his beloved mountains, *The Yosemite*, and in 1918 and 1950, respectively, *Steep Trails* and *Studies in the Sierra* were posthumously published.

Muir was an extremely influential environmental writer and activist, keeping company with such important figures as Ralph Waldo Emerson and Theodore Roosevelt and consistently pushing for the preservation of forests and wildlands. Muir's greatest failure and last great environmental battle was similar in many ways to Austin's defeat in the Owens Valley. Along with thousands of other Americans, Muir worked unsuccessfully to save the Hetch Hetchy Valley from a destructive dam designed to supply San Francisco with water. In 1909, he published a call to action on behalf of the imperiled valley titled *Let Everyone Help to Save the Famous Hetch-Hetchy Valley and Stop the Commercial Destruction Which Threatens Our National Parks*, and he continued to be active in the valley's defense until his death in 1914.

Muir continued to write throughout his career, publishing works on natural history and remaining active in environmental issues affecting his beloved "Range of Light." His literary reputation continues to grow, as his unpublished manuscripts, journals, and letters have enjoyed one of the most vigorous series of posthumous publication of any western American writer.

Gary Snyder (1930–)

From the Yosemite Valley, the PCT makes its way to the northwest, past Lake Tahoe and into the northern-most portions of the Sierra Nevada and the heart of the Klamath Mountains. Moving toward the western side of the Sierra, the PCT enters moister climates, winding its way through moss-covered California black oak, Douglas fir, bracken fern, and mountain misery, or, as the native Wintu and author Gary Snyder call it, "kitkitdizze."

Gary Snyder—logger, fire lookout, trail crew member, and contemporary environmental poet, essayist, philosopher, and activist—makes his home on the San Juan ridge of the Yuba watershed, just west of the PCT's trail corridor. A native of the Pacific Northwest, Snyder grew up on a small farm in Oregon and spent much of his boyhood rambling through the forests and mountains of Oregon, Washington, and California. Early in his life, he witnessed the wanton destruction of his beloved western forests and found a love for the study of Native American culture and lifeways, mountaineering, and ecology. A member of the Beat generation and a participant in San Francisco's famed Six Gallery Reading in October 1955, Snyder has always sought personal and cultural transformation through his poetry and philosophy. In 1956, Snyder moved to Japan to study Zen Buddhism and Asian languages and lived abroad almost continuously for the next twelve years. Since returning to the West, Snyder's poetry has fused ecological insights and Native American wisdom with Buddhist teachings and practice to offer an alternative paradigm for Americans who wish to "reinhabit"—or become native to—their own home places.

Snyder's first two books of poetry, *Riprap* and *Myths & Texts*, were published in 1959 and 1960, respectively; both relied heavily upon his experiences growing up in the Pacific Northwest, exploring such issues as trail construction, wilderness travel, logging, and forest fires and the stories that shape our relationships to the natural world. *Riprap* was republished in 1965 under the title *Riprap & Cold Mountain Poems* and included Snyder's own translations of the works of Chinese poet and hermit Han Shan. By 1975, when Snyder was awarded the Pulitzer Prize for his 1974 publication, *Turtle Island*, his literary career and activist reputation were both firmly established. A major collection of Snyder's poetry, *No Nature: New and Selected Poems*, was published in 1992, and in 1996 he completed *Mountains and Rivers Without End*, a single long poem, more than twenty-six years in the making.

Snyder's literary work also includes a number of essay collections and prose pieces that explore issues in mythology, poetry, and ecology and advocate cultural and political transformation. In 1969 he published *Earth House Hold: Technical Notes and Queries to Fellow Dharma Revolutionaries* and *The*

Old Ways: Six Essays in 1977; both illustrate Snyder's fusion of Eastern and Western philosophies and lifeways and his continuing preoccupation with finding sustainable cultural mythologies for Americans to live by. Snyder's most recent works of prose, *The Practice of the Wild* (1990) and *A Place in Space: Ethics, Aesthetics, and Watersheds: New and Selected Prose* (1995), continue to explore the vital connections between the stories we tell in our culture and the lives we lead on our land.

: : :

The work of these three writers spans the century during which California's crest trail came into being, ranges over each of the three distinct ecoregions the trail passes through, and exemplifies the shifting values and attitudes that have led Americans to preserve such a unique part of our cultural history and natural heritage. Without the works of such environmental writers and thinkers, and without the opportunity for recreating in such awe-inspiring wildlands, we would be much poorer as a people. Through wrestling with the challenging ideas of such visionary thinkers as Austin, Muir, and Snyder and exploring the rugged and beautiful wildlands of California's crest, we have gained a deeper sense of who and where we are—and, most important, how to live here.

ENVIRONMENTAL EDUCATION, ECOCRITICISM, AND ECOLOGY

In order to study the California crest and the literature written about it, we must have some familiarity with the development of, and interactions between, two separate fields of inquiry: ecology, the study of the interrelationships among living organisms and their environments, and ecocriticism, the study of environmental themes in literature and literature's role in human ecology. Both fields have followed a pattern of development that was very similar to the construction and establishment of the PCT itself. This is due primarily to the fact that the development of all three was intricately tied up in the growth of the popular American environmental movement. The science of ecology as well as the study and production of environmental literature both served to inform and inspire the American environmental movement. At the same time, however, it was the rise in outdoor recreation and popular environmental awareness that brought both fields from the dusty bookshelf of academe and thrust them into the limelight of public attention and social relevancy.

In many respects the PCT and the authors considered in this study have played significant roles in awakening America's environmental consciousness. For many Americans, hiking sections of the PCT and exploring its environs in the Sierra Nevada or reading the works of Austin, Muir, and Snyder has constituted a type of informal, yet highly effective, environmental education. It seems appropriate therefore to unite these authors and this trail in a more formal enterprise aimed at increasing our awareness of environmental issues and our ability to solve them. In order to explore the work of these environmental authors and the natural environments that inspired them, we will need to use the insights and methods of both ecocriticism and ecology.

Ecocriticism and Environmental Literature

From Alvar Núñez Cabeza de Vaca's accounts of traveling on foot from Florida to Mexico and early Puritan responses to the "howling wilderness" of the American continent to the travel writings of William Bartram and the Emersonian and Thoreauvian traditions, American authors have a strong tradition of engaging with the natural world and exploring how we move through, live in, and perceive it. This long-standing tradition of physically and imaginatively exploring the American environment through literature has enjoyed a virtual explosion in the past decade. The number of relatively new nature writers now publishing and receiving critical attention is almost as astounding as the quality and diversity of approaches being taken. Likewise, since the 1970s interest in outdoor recreational activities has increased sharply. In the twenty-first century, a growing number of Americans have become interested in reading about and spending time in our natural areas and wildlands. This increase is closely tied to both the escalating severity of environmental problems and our slowly dawning awareness of how these problems threaten the quality of our lives.

Ecocriticism—the study of the relationships among literature, culture, and environment—was established in response to the increasing popularity and cultural significance of environmental literature, as well as the growing recognition among literary scholars and educators of the importance environmental values play in the environmental crisis and the efficacy with which literature represents and reinforces those values. As a distinct field, ecocriticism can be traced from Joseph Meeker's *Comedy of Survival* (1972) and William Rueckert's essay "Literature and Ecology: An Experiment in Ecocriticism" (1978) to such works as Annette Kolodny's 1975 book, *The Lay of the Land: Metaphor As Experience and History in American Life and Letters* and Frederick Waage's *Teaching Environmental Literature: Materials, Methods, Resources,* published in 1985. Ecocritical practice, however, has a tradition stretching back to the eighteenth century, as David Mazel notes in *A Century of Ecocriticism* (2001). Meeker and Rueckert define the practice of ecocriticism as the study of biological themes and relationships that appear in literary works and the application of ecological concepts to literature, as well as the study of the role literature plays in the ecology of the human species.

Ecocriticism emerged from obscurity in the 1990s, however, because it was during this decade that the field grew from an eclectic approach to literary criticism followed by a number of geographically and professionally isolated scholars to a distinct field with its own professional association, journals, book collections, and academic positions. In 1990 the University of Nevada, Reno, created the first academic position in literature and the environment, and shortly thereafter, in 1992, the Association for the Study of Literature and Environment was formed and Scott Slovic was elected its first president. A year later Patrick D. Murphy established the journal *ISLE: Interdisciplinary Studies in Literature and Environment.* By the mid-'90s, ecocriticism was taking shape as a significant field.

The development of ecocriticism as a method of critical practice should be seen as continuing the expansion of literary criticism that has been ongoing since the 1950s. Since that time the development of such schools of criticism as feminism, postcolonialism, Marxism, and multicultural and cultural studies has sought to enlarge the literary canon and offer more diverse approaches to the study of literature and its relationship to human culture. Although these schools have succeeded in recovering the lost voices of African and Native Americans, laborers, and women, as the editors of *Reading the Earth: New Directions in the Study of Literature and Environment* note, "the 'voice' longest neglected has been that of our physical environment, the voice of nature, which cannot speak through conventional means" (Branch et al. 1998, xii). Like its predecessors, ecocriticism seeks to enlarge the canon and the scope of literary investigation. However, unlike other fields of literary criticism, ecocriticism also attempts to include the non-human natural world as well as our environmental values and attitudes within the realm of exploration and study.

As Richard Kerridge defines the field in *Writing the Environment: Ecocriticism and Literature,* ecocriticism represents "environmentalism's overdue move beyond science, geography and social science into 'the humanities'" (1998, 5). Thus, ecocritics offer new insights into the root causes of environmental problems and, through their study of works of environmental literature that engage and express our environmental values and beliefs, seek to identify the sources of transformation necessary to solve such problems.

In order to successfully achieve this goal and understand works of environmental literature, however, ecocritics must gain some facility with the ecological sciences. Because ecocritics often study interdisciplinary texts that refer to the natural world, many have come to see the environmental sciences as an integral part of their approach. In his interdisciplinary study of Appalachian literature, *Story Line: Exploring the Literature of the Appalachian Trail,* Ian Marshall notes that

> [t]o study the interrelationships between living things, and between
> them and their habitat, requires some acquaintance with such fields
> as biology, physics, geology, anthropology. . . . I find that science can
> indeed be a useful tool for the study of literature, at times helping to
> resolve critical problems, often clarifying my understanding of a princi-
> ple of life that once engaged a writer's attention. (1998, 6)

For Marshall as well as other critics, such an approach seems to be required by the inherent interdisciplinarity of the texts they study. John Elder comments on this unique aspect of environmental literature, observing that "scientific awareness" in this genre "is augmented and fulfilled by human emotion and personal history. Similarly, verse is informed, its systems of metaphor generated, by the insights of science" (1985, 162). A critical approach informed by science, then, is required by the subject of study itself.

The problem ecocriticism faces today is that a clear methodology for engaging in interdisciplinary literary scholarship has not yet been developed. Many of the same critics who praise interdisciplinary scholarship do little more than borrow a key term, phrase, idea, image, or metaphor from a companion discipline when it seems convenient. Although such a practice does cross disciplinary boundaries, it is not sufficiently critical enough to warrant the praise accorded it in theory. John Tallmadge notes this problem in "Toward a Natural History of Reading," in which he laments the fact that although ecocritics have made substantial claims of interdisciplinarity, their "underlying method has generally been that used by other [literary] schools, namely, close reading of a primary text, mediated by close reading of other, chiefly literary texts. In other words, the 'eco' refers more often to the content of the work or the purpose of the critic than it does to the critical method itself" (2000, 34). Tallmadge suggests that the methodologies employed by ecocritics are not fulfilling in practice what they promise in theory. A better approach would be to adopt from other disciplines the methodologies for gathering data, testing conclusions, and applying solutions. Though it would necessitate moving beyond the text, this technique would more successfully fulfill the promise of interdisciplinary thinking and more fully benefit from its many advantages.

Ecology and Environmental Education

During the sixty years from the time the Pacific Crest Trail was first proposed to the date of its completion, monumental shifts occurred in how Americans perceived, valued, and behaved toward our public lands. From the establishment of the Wilderness Society in 1935 to the passage of the Wilderness Act in 1964, western Americans would come to define themselves, and their land, in much different terms than before. The passage of the Wilderness Act stands as a watershed moment in American environmental history, similar, in many respects, to the cultural transformation occurring near the turn of the nineteenth century. During the late 1960s and early 1970s Americans became aware of the new science of ecology—the study of relationships among species and environmental systems—and began to recognize a few of the implications of ecology's first law: that all living beings are interdependent and interrelated. The first Earth Day was held in 1970, and the next twenty years witnessed an incredible increase in environmental concern and a massive rise in outdoor recreation, until outdoor recreation (more so than any extractive industry) emerged as the primary economic activity on our public lands (Abramovitz 1998, 7). With the increased availability of 7.5-minute U.S. Geological Survey maps, a host of innovations in the construction and marketing of outdoor gear, and the rise of trail guidebooks and popular magazines such as *Outside* and *Backpacker,* a virtual revolution in outdoor recreation began to take place in the '70s and continued unchecked through the beginning of the twenty-first century.

In a manner similar to the development of ecocriticism as a distinct scholarly field, the growth of ecology, as an academic and popular movement, was primarily a post-1960s phenomenon that also enjoyed tremendous development in the 1990s. Although the science of ecology has much deeper roots than ecocriticism as a popular movement allied with environmental education, conservation, and outdoor recreation, its greatest advances took place in the latter half of the twentieth century.

The term *ecology,* or *oeckologie,* was coined in 1866 by Ernst Haeckel to describe a branch of scientific investigation that he believed should exist. Although ecological questions had been explored through other scientific disciplines, Haeckel recognized the need to develop a coherent field of "ecological" inquiry. By the 1890s a few biologists had begun to think of themselves as ecologists, but a unified discipline did not yet exist. Still, the turn of the century saw the publication of a number of seminal texts in ecology, including such works as E. Warming's *Oecological Plant Geography* (1895) and F. E. Clement's *Research Methods in Ecology* (1905), the latter being the first U.S. book on the subject. Additionally, in 1913, Charles C. Adams and Victor Shelford, both pioneers of the field of U.S. animal ecology, published, respectively, *Guide to the Study of Animal Ecology* and *Animal Communities in Temperate America.* As Robert P. McIntosh notes in his history "Ecology Since 1900," "[b]y 1920 self-conscious ecology was reasonably well established and recognized as an academic discipline in America, although it was hardly known to the general public" (1977, 356).

The field continued to develop internally through the 1950s, remaining largely descriptive in nature and lacking the applied and theoretical developments that would come in the latter half of the century—developments that would lead to ecology's increasing social significance and critical legitimacy. Although practitioners in the field had established their own professional society and publication outlet by the 1920s, they would not be successful in gaining significant national attention, funding for research, and social relevance until after the 1960s.

McIntosh notes the significant lag time between ecology's emergence as a legitimate scientific field and the public's recognition of the social, political, and economic implications the field has to offer: "Outside of academic and limited professional circles ecology was little known, and its potential importance for human well-being was not recognized, although it had been a tenet of ecologists from its very beginnings. Perhaps the really significant development in ecology was its emergence from obscurity" (368). Especially when considered as an applied instead of theoretical science and as an educational tool for affecting cultural change, as it is in this study, ecological education did not begin to make substantive impacts upon public perception and policy until the dawning of the environmental movement.

The emergence of a popular environmental movement in the United States can be traced back, as historian Samuel P. Hays has noted, to the expansion of outdoor recreation in the late 1950s and early 1960s (1998, 343). This early stage of the American environmental movement was characterized by a concern for protecting natural landscapes primarily for human recreation, resulting in the passage of such bills as the 1964 Wilderness Act and the Wild and Scenic Rivers Act and National Scenic Trails Act of 1968. The 1960s and 1970s also saw dramatic increases in public concern over air and water pollution, as well as wildlife and biodiversity issues. By 1973, three separate Clean Air and Clean Water Acts had been passed, and the number of Americans who watched wildlife for enjoyment had for the first time surpassed the number who hunted for recreation (344).

It was during this period in U.S. history that the "new" science of ecology began to develop an increasing emphasis on human disruptions of natural ecosystems, applied solutions to ecological problems, and thus began to significantly affect policy and resource management decisions. McIntosh concludes, "In spite of abortive efforts in the 1930's and 1950's, it is only in the 1970's that there seems to be a determined effort to develop a general ecology incorporating the complex of human affairs" (1977, 368). Although finding ways to incorporate the "complex of human affairs" into the ecological study of natural systems did thrust the ecological sciences into the limelight of public awareness, it also presented practitioners, especially those with a concern for the "purity" of the field, with a number of problems.

The primary problem for ecologists has resulted from the efficacy with which the insights of their field can be applied to existing environmental problems that are in need of social and political solutions. McIntosh observes, "Ecologists have increasingly been involved in matters that are beyond their training and are called upon to interact with other scientists, engineers, lawyers, economists, and other social scientists, as well as diverse governmental agencies at local, state, federal, and even international levels" (368). The ecologist's role as expert authority has, in many instances, thrust him or her into fields that are distinct from the discipline and the types of issues ecology is capable of commenting on.

This problem will continue to worsen as the environmental crisis escalates. As environmental problems compound, we will increasingly need ecologically informed policies and environmentally educated citizens. As Joel Cracraft and Francesca T. Grifo assert in *The Living Planet in Crisis: Biodiversity, Science, and Policy,* "The results of science must be digested and interpreted in a broader setting, one that moves our value systems from those anchored squarely in maintaining or expanding our cultural hegemony over the economically disadvantaged to one that recognizes a shared destiny for the planet" (1999, xx). In order for ecologists to succeed in presenting the insights of their field to a broader audience, they must be trained in the rhetorical methods most effective for such audiences and have some understanding of the preconceived knowledge, values, beliefs, and attitudes held by those they would reach. In "Perspective: Scientists' Public Responsibility," Strachan Donnelley argues that scientists

> have a professional and human responsibility to educate us citizens, to help us get our heads screwed on right and meet our long-term responsibilities to humans and nature. The latter task in public education may prove as formidable, challenging, and practically important as scientific exploration itself. The gauntlet of public education is thrown down and ought not to be ignored. Our citizen ignorance is an integral part of the living planet in crisis. (1999, 300)

The importance of preparing future ecologists to work effectively with the public and of educating our citizenry about environmental issues cannot be overemphasized. The U.S. environmental movement has primarily been a citizen-led movement that successfully forced governments, industries, and "experts" to comply with public opinion and with the insights of the "frontier" science of ecology. As Hays notes, "The prevailing pattern [of the American environmental movement] was one of public thrust and managerial reaction, of public impulses pushing managers further and faster than they thought wise. Hence, agencies acted and reacted somewhat reluctantly, defensively, seeking to parry and hold off rather than to serve as vigorous agents of environmental change" (1998, 368). Such institutional inertia can be overcome, as history teaches us, only through an active, engaged, and ecologically educated citizenry. In order to educate and activate that citizenry effectively, we will need both the scientific and the humanistic approaches found in the ecological sciences and ecocriticism.

Ecological Literacy

It is my hope that, by combining ecology and ecocriticism, by joining California's tales with its trails, we may become truly literate in reading our own western landscape. The term *ecological literacy,* first coined by David Orr, refers to the ability to read and interpret a natural landscape in the same way that one reads and deciphers a text. Whereas literacy rates in the United States have increased markedly with public education and industrialization, our ecological literacy has plummeted significantly. This ecological ignorance, or illiteracy, I believe, is the primary cause of the current environmental crisis and our failure to respond appropriately to it.

One of the most powerful demonstrations I ever witnessed of this type of ecological literacy was provided by David Charlett, a botanist from the University of Nevada, Las Vegas. We were taking a group of field students to a research site in the eastern Sierra Nevada called Little Valley. In preparation for my portion of the class, I had been reading volumes about the natural and cultural history of the valley. David, on the other hand, a guest instructor from down south, arrived in the valley with no prior preparation. On our first day, we followed a small creek through the center of the valley, admiring the mix of lush meadows and lodgepole and fir forests. As we hiked, David began lecturing me on the history of the valley, as if he was reading an invisible script taken directly from the pages of researched sources I had been so diligently studying.

"Well, it looks like this valley was clear-cut, at least once. And then of course it was grazed pretty heavily," David said as he surveyed our surroundings. "I would say it was clear-cut around the turn of the century, then grazed, sheep primarily, for at least another fifty to seventy years, and then left alone for a while."

I was amazed by the accuracy of his observations, all of which accorded with my own research. Then he stunned me by adding, "Oh, yeah, look at this, the stream was channelized as well. Wow, they were pretty busy up here."

Finally, unable to contain myself, I asked him to explain how he was able to simply look the valley over and know its entire history. For an answer, I got an impromptu lecture in ecological literacy. David explained that the large forests rising up the slopes surrounding the valley were made up of single-aged stands of trees, all of which were less than one hundred years old. This, he explained, is common in the Sierra Nevada and is evidence of the clear-cutting performed all across the range during the Comstock era. In and surrounding the meadow areas, however, we observed much smaller even-aged stands of trees that were only a couple of decades old. This, he explained, was the result of stockmen grazing sheep in the grassy areas while the bare slopes naturally became reforested. Later, after a few decades of grazing, first successional trees like lodgepole pine were able to move back into the meadows once the animals were removed. The channelization of the stream was evidenced by still existing hills of sand and sediment piled up during the work and other scars still perceivable in the soil.

Such forms of ecological literacy do not necessarily take years of botanical training to develop. I hope to demonstrate that by exploring the writings of Mary Austin, John Muir, and Gary Snyder and studying the Sierra Nevada wilderness directly, we can help ourselves, and our students, to become ecologically literate—to be able to read and respond more appropriately to our own home places. Although we are currently engaged in reading the stories of others, we cannot escape the fact that we are also writing our own, inscribing ourselves onto the land for future generations to read. The real question for those of us who have read the trail is: What kind of story do we wish to tell? Will it be a story of continued ignorance, conquest, and degradation, a heroic tragedy in which all the characters die in the end? Or will we choose to walk a different path and enact a different story, one of understanding, restraint, and hope? The curious thing about such stories is that because we believe in them and enact them in the world, they have an uncanny tendency to come true. One day we will have to explain this truth to our children and justify why we chose to write the story they will be forced to live.

CHAPTER TWO

Environmental Education
and the Ecological Crisis

The mountains speak with multiple voices, addressing each of us in the dark of our
minds according to our own needs, issues and aspirations. . . . [T]he mountains'
greatest power is transformation. And the mountains' gift is . . . the power to tell
our stories and so, speaking and listening to one another, enter into community.

JOHN TALLMADGE,
Meeting the Tree of Life

Crawling through the sand and dust on hands and knees, her eyes wide and
face aglow with excitement and wonder, a field-studies student exits a small
cave, gingerly carrying a handwoven Paiute basket. The ancient relic has
been amazingly well preserved by the high year-round aridity of the Great
Basin Desert and the long, patient protection of the small alcove in which it
was hidden. I have seen similar artifacts in museums, their walls collapsing
and plant fibers disintegrating as they turn slowly into dust. This particular
find, however, still appears watertight under close inspection. The tiny par-
allel teeth marks of a kangaroo rat are noticeable on the rim, but the willow-
shoot and yucca-fiber construction is still tight and solid. Some form of
black lichen grows on the outside of the bowl, while the inside is full of dust,
surrounded by history and filled with mystery. At some point in time, the
bottom of the bowl was replaced with a larger square-shaped patch, sewn
expertly in place.

We are surrounded by pinyon-juniper forests. The pinyon pine, *Pinus monophylla,* was a tremendously important food source for the indigenous cultures that once lived here. Perhaps this basket was used to roast and winnow the large nutritious nuts of the desert pine, and eventually the original bottom burned through. I can imagine women and children tossing the nuts into the air with red-hot coals from the fire and quick, deft movements of the wrist.

The students and I marvel at the skill and artistry exhibited in the bowl's construction. One student quietly remarks, "You know, I don't own a single thing that was made with such care and skill." Another laments, "I couldn't even make a bowl or a basket if I tried. Actually, I can't really make anything at all, now that I think about it." We talk quietly about the differences between possessing skills and owning possessions and try to imagine the people, the lives, and the culture that once thrived here, in the Great Basin and Mojave deserts.

All that is left now are faint traces of a rich history written indelibly on the enduring landscape. I am reminded of the pictographs that have been left to hang cryptically on the canyon walls of this wide desert land. Although some have been successfully interpreted, the meanings of most have been lost to us. Somewhere buried deep under layers of time, an entire lifeway, a complex of cultural and personal wisdom, lies silent and secret.

As we place the bowl reverently back into the high cave, it is easy to imagine the passing of our own culture, to step back from our historically confined perspectives and wonder what future generations will discover about us. Standing in such a place it is easy to imagine students of the future discussing the lost civilizations of the Americas with the same awe, mystery, and trepidation we find in our voices as we speak of the Anasazi who once lived here. As we survey the rugged lands about us, though, we cannot help but imagine how much greater will be our progeny's sense of loss. We are losing much more than the rich diversity of human cultures, languages, and lifeways that followed their different lines of evolution from distinct ecoregions all over the globe. Today, we are witness to such a rapid eradication of biodiversity, massive disruption of the planet's life-support systems, and permanent despoliation of natural ecosystems that the very future of biological evolution seems to be threatened.

Our current ecological crisis, with its global proportions and increasing severity, calls into question not just the survival of particular cultures, but also the continued existence of the human race itself and many of the life-forms we have come to hold dear. We have evolved together for millennia, caught in a constant cycle of interdependent competition and cooperation. Unfortunately, those of us alive today are witnesses to and perpetrators and victims of the greatest loss of life that this planet has seen since the cataclysmic extinction of the dinosaurs more than sixty-five million years ago.

The litany of loss is mind numbing and difficult to comprehend. We know that one in every four mammals is in danger of extinction and that two out of every three bird species and one-third of all fish are in serious decline worldwide, while recent declines in insect populations have been so dramatic and rapid that scientists have not yet been able to calculate them. As we hike the California crest and fish in the Sierra Nevada's free-flowing streams, I am forced to remember that California's state mammal—the grizzly bear proudly displayed on its flag—was long ago purposefully extirpated from its home range and that ten of the eleven western states, including California, have endangered fish as their state fish.

Long stretches of the Pacific Crest Trail lead us through soaring ponderosa and sugar pine and past massive sequoias and redwoods, reminding us that animals are not the only living beings dying at an alarming rate. Our studies in environmental history remind us that only 1 percent to 5 percent of the original forests in the United States remain and that 95 percent of the Sierra Nevada's forests were clear-cut during the Comstock era. Each year the world loses a forest the size of Honduras and is thus much poorer in biodiversity, natural resilience, and the ability to absorb carbon, regulate climates, produce fertile soil, and supply fresh water. Such irreversible losses have caused the average temperature of the earth's surface to rise by 1.2 degrees Celsius since 1870, resulting in the well-documented effects of global warming and climactic change that cause us to lose more than two hundred thousand acres of cropland each year to desertification (Flavin 1998, 12).

Similarly, soil losses in logged temperate forests soar from the natural rate of roughly 0.05 tons of soil each year (far less than what is replaced by natural soil-building processes) to more than 17 tons per year (Abramovitz 1998, 13). Not far from the northern reaches of California's crest trail lies the small logging town of Stafford, which was buried on New Year's Eve 1996 by a massive mud slide originating in a Pacific Lumber clear-cut above the town. The following year, more than ten thousand people were killed worldwide by human-exacerbated flooding, a death toll that has been slowly rising throughout the twentieth and twenty-first centuries ("Fire, Flood, and Drought" 1998, 37).

As we trudge up and down the trail's steep switchbacks, march steadily across the open meadows, and ford the icy streams, we are reminded how seldom we have the opportunity in our everyday lives to engage in our most important evolutionary adaptation, in our oldest evolutionary home: walking in wilderness. Even in the national forests we pass through, roads far outnumber walking trails, as if the car, not the foot, was the basic unit of human locomotion. There are enough miles of roads in these publicly owned forests to circle the globe fifteen times, whereas the combined total of all our national parks is only slightly larger than the 150,000 square kilometers of the United States that are paved over by roads and parking lots ("Driving Up CO2" 1997, 39). Most Americans live in urban and suburban environments comparable to Los Angeles, where 70 percent of the city's surface area is dedicated in some form to the automobile (that is, roads, parking lots, and so on) and only 5 percent is dedicated to parks and open spaces ("Road Rage" 2000, 11).

Regardless of where we live on this planet two things are sure: First, opportunities for experiencing, understanding, interacting with, and coming to value the natural world are decreasing. And second, the natural world itself is losing its capacity to support human and nonhuman life as we have come to know it. Unfortunately, both of these trends are due, primarily if not entirely, to the actions of the human species. Although this places tremendous responsibility on present and future generations, it also represents our last and greatest hope. If the origins of environmental problems are found in human culture, then it is reasonable to assume that the solutions lie there as well. Global warming and climactic change, for example, will be much more difficult to solve if they are primarily caused by a natural million-year planetary cycle than if they are the result of increased carbon emissions from the burning of fossil fuels and decreased carbon absorption from the clear-cutting of forests. From this perspective, then, we can say without irony and with some degree of accuracy that the bulk of environmental problems facing us today are *fortunately* caused by human activities.

THE ECOLOGICAL CRISIS
AS EDUCATIONAL CRISIS

As the contemporary ecological crisis has forced us to grudgingly recognize, the survival of our way of life, our social institutions, and the human race itself will depend upon our ability to transform human culture so that we may live within the planet's finite carrying capacity and no longer disrupt the natural biogeochemical cycles that sustain us. The ability to develop the necessary economic, political, technological, and cultural systems required by the need for sustainability will depend upon a competent and educated citizenry that is informed about both the limits of the natural ecosystems upon which we depend and the variety of ways in which human cultures have developed (or may develop) sustainable relationships with those environments. Such a cultural transformation requires that we recognize, as David Ehrenfeld observes in *Greening the College Curriculum,* that "ecological ignorance is dangerous. . . . [G]aining an environmental understanding *must* be an essential goal of every student's education" (1996, ix; emphasis in original). Regardless of our political inclinations or disciplinary fields, the current planetary crisis dictates that human survival depends upon our ability to understand the causes of environmental problems, as well as our capacity to develop original and effective solutions to them.

In order to accomplish both of these goals, we must first recognize that the environmental crisis represents more than a merely ecological phenomenon to be studied by the scientific method alone. Because most of our current environmental problems are the result of human disruption of natural cycles and systems, and because the most significant effects of this disruption to us will be social and personal, the environmental crisis is, as Bill Devall and George Sessions note in *Deep Ecology,* "a crisis of character and of culture" (1985, ix). In "Changing the Dominant Cultural Perspective in Education," C. A. Bowers notes this cultural basis of environmental problems, observing that "the aspects of the ecological crisis that can be attributed to human behavior are cultural in nature and are directly related to modern ideas and values that are the basis of knowledge learned in . . . education" (1999, 161).

Bowers is not alone in his recognition that our current educational system is responsible for compounding environmental problems and our failure to effectively respond to them. Similarly, David Orr asserts, "The disor-dering of ecological systems and of the great biogeochemical cycles of the earth reflects a prior disorder in the thought, perception, imagination, intel-lectual priorities, and loyalties inherent in the industrial mind. Ultimately, the ecological crisis is a crisis of education" (1996, 9). As Orr notes, our edu-cational system is implicated in the current environmental crisis and is part of the problem rather than part of the solution.

There is an old saying in addiction recovery programs (which focus on solving life-threatening problems through changing personal behaviors): that the definition of insanity is repeating the same behavior again and again but expecting different results. Such a dictum can be profitably applied to our current life-threatening problems—such as our addiction to fossil fuels and technology, unexamined belief in continual progress, stubborn anthro-pocentrism, and unassailable belief that we can transcend the finite limits of natural systems. Although these basic tenets of the modern industrial mind have been successful within a seemingly boundless world of environmental health and wealth, they are not appropriate for living in a world that is rap-idly approaching its natural limits. As Orr notes, "The kind of education that enabled us to industrialize the earth will not necessarily help us heal the damages caused by industrialization" (8). If we are to avoid the insanity of endlessly reproducing the same form of industrial education that created the current ecological crisis, while fruitlessly hoping for different results, we must begin to rethink the process of education on a variety of levels. In fact, we must begin to question many of the basic premises and assumptions upon which the modern worldview and our current humanistic educational system rest. We will be required to reconceptualize our most basic relation-ships with the natural cycles and systems that sustain us; to reformulate our notions of disciplinarity, pedagogy, and how knowledge is produced; and to reevaluate our assumptions of educational and scientific objectivity.

Such a process will entail changing our current forms of education on a variety of levels, the most basic of which will necessitate a serious, concerted examination of the anthropocentric values implicit in much of our contem-porary worldview and enlightenment-based educational system. In *Deep Ecology*, Bill Devall and George Sessions argue that because the basic assumptions underlying the "humanistic anthropocentrism of Western lib-eral arts" education are so deeply implicated in our current ecological crisis, they "cannot conclude that contemporary education is ignoring values. Education is surely teaching values both explicitly and implicitly; it is teaching the worldview and values of the scientific/technological society" (1985, 182). Within this worldview, the earth is seen almost exclusively as a collection of inanimate and virtually infinite natural resources and is valued solely as a storehouse of inexhaustible economic wealth. The problem with allowing such a system of values to remain firmly entrenched in, and to be reinforced by, our educational system is that it contradicts everything that the science of ecology and the trajectory of human history have shown us to be true about the world and our place within it.

The question becomes, then, not *whether* we should incorporate values-based instruction into our curriculum, but, rather, *what* values we should include (by default or conscious decision) in that curriculum. As Gregory Smith and Dilafruz Williams note, "All education . . . inevitably takes some moral point of view—whether it is promoting the values of the market and technology or values premised on the maintenance of caring relationships with other people and the earth" (1999, 16). The sobering facts of the escalating environmental crisis necessitate that we incorporate a new system of values into every aspect of the educational enterprise, training students to be competent and informed citizens capable of thinking about and working for the welfare of their larger human and nonhuman communities. From this perspective, schools and universities can be seen as potential leverage points for effecting the social change necessary for responding to the environmental crisis rather than as unintentional environmental culprits pushing us toward self-destruction and eventual extinction.

In order to be successful, such a process of environmental education will have to involve all of the disciplines, emphasize the knowledge and skills required to solve existing environmental problems, and develop new lifeways and socioeconomic systems that no longer exacerbate such problems. The skills and knowledge associated with these requirements of sustainability have been termed by David Orr "ecological competence." Orr argues that "[e]cological competence implies a different kind of education and a different kind of educational experience that develops the practical art of living well in particular places" (1992, 84). An educational system that seeks to develop ecological competence in its students will need to incorporate the study of environmental values, beliefs, and aesthetics into the more traditional study of natural systems and environmental economics and policy. It will also require the inclusion of experientially based learning and practice in the hands-on application of solutions to social and environmental problems. The traditional association of environmental education with the sciences perpetuates the belief not only that science and technology will unfailingly provide solutions to environmental problems, but also that nonquantifiable phenomena such as our environmental values, beliefs, and aesthetics have no significant bearing on existing environmental problems or their solutions.

In order to reform our educational system, and thereby our society so that we can successfully respond to the contemporary environmental crisis, we must fully incorporate the humanities into environmental studies and recognize that meaningful social and personal transformation will result from changes in our values and beliefs as much as from developments in our knowledge and technology. In *Preparing for the Twenty-first Century,* historian Paul Kennedy concludes, "[T]he most important influence on a nation's responsiveness to change probably is its social attitudes, religious beliefs, and culture" (1993, 16). The role of the humanities, then, is crucial because the social attitudes and religious beliefs of a people are recorded and represented most exhaustively and accurately in their literature.

UNITING THE ENVIRONMENTAL SCIENCES AND HUMANITIES

Recently, many educational institutions have begun to take tentative steps in this direction, by developing courses in the environmental arts and literature as well as by establishing interdisciplinary environmental studies programs. Most of these efforts, however, have not forayed far enough into interdisciplinarity to benefit from its many advantages, nor have they fully recognized that an environmental education cannot simply stop after imparting information; it must also alter students' basic worldviews, values, and actions if it is to be effective. This represents a distinct change from how education has traditionally been viewed in this country. Most environmental educators, ecocritics, and ecologists agree, sharing the conviction that the most significant purpose of their field is to aid us as a society in responding appropriately to the environmental crisis that currently threatens us.

Whereas the methods and discipline-specific goals of each field are quite distinct, this larger community-oriented aim of moving society from self-destruction toward sustainability is shared by both ecocriticism and ecology. It is my contention that each field can more successfully achieve this metaobjective of cultural transformation through education by learning from and applying the approaches used in its companion discipline. In order for ecologists and environmental scientists to be successful in communicating the insights of their fields to the public, they must be trained in the environmentally oriented humanistic disciplines, with special attention paid to communication (that is, literature, composition, rhetoric, speech, and journalism). Likewise, for ecocritics and instructors of environmental literature to adequately study environmental texts and effectively reeducate students, we must be well informed in the ecological and environmental sciences, namely, ecology, geography, biology, and toxicology.

I would like to suggest that the disciplinary and methodological gap between these two fields is not as wide as most scholars assume and that the benefits of bridging it far outweigh the potential difficulties involved in the attempt. Whereas the "purest" forms of literary criticism are solely concerned with illuminating a particular text and the "purest" forms of environmental science focus on the scientific study of a place or thing, these approaches are not mutually exclusive but in fact exist on either end of a spectrum of approaches to environmental texts and issues. Viewing each field as representing different sites along the same spectrum is particularly informative as we trace some of the most recent advances in each discipline—advances that have actually brought them both closer to the center of this wide spectrum than in the past.

One might graph each field and its associated disciplines in this way: On the left side of the spectrum are the traditional fields of literary criticism, such as new criticism, formalism, structuralism, and a host of other approaches to literature that are primarily, if not exclusively, concerned with exploring the meanings and structures of literary texts and their relationships to other texts. On the right side of the spectrum are the "hard" environmental sciences, such as toxicology, hydrology, botany, geology, conservation biology, and a number of other scientific approaches to studying species, features, and systems of the nonhuman environment. Closer to the center of the spectrum, but still falling on the left side, we find ecocriticism and other humanities-based approaches to environmental issues, such as environmental history, ethics, and aesthetics. These fields, like literary studies, are often concerned with the study of texts (literary and nonliterary) and other modes of cultural production while also exploring their effects on human and nonhuman communities. In short, they aim to illuminate, to some degree, both environmental texts and environmental issues. Similarly, situated on the right side of the spectrum but moving near the center, we find the "soft" environmental sciences, such disciplines as human ecology, environmental policy, environmental economics, and the rising number of interdisciplinary environmental studies programs. These fields, though still relying heavily on the environmental sciences, have begun to incorporate some humanities-based approaches to environmental issues so that the realm of human action and belief can be brought within the scope of investigation.

Ecocriticism has succeeded in using interdisciplinary investigations of environmental literature that illuminate not only texts but also the issues they explore, just as the field of environmental studies has begun to recognize the efficacy of incorporating investigations of environmental aesthetics and ethics into its science-based curriculum. The goals of these two fields, then, are much closer on the spectrum than has been traditionally assumed. I contend that through an interdisciplinary field-based approach to environmental texts and issues we can occupy a middle ground on this spectrum, one that provides scholars and students with a more holistic understanding of environmental texts, issues, and places than does an ecocritical or environmental studies perspective alone. By adopting some of the field-based approaches used in the environmental sciences, ecocritics can discover new things about environmental texts while also learning more about the specific environmental issues and particular natural environments that form the subjects of those texts. Likewise, by incorporating the study of works of environmental literature into environmental studies curricula, environmental scientists can better understand the complex relations between their particular sites of research, or specific environmental issues, and the human values, beliefs, and aesthetics that directly affect them. Through interdisciplinary field-based approaches to environmental issues and texts, we can occupy this fertile middle ground between the disciplines, a liminal area that in ecological terms is known as an "ecotone." Ecotones—areas where distinct ecosystems meet and overlap—are areas of high biodiversity and natural resilience, places rich in life and possibility. Regardless of our particular fields, as environmental scholars and educators we would benefit from inhabiting this rich transition zone between disciplines so that we may more effectively avail ourselves of the abundant resources each field has to offer.

Because of the inherent interdisciplinarity of environmental texts, ecocritics have traditionally been lavish in their praise of interdisciplinary studies, arguing that such approaches are necessary for the adequate exploration of environmental literature. However, I contend that ecocriticism has not taken interdisciplinarity far enough as a critical methodology and tends to use it informally, when it is convenient, rather than as a formal critical practice.

Similarly, though environmental educators and scientists have tended to support interdisciplinary investigations of environmental issues, historically this has excluded humanities-based approaches, relying instead on the different disciplinary perspectives offered within the sciences themselves. Environmental science has been slow to recognize the need for, and efficacy of, moving outside the larger scientific field to include the historical, philosophical, literary, and aesthetic perspectives offered by the humanities. Thus, a new approach seems to be called for within both disciplines, an approach that can fully explore, and effectively respond to, the complex of natural and cultural interactions that have caused, and continue to exacerbate, the current environmental crisis.

ECOCRITICISM AND THE NEED FOR FIELDWORK

In *Wanderlust: A History of Walking*, Rebecca Solnit explores the importance of walking as a method for experiencing the natural world and connects it with the experience of reading. She writes, "If the body is the register of the real then reading with one's feet is real in a way that reading with one's eyes alone is not" (2000, 70). "Reading with one's feet" calls for the scholar to use some form of fieldwork, some manner of direct engagement with the natural world represented in a work of literature as a means of informing scholarship. Likewise, as an instructor, one may find it necessary to expand one's pedagogical practice to include field-based experiences for students struggling to understand the relationships between the texts they read and the world they inhabit.

Solnit notes many interesting affinities between texts and trails that suggest the notion of exploring literary landscapes with one's feet is less radical than it might seem: "Just as writing allows one to read the words of someone who is absent, so roads make it possible to trace the route of the absent. Roads are the record of those who have gone before and to follow them is to follow people who are no longer there" (72). From this perspective, books and paths are exactly that—markers to show us where other minds and feet have been—so that we may retrace their intellectual and physical journeys ourselves.

In fact, most people experience the natural world through reading books about it and walking on paths that have been constructed in it. This does not mean that the places they go, the new things they discover, and the ideas they come across are less beautiful, less worthy, less novel, or less valuable just because others have visited that place or idea before. Rather, it is in part because those places have been visited, because those ideas have been espoused by others, that they come to have an important place in our culture. Simplicity resonates with us not only because it is a good idea but also because it was so eloquently articulated by Thoreau in *Walden*. Freedom is not a new idea for us, or Edward Abbey, nor is it important to Americans today because each of us invents it as a value, but rather because it is a shared value of our culture, a part of our history that resonates with the power of the men and women who lived and espoused it before us.

As my students and I learned during a recent field-studies class, the Pacific Crest Trail is a part of our National Scenic Trails System not because it offers one the opportunity to go where no human has been before. Rather, it is important largely because it was built, protected, and hiked by many before us. As we noted, it did not matter that others had hiked that section of the trail before us or soaked their sore muscles in Iva Bell hot springs as we did. Never having traveled that section of trail before, it presented a narrative new to us. What we would find around the next bend was still a mystery, no matter how many had discovered it before.

In this sense, for the reader or traveler, books and trails share many of the same salient characteristics. Ideas and places function in the same manner for the traveler or thinker. As Solnit notes, "This is what is behind the special relationship between tale and travel, and, perhaps, the reason why narrative writing is so closely bound up with walking. To write is to carve a new path through the terrain of the imagination, or to point out new features on a familiar route. To read is to travel through that terrain with the author as guide" (72). And we may add to Solnit's comparison that in the process of unifying the tale and the trail, by connecting the reading with the walking, we are able to use the book as a guide on the trail and our experience on the trail as a guide through the book.

During field-studies classes, when the opportunity for such synthesis is offered, we find that reading the text shapes our perception of the trail and our experience on it, just as hiking the trail shapes our perception of the text and our experience reading it. Such attempts to unify the tale and the trail recognize and respond to the way readers read and walkers walk, or, more accurately, the way readers walk and walkers read.

This approach, however, offers a number of challenges to the traditional literary scholar because the object of study centers upon an author's relationship to a very real, and often distant, extratextual environment. Because these extratextual environments figure so prominently in the works of nature writers, the traditional practices of the literary scholar may not be adequate for complete understanding. A careful study of such works will often entail that the scholar adopt a number of research methodologies that seem to be at odds with traditional literary scholarship, such as the scientific study of natural ecosystems and processes or self-reflective and direct observation of how living in and moving through such landscapes affects the traveler's attitudes and perceptions. Adopting such field-based methodologies as a supplement to, rather than a substitute for, traditional textual research can enable the scholar to compare environmental texts with the extratextual environments to which they refer. In addition, the critic can compare the author's literary representations with his or her own experiences in the real world.

Learning the methodologies of other disciplines, however, and becoming familiar with their key concepts and theories requires a tremendous amount of time and effort on the part of the critic. In addition, taking to the field requires that the critic learn a host of field-based technical skills. Simply traveling to and living in some of the environments these authors write about can be a difficult and challenging experience. Even if the field scholar already has the technical skills necessary and is familiar with the appropriate methods and ideas of other disciplines for engaging in place-based literary studies, these approaches still absorb a great deal of the scholar's time and money. However, these challenges, though often representing significant obstacles for literary scholars interested in field-based interpretation, are probably not the primary reason more scholars are not attempting it. The most significant disadvantage of place-based scholarship for the literary scholar is that he or she has been trained only in textual analysis and is asked to develop or experiment with new methods of study in order to succeed. Much like the contemporary ecologist who is asked to participate in public policy hearings and resource management decisions that fall outside his or her specific discipline, place-based ecocriticism requires the literary scholar to gain facility with a variety of skills and methodologies in which he or she has not been professionally trained. In addition, the time required for such field-based investigations appears to supplant the time needed to engage in traditional textual research. Literary field studies, then, seem to ask scholars to question and replace much of what they have been taught and come to hold of professional value.

Therefore, such forms of fieldwork have not traditionally been seen as necessary or even viable forms of practice for the literary scholar and instructor. Within the field of literary studies, it has been tacitly assumed that because the object of study is a text, all necessary information will likewise be found in texts. Such forms of textual primacy are inadequate, however, for the study of texts that focus so pointedly upon extratextual environments and our responses to them. In *Story Line,* a place-based study of the literature of the Appalachian Trail, Ian Marshall laments the singularly textual approach, observing that "literary critics in general have neglected fieldwork. If the evidence they seek is not in the library, they don't want to know about it" (1998, 145). The primary problem with such a textually confined methodology is that it fails to include within the realm of investigation some of the most salient features of environmental texts, namely, the particular environment informing and inspiring the work.

In *The Environmental Imagination,* Lawrence Buell notes, "These are the characteristic results of a metropolitan-based enterprise of academic criticism for which it easily becomes second nature to read literature about nature for its structural or ideological properties rather than for its experiential or referential aspects" (1995, 36). By engaging ourselves, and our students, in field-based explorations of environmental texts and their extratextual environments, we can more readily investigate the experiential and referential aspects of these texts. Such a process is key for understanding the work of nature writers because a vast majority of them are explicitly engaged in the referential and experiential and therefore view ideology and structure either to be less significant than the characteristics of the environments they write about or to grow organically from those environments. Field studies offer us the opportunity to explore the important interconnections between environmental texts and their extratextual environments so that we may come to understand not only the text itself, but also its relationships to the reader and the world.

ENVIRONMENTAL EDUCATION AND FIELDWORK

For educators interested in developing "ecologically competent" or "ecologically literate" students, field experiences offer tremendous opportunities for connecting course curricula with local environmental issues. Such experiences ground discussions of ecology and environmental values in the real world. As David Orr notes, "Ecological literacy is becoming more difficult, I believe, not because there are fewer books about nature, but because there is less opportunity for direct experience of it" (1992, 89). Frank Trocco recognizes this problem, arguing that environmental education is, in fact, "re-education" because we already have learned a great deal about the environment from our culture, and "most of this information is incorrect and based on unquestioned assimilation. . . . [R]eeducation aimed at modifying this information is much more difficult than education, because you are not merely filling a receptive space but first pushing out (often painfully) previously learned and accepted data" (1985, 138). Those of us who teach classes in environmental literature and science are often made painfully aware of just how much inaccurate information about the natural world our students already "know."

The primary problem with our students' environmental knowledge is that it is not based on direct contact with, and experience in, the natural world, and it is not founded upon the insights of the ecological sciences. The majority of what our students "know" about the world is assimilated uncritically from our larger society, from the market-driven forces of our media and productions of popular culture. In fact, most Americans spend the majority of their lives in human-created environments and have little opportunity or encouragement to experience, much less study, the natural world directly. If we are to be successful in reeducating an ecologically illiterate public, we must reconsider the environment in which that reeducation will take place.

As Frederick Waage points out in *Teaching Environmental Literature,* "[D]ecisions about educational environment are as significant as decisions about curriculum" (1985, 5). The ease with which we teach environmental issues in settings isolated from any direct experience of natural environments is extremely problematic. Expecting our students to alter their anthropocentric notions of the natural environment, the earth's biogeochemical cycles, wilderness areas, ancient forests, or endangered species without giving them some experience (perhaps for the first time in their lives) of the reality of these things is unrealistic and self-defeating. As David Orr asserts in *Ecological Literacy,* "[S]tudents taught environmental awareness in a setting that does not alter their relationship to basic life-support systems learn that it is sufficient to intellectualize, emote, or posture about such things without having to live differently" (1992, 91). Ecocritics and environmental educators alike would do well to recognize that this is what most students take from our courses, because this is exactly what the majority of us do today.

If we are serious about teaching ecological sustainability, we must expand our pedagogical practices just as ecocritics have expanded the literary canon. In recognition of both the literary and the social implications of how we teach environmental literature, Waage argues that "[t]he ideal situation, then, is one in which the student is immersed for some time in a physical environment as close as possible to that of a particular work or group of works" (1985, 7). Such a process not only teaches students more about the texts and issues they are studying, but also affords them the opportunity to explore the natural world and their interrelationships with it directly. In John Elder's collection *Stories in the Land,* Kurt Caswell sums up the motivations of the environmental field-studies instructor quite well:

> I thought then that, as a teacher, the single most powerful tool I have in helping to heal the fractured relationship between people and nature is

simply to guide students in their classroom studies and provide opportunities for authentic experiences on the land. The combination of these two key elements will help students define themselves in the context of their communities and the natural world. In trying to reawaken the human spirit to a better way of living on earth, this is a good place to begin. (1998, 30)

As environmental educators, we shoulder the weighty burden of training future citizens, teachers, policy makers, and natural resource managers. If they are allowed to maintain the same anthropocentric and nearsighted perceptions that gave rise to our current ecological crisis, then they will be incapable of solving the increasingly urgent problems we now face. Their failure will, in part, be ours.

ENVIRONMENTAL SCIENCE, VALUES, AND ETHICS

Environmental studies programs, both inside and outside of universities, traditionally make much better use of the advantages of field-based methodologies than do green literary studies. However, environmental education often fails to achieve its goal of reeducating students with regard to their relationship to the natural environment because its scientific focus neglects important issues of environmental values, beliefs, attitudes, perceptions, aesthetics, and ethics. Environmental education is limited by this scientific focus in the same way that ecocriticism is limited by its emphasis on textuality. Most environmental studies programs emphasize scientific approaches to environmental issues (the collection of quantitative data and use of "objective" observational research) while marginalizing humanities-based explorations of those same issues (such as gathering qualitative information and exploring subjective responses to the environment).

Although the scientific approach has proven the most effective method of studying the natural world, it remains incapable of exploring many of the underlying causes of environmental problems and engendering action on their behalf. We tend to place great authority on quantifiable data and scientific research, but we do not, as many psychologists have noted, tend to take action based solely upon these forms of "objective" knowledge.

Especially when it comes to such value-laden issues as the environment and the effect our lifestyles have on it, we generally justify our existing behavior, or change that behavior, based upon emotionally charged values, beliefs, and attitudes rather than on objective information. Unless we include the critical investigation of these "subjective" phenomena—the majority of which are difficult if not impossible to quantify with the scientific method—in our environmental studies programs, some of the most important factors affecting environmental issues will be omitted from our analysis.

Such an omission is particularly problematic for those studying complex environmental issues and systems. As the first law of ecology informs us, all beings are interdependent and interrelated; we cannot, despite our disciplinary history and fervor, divide environmental issues into their respective disciplinary categories, studying the physical, biological, chemical, historical, and cultural aspects of a particular issue or place as if they were completely separate and unrelated. As David Orr notes in "Reinventing Higher Education," "The great ecological issues of our time have to do one way or another with our failure to see things in their entirety" (1996, 11). For environmental studies programs to successfully respond to these contemporary ecological issues, we must begin to incorporate interdisciplinary approaches into our practice that will enable us to study environmental issues in their entirety and recognize their inherent complexity. As long as environmental educators continue to privilege the sciences over the humanities, our understanding of the complex relationships between human culture and nonhuman nature will remain limited and incomplete.

Environmental educator John Elder agrees, stating in *Stories in the Land: A Place-Based Environmental Education Anthology* that "[r]ather than assuming that science and the humanities must remain forever discrete, environmental education needs more boldly to inhabit the ecotone where they join and comingle, where something new may evolve" (1998, 8). Such an evolution will result in a new generation of environmentally literate students and scholars who are capable of studying both ecological systems and their intersections with human culture. The contemporary ecological crisis, with its ever escalating nature and global proportions, requires just such a partnership: membership in both science- and humanities-based disciplines and citizenship in both human and nonhuman communities.

Although some proponents of the "objectivity" of the scientific method may bristle at such a recommendation and argue that science's role is merely to understand how the world works and to document changes in its natural systems, I believe that the severity of the current ecological crisis requires us to take a much more utilitarian view of the purposes of scientific study and education. Though I have known conservation biologists who were content to graph the decline of a particular species and, in the name of objectivity and noninterference, do nothing more than act as a witness to its extinction, I believe we have an ethical and professional responsibility to intercede on behalf of imperiled wildlands and species. This holds doubly true in cases where human interference is responsible for the decline in the first place. Likewise, as recent advances in the field of quantum physics have demonstrated, such beliefs in the "objectivity" of science and the separation of the observed from the observer are fallacious. Similarly, studies in the history of environmentally oriented scientific debates have demonstrated that "objective" scientists often take opposing positions on a particular issue based upon their personal values and institutional affiliations rather than on differences in the observed data. Science, then, cannot be practiced in a moral vacuum because it is never capable of pure objectivity.

There is a moral imperative, I believe, for anyone documenting a particular injustice, especially if that injustice threatens his or her own life and the lives of others, to actively resist it. Gregory Smith and Dilafruz Williams note this problematic aspect of most scientific approaches to environmental issues, lamenting the fact that "classes in environmental education focus on scientific analysis and social policy—not cultural change" (1999, 3). Because environmental problems are, as I have argued, cultural problems at their roots, those of us who witness environmental destruction and degradation are morally obligated to seek cultural change. This, of course, requires that we understand the aspects of culture that produced the problem in the first place and that we are capable of modifying our own, our students', and our society's behavior so the problem can be solved.

In order to effect cultural and personal change, however, we must move from the "objective" scientific realm into the "subjective" world of values, perceptions, attitudes, beliefs, persuasion, propaganda, and rhetoric—in other words, into the domain of the humanities. As many cognitive and behavioral psychologists have noted, "[E]xposure to facts alone is not enough to turn people toward environmental action. The facts can actually turn people away from meaningful engagement with the issues" (Kaza 1999, 145). According to Stephanie Kaza, what is required to connect a growing environmental awareness developed through scientific study with a commitment to change ecologically disruptive behaviors "is to overcome patterns of avoidance and psychic numbing while generating compassion and commitment to act" (146).

Such a process can be initiated only through a humanities-based approach that can investigate personal behaviors and the values that support them directly. Of course, such investigations do not fall within the realm of science, and because of their moral basis they are often considered suspect by proponents of the "objectivity" of the scientific method. Whether or not environmental educators incorporate such value-laden investigations into their primarily scientific curriculum, we should recognize, as historian Donald Worster does, that "science is always, in some measure, involved in matters of value and moral perception" (1977, xii). The question environmental educators and scientists need to ask is not whether science should take a moral stance, but rather *which* moral stance it should take.

Once we recognize the benefit of exploring values and ethics alongside the scientific analysis of environmental issues and the advantages of incorporating humanities-based approaches into environmental studies curricula, the efficacy of studying works of environmental literature becomes readily apparent. As geographer Yi-Fu Tuan notes in *Topophilia*, "The forceful and precise articulation of environmental attitudes requires high verbal skills. Literature rather than social science surveys provides us with the detailed and finely shaded information on how human individuals perceive their worlds" (1974, 49). By introducing students to a variety of literary texts—works that demonstrate varying environmental attitudes from the anthropocentric and utilitarian to the biocentric and aesthetic—we can expose not only the values that produced the current environmental crisis, but also those that seek, in different ways, to solve it.

Likewise, such literary investigations serve to expose each student's own preconceived and culturally received environmental attitudes to critical examination. Vernon Owen Grumbling comments on this particular value of including literary works in the discussion of environmental issues:

> Because literature works through value-laden images and offers itself to the interpretation of the reader, its peculiar value is to personalize the moral and aesthetic issues that inevitably arise in exploring conservation of biodiversity and sustainable development. Those teaching in disciplines other than literature can easily "borrow" a particular literary text as a means of stimulating students to respond in personal terms to the environmental consequences of attitudes and behaviors. (1996, 151)

Coupled with the authority of scientific research and direct experience of the natural world, such an approach can be particularly powerful and edifying for the environmental field-studies student. Considering the ethical and utilitarian goals commonly held by environmental educators—the desire to respond effectively to the environmental crisis through educational, personal, and cultural transformation—an interdisciplinary field-based approach to environmental studies is required.

INTERDISCIPLINARY FIELD-BASED APPROACHES

We often focus upon differences between scientific and humanities-based research, but both methods of studying the world share many affinities. Although their particular methodologies are quite distinct, both are concerned, for example, with describing, exploring, and discovering some small portion of the "truth" about our world and our place in it. Like the proverbial blind men describing different portions of the elephant's anatomy, the sciences and humanities are limited by methodology and perspective so that a complete and accurate picture of the world cannot be drawn from one discipline alone.

I have offered a few questions below as examples of the manner in which an ecocritic might approach environmental texts through an interdisciplinary field-based methodology, as well as how the environmental studies practitioner might include literary works in the investigation of environmental issues and natural environments.

Questions focusing on the text:

1. How does my experience in this place (or with this activity) compare with the author's recorded experience, or how does it modify my interpretation of the text?
2. What can I discover about the author's methods and rhetorical choices by emulating them myself in my own writing?
3. How might the author's experience in this place have affected him or her (choices, aims, methods, ideas, and so on) and the text itself (images, metaphors, composition, revision, publication, information, and the like)?

Questions focusing on the place:

1. How has this place changed since the author wrote about it?
2. What other information can I gather about features of this place through direct observation or interdisciplinary research?
3. How has the text or author affected this place?

Questions focusing on the text and place equally:

1. What correspondences do I see between the text and the place?
2. Is the author's representation of this place accurate in comparison with my own observations?
3. What values do we find in the text? What values accord with this place? Are they convergent or divergent? Why?

Questions about the audience (reader or recreationalist):

1. How does the text affect my (or others') environmental beliefs, values, attitudes, and actions? And, separately, how does the place affect my (or others') environmental beliefs, values, attitudes, and actions?
2. How does my combined experience with both the text and the place affect my environmental beliefs, values, attitudes, and actions?
3. What are the differences between questions 1 and 2?

Not meant to be exhaustive, this sampling of critical questions should offer field scholars and students a place from which to begin their interdisciplinary explorations of environmental texts and issues.

Depending on the scholar's aims and the questions he or she seeks to answer, there are three basic methodologies for engaging in place-based interdisciplinary ecocritical investigations or for incorporating works of environmental literature into environmental studies curricula. I term these three approaches to field studies as follows: *place-based, regional,* and *practice-oriented.*

Place–Based Field Studies

The first field method takes place in situ, in the exact location about which the text being studied or used was written. I term this method *place-based field studies,* as it focuses on the particular places emphasized in environmental texts. With this approach the student or scholar may explore the correspondences between the text and the place or investigate the differences between literary representation and reality. Or the scholar may choose to compare the author's experience with his or her own experiences, or how the place has changed, or its effect on the text, or even the text's effect on the place. Such a process, for example, might incorporate interdisciplinary field studies of Walden Pond and its environs into the study of Thoreau's *Walden.* Or the environmental educator may use readings from *Walden* to aid students in understanding the historical and cultural significance of Walden Pond's ecosystems. Similarly, one might choose to study parts of John Muir's *Mountains of California* or *My First Summer in the Sierra* by finding the exact locations referenced in each work.

Walking with Muir Across Yosemite (1998), by Thomas Vale and Geraldine Vale, represents one such approach for the environmental scientist. The Vales use Muir's work primarily as a historical document to study forest succession rates and the effects of fire suppression on forest composition. Ecocritic, biographer, and historian Cherry Good uses a similar approach in *On the Trail of John Muir* (2000), visiting a series of sites important to Muir, from his boyhood home in Scotland and his father's farm in Wisconsin to his own home in Martinez, California, cabin site in Yosemite, and glacial explorations in Alaska.

Regional Field Studies

The second field approach does not require the student or scholar to travel to the exact location written about in a particular literary work, but rather requires him or her to find a bioregion similar to the one represented in a particular text. Likewise, environmental educators exploring a specific envi-

ronmental issue or ecosystem do not necessarily have to find a piece of literature dealing with that particular place or issue; rather, they can benefit from
using literary works that explore related issues and similar landscapes. I term
this approach *regional field studies,* because it emphasizes regional similari-
ties between environmental texts and their extratextual contexts.

For the ecocritic or student of environmental literature studying the
works of such writers as Mary Austin or Edward Abbey, for example, some
sort of experience in, and study of, arid ecosystems may be particularly edifying. Even if these field-based experiences do not take place in the exact
location discussed, or even the same specific type of ecosystem, much can
be gained from experiencing, traveling in, and studying similar arid landscapes. One may still expect to find many of the same species and natural
processes and that much of the physical and aesthetic experience will remain
the same whether one is in the Escalante canyons or the Great Basin or
Mojave deserts or reading *Desert Solitaire* or *The Land of Little Rain.*

Likewise, for environmental studies practitioners working in the southwestern deserts and arid regions of the Intermountain West, exposure to the
writings of these desert authors serves to illustrate, and perhaps alter, many of
the cultural and aesthetic perceptions we have of desert landscapes, introduces
readers to a variety of species and ecosystemic processes, and offers insight
into past and present cultural interactions with such landscapes. One need not
travel to Arches National Park or the Owens Valley, or find an environmental
author who has published on one's own particular species or site of study, in
order to benefit from such an interdisciplinary approach because many of the
key issues in such texts and places will naturally overlap. Issues such as the
availability of water; floral, faunal, and cultural adaptation to harsh environments; and common aesthetic attitudes toward desert climates share significant affinities in similar natural environments and literary productions.

Practice-Oriented Field Studies

A third useful approach for uniting the study of environmental texts and
natural environments entails emulating a particular author's methods in
order to shed light on the text being studied or in order to learn more about
one's relationship with a particular place. For this approach, it does not matter whether one's field experiences take place in a landscape that is very similar to or quite different from that treated by the author being studied. The

author's methods and practices, rather than the location, are of primary importance. I call this approach *practice-oriented field studies,* because it emphasizes the practices used by the author over the particular region or place in which the text was composed.

For example, an ecocritic might keep an almanac of his or her own backyard or engage in some form of ecological restoration while studying a work like Aldo Leopold's *Sand County Almanac.* By using Leopold's methods as a model for our own practice, we may learn more about how the text was produced, the development of his ideas, and our own home bioregion. Similarly, we might use the models for bioregional practice offered in Gary Snyder's prose and poetry to invigorate our own efforts, or those of our students, in environmental activism and reinhabitation. Engaging in such practices offers the ecocritic rich opportunities for understanding the personal, political, and ecological contexts in which Snyder's work was written.

Likewise for the environmental scientist, engaging in activism or attempting to understand ecopoetry that, like Snyder's, explores personal, spiritual, and cultural meanings of particular species offers rich insights into the larger contexts in which the ecologist's discipline-specific studies take place. As Barry Lopez demonstrates in *Of Wolves and Men,* a complete understanding of *Canis lupus*—its current status, role in natural ecosystems, and potential for recovery—is impossible without also coming to grips with the role it has traditionally played in our cultural imagination and our own misguided efforts at predator eradication.

THE FOUR KEY ELEMENTS

Regardless of which approach we choose to take, such interdisciplinary field-based investigations can be used to augment traditional scholarship and pedagogy and offer a more complete understanding of environmental texts and their extratextual environments. The possibilities for engaging in such interdisciplinary field studies are virtually endless, but they should include some combination of the following four key elements: the utilization of the *natural sciences* to study particular places, species, and systems; the use of the *environmental humanities* for the study of ethics, art, literature, history, and their interrelationships with the natural world; an increased depth of *self-knowledge* and critical examination of our own culturally received environmental attitudes, beliefs, values, and behaviors; and some form of *worldly experience* in the natural environments being studied and with the practices required to respond to the contemporary environmental crisis.

These four principles are plotted in the following diagram as the four cardinal points on a compass, for to know who we are, we must first know where we are. There is nothing more fundamental than the ground beneath our feet, nothing more miraculous than its ability to sustain life, and nothing more necessary than our efforts to defend it.

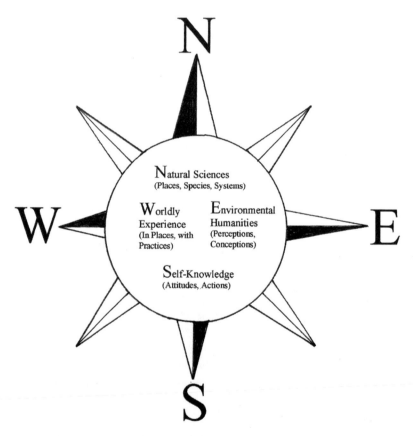

The Four Key Elements

CHAPTER THREE

Mary Austin in the Land of Little Rain

There was something else there besides what you find in the books; a lurking, eva-
sive Something, wistful, cruel, ardent; something that rustled and ran, that hung
half-remotely, insistent on being noticed, fled from pursuit, and when you turned
from it, leaped suddenly and fastened on your vitals. This is no mere figure of
speech, but the true movement of experience.

MARY AUSTIN,
Earth Horizon

My wife and I have been hiking through the heat all afternoon, across the
sagebrush flats and past the few pinyon pines that dot the hillsides. We rise
above the Owens Valley along a stretch of the southern Sierra Nevada, the
great range standing to the north and west of us, while the wide arid lands of
the Great Basin and Mojave deserts disappear into the distant horizon to the
east. The sun pounds down from above, burning, incessant, and merciless.
No clouds. Barely a breath of wind. Nothing it seems but an overpowering
golden glow emanating from an endless pale-blue sky to rule over this
burned land. I am reminded of Mary Austin's fitting descriptions of living in
this land, where "the air breathes like cotton wool" (1997, 31).

Water is sucked out of our pores as we hike, the sweat drying on the skin
so quickly that I begin to believe that dehydration could become an audible
exercise here, in this land of little rain. Yet one feels strangely calm here; a
serene silence lies over the land, settling slowly as we walk on the soul. Mary
Austin must have felt it, too, on her journeys through this haunting and

beautiful country. In *The Land of Little Rain*, she notes that this is "[a] land of lost rivers, with little in it to love; yet a land that once visited must be come back to inevitably" (5). Yesterday, we had to hike an extra four miles just to find water, since the seasonal stream we had planned to camp at was dry. There are no guarantees in this wide simmering land, I reminded myself, marking another of Austin's "lost rivers" on my map along with the time of the season during which it had leaped its banks and vanished into the sky. Here one can lose rivers and springs in a maze of both space and time.

The search for water, an endlessly repeated quest in such a place, tutors us as we strive to become literate in reading the landscape. The land continues to give us cryptic signs of the sweet liquid life we seek: a game trail, a distant shade of green, or the flocking of birds. Signs. They point the way to water; if we read them correctly and have the patience to keep reading and walking, we know we will get there—not soon, but eventually—to the blessed banks of some secret spring, or the tasty trickle of a sweet-water creek, or even, perhaps, the full-bodied roar of a river like the Kern.

As we explore the country and reread passages from Austin's work, I am amazed by the accuracy of her descriptions, the fidelity of her representations of experience to my own experiences, and the uncanny manner in which her prose seems to capture the unique character of this wild and strange land. Although a century has passed since Austin lived and wrote in this rugged region, many of the things she describes in her fiction can be found in the desert today. In "Lost Borders," she instructs her readers in the realities of desert travel: "[W]here you find cattle dropped, skeleton or skin dried, the heads almost invariably will be turned toward the places where water-holes should be" (1987, 43). Almost one hundred years later, trekking with a group of students through the Silver Peak Wilderness Study Area in the central Great Basin, I was haunted by the accuracy of Austin's description as we stumbled upon a mummified cow carcass. Complete with a plastic ear tag, white grinning skull, and sun-dried hide, the cow's remains appeared as if they had literally jumped off the pages of Austin's book and taken shape on the ground before us. In order to test her knowledge of the desert further, I took a bearing off the cow's exposed skeletal nose and began searching for the spring that Austin assured me must be there. A little more than a mile later, I came upon a small mud-bottomed spring, surrounded by willow and wild rose, just as she had promised.

Mary Austin's unique ability to accurately represent the land, people, and wildlife of the southern California region has been widely acknowledged. Marjorie Pryse notes that Austin always "remains faithful to literal accuracy in her natural description" (1987, xiv). Austin's fidelity to the manner of life and quality of experience endemic to the American Southwest represents one of the most important aspects of her fiction as well as one of the most consistent preoccupations of her writing life. As she laments in "Lost Borders," "I was sore then about not getting myself believed in some elementary matters, such as that horned toads are not poisonous, and that Indians really have the bowels of compassion" (1987, 158). Austin's anger at not being believed about things she had experienced herself caused her to strive for an extraordinary degree of authenticity in her writing. She complains in "Regionalism in American Fiction" that "[o]ur Southwest, though actually the longest-lived-in section of the country, has not yet achieved its authentic literary expression in English" (1996b, 134). The resolution of this problem became one of Austin's most persistent ambitions and perhaps one of her greatest accomplishments.

Austin's descriptions of the rugged lands, sparse wildlife, and colorful characters of the Southwest often focus upon the phenomenological, attempting to put into words the actual experience of the thing described rather than the rational explanation of it. In her description of the extremely effective camouflaging techniques of horned lizards, for example, Austin relates her observations as they are experienced by one who has just witnessed the uncanny ability with her own eyes: "Now and then a palm's breadth of the trail gathers itself together and scurries off with a little rustle under the brush, to resolve itself into sand again. This is pure witchcraft. If you succeed in catching it in transit, it loses its power and becomes a flat, horned, toad-like creature, horrid looking and harmless, of the color of the soil" (1997, 98). Rather than begin her description with the intellectual rationalization of the event—the ability of horned lizards to blend in with the sand—Austin relates the event as it is experienced by the senses. As we explored Austin's country, we came across a number of horned lizards and other similarly camouflaged reptiles. Each time one scurried from its hiding place in the sand, even though our previous experience had taught us the truth behind the illusion, we were caught momentarily by the inexplicable experience of actually "seeing" the sand animate itself, slide across the trail, and then slowly resolve into the recognizable shape of *Phrynosoma platyrhinos.*

In other descriptions of the region, Austin's detailed knowledge of the habits of local plant and animal species adds both a factual accuracy to her observations and an immediacy of significance that could save one's life. In the opening passage of the chapter "The Mesa Trail," Austin describes the trail's route by noting that "[i]t strikes diagonally across the foot of the hill-slope from the field until it reaches larkspur level" (92). Such a description, for someone knowledgeable about the botany of the area, is as accurate as giving the trail's precise elevation, a very common method used by modern-day guidebooks to aid reader-travelers in navigation. Tall larkspur, or *Delphinium glaucum,* a three- to six-foot-tall brilliantly blue and purple, easily distinguishable flower is limited to an elevation range of five thousand to ten thousand feet. The trail Austin describes begins at Naboth's field at an approximate elevation of forty-one hundred feet. It then climbs nine hundred feet in elevation in a southwesterly direction until it reaches the five thousand–foot mark and turns directly south, neither losing nor gaining elevation for quite some time. Without the aid of modern altimeters and GPS units, Austin is able to use her own intimate knowledge of the flora and fauna of the region to provide just as precise directions as any contemporary guidebook could.

Likewise, Austin's descriptions of desert plants are as accurate as those within any contemporary field guide. She describes one of the most common plants of her region—one that is easy to overlook because of its uniformity across the landscape—with the precision of a professional botanist and the lyricism of a poet:

> Sagebrush, the silvery pubescent *Artemisia tridentata,* is no sage, nor yet brushy as are the spined and brittle members of the chaparral. It has a twisty woody base and herbaceous tops, well feathered with gray-green velvet leafage, and grass-like tips of self-colored, aromatic seed. "Tridentata" it is called because of the three-lobed leaves, and "Artemisia," being sacred to young Artemis, hung up in her temple in votive wreaths. Always there is about sagebrush that virginal suggestion, shy-colored, fresh-smelling, sufficient to itself. (1927, 171)

One who is familiar with this common and aromatic shrub of the West will instantly recognize the aptness of both Austin's objective observations and subjective associations. Additionally, Austin employs almost every conceivable rhetorical strategy here to convey the fullest description of the plant possible. She describes it in both negative and positive terms (that is, what it is not like as well as what it is like); records finely shaded details in color, shape, and smell; and offers less objective but perhaps equally useful subjective associations commonly attributed to the plant.

In a similar manner, Austin displays a close knowledge of animal behavior and the ability to read wildlife signs correctly in her description of the water trails of the Ceriso. She notes that "[b]y the end of the dry season the water trails of the Ceriso are worn to a white ribbon in the leaning grass, spread out faint and fanwise toward the homes of gopher and ground rat and squirrel" (1997, 17). She then admonishes readers to get "down to the eye level of rat and squirrel kind" if they are to perceive the trails in detail. The "fanwise" description, easily passed over by those without a close knowledge of arid regions, relates an exceedingly important detail about both animal trails and the availability of water in the desert. Although animals forage, rest, and den in a wide variety of manners and places, they all (at least the animals that need it) water at the same spots, which are usually limited in number and widely dispersed in desert regions. From a bird's-eye view, the web of crisscrossing trails made by different species converges on the same sources of water. Thus, whenever two trails meet, the diverging prongs of the fork almost always face away from water, whereas the bottom of the V points toward the nearest water source like an arrow. As Austin well knows, such forms of precise place-based knowledge can mean the difference between life and death for the desert traveler. A few paragraphs later, she warns readers: "Venture to look for some seldom-touched water-hole, and so long as the trails run with your general direction make sure you are right, but if they begin to cross yours at never so slight an angle, to converge toward a point left or right of your objective, no matter what the maps say, or your memory, trust them; they *know*" (19; emphasis in original). As Austin demonstrates, knowing in the desert entails relearning what our culture has let us forget and finding mentors in the movements of animals and teachers in the habits of trees.

Such descriptions are easy for the literary scholar, working in an air-conditioned office and drinking coffee, to ignore; however, after spending a ten-mile day on the trail and coming upon a dry creek bed where one planned to find water, these textual passages become much more significant. The quest for water, in Austin country, underlies everything that one does and sees. It dictates the types and numbers of native plant life, directs the pattern of game trails, and haunts the thoughts of every desert traveler. Whether one is reduced to relying on a few precious mouthfuls of water trapped in a *tinaja* or is lucky enough to find a bubbling spring of sweet water seeping out of the ground, the presence or absence of water can mean the difference between life and death. Even today, with topographic maps, maintained trail systems, and developed springs for backcountry travelers, it is still as Austin described it: "Not the law, but the land sets the limit" (3).

Even at a developed Bureau of Land Management (BLM) spring used by PCT hikers, for example, I was reminded of the paradoxical nature of the desert so often described in Austin's writing, where both life and death are so often present together. At the same time that we were filling our bottles with life-giving water, I could not help but wonder about Giardia, E. coli bacteria, and a host of other contaminants that might be living in that spring. At the time, I was recovering from a bout of Giardia contracted on another field-studies expedition, and although I was aided by a modern-day water filter, my recent illness made me even more conscious of the very real and ever present dangers that must have faced Austin and other desert travelers during her time. Such dangers, although now mitigated by a web of roads and trails, developed springs, and technologically advanced camping gear, still exist over much of the Southwest. They serve to remind the ecocritical field scholar that Austin's representations of the natural world—along with their associated questions of accuracy—retain a significance that goes well beyond the artistic and linguistic. Maintaining the accuracy of her descriptions was not only an artistic principle for Austin, but also a practical necessity.

THE PROBLEMATICS OF LITERARY REPRESENTATION

Although Austin's descriptions of the Southwest display a remarkable degree of accuracy, we cannot assume, as poststructuralists often point out, an unproblematic mimesis between the text and the place it is meant to represent. No matter how accurate the picture painted in words, it still fails to replace or re-create the experience of actually "being there," simply because words can describe only things; they are not the things themselves. This distancing effect of language was not unforeseen by Austin, however. Like many other nature writers, Austin was self-consciously—almost painfully—aware of the limits of linguistic representation and often emphasized them in her work.

Austin is often quite direct in discussing the difficulties involved in trying to accurately express her observations of, and experiences in, the southern California region in words. She prefaces *The Land of Little Rain* by stating, "[T]here are certain peaks, cañons, and clear meadow spaces which are above all compassing of words," and warns readers directly that "if you do not find it all as I write, think me not less dependable nor yourself less clever" (xvi). Austin clearly recognizes the limits of her ability to re-present the reality of the desert Southwest in a book. However, because she is engaged in an attempt to translate some semblance of her experiences there for readers, she simply confronts the problem directly and honestly so that readers become aware of it as well. By emphasizing the limits of language, Austin destroys its usual transparency for readers, forcing them to recognize that what they are experiencing is not the desert itself, but a textual representation of it.

In "The Friend in the Wood," Austin admits the distance between her experiences of the desert and her literary expressions of those experiences, while also emphasizing the craft she puts into those "inadequate" literary representations. She confesses, "By this time I had realized that the illuminations which came from those silent sessions in the wild were the sort of which set in motion the search for words, for nice distinctions of definition, for intricate unfoldings of smooth-pointed buds of suggestion" (1990, 196). Even as she foregrounds the literary craft and choices involved in the linguistic representation of her home region, Austin admits that as careful as those choices are, as accurate as she tries to make her descriptions, they are still merely "suggestions" of meaning.

Austin's initial experiences in the region helped her to understand the limits of language and to recognize the importance of exposing those limits to her readers. As Shelley Armitage notes, "Initially, [Austin] felt the rigors and bleakness of the desert denied her a vocabulary and her mysticism: This was a 'wordless wilderness' for which her reading of Hugh Miller, Emerson, Tennyson, and the Romantic poets hardly prepared her" (1990, 8).

As she notes in her autobiography, Austin, the newly transplanted emi-

grant and nature writer, was in desperate need of what she called "a vocabulary expressive of experience" (1932, 265). Such a vocabulary was to be found
not in the annals of literature but in the land itself. In *Earth Horizon*, Austin
catalogs a variety of things in the region upon which she kept "voluminous
notes" as she began to learn how to write about the West. Her attention to
detail, concern for accuracy, and emphasis on language are evidenced as she
writes, "Along with these things, there were collections of colloquial phrases,
Spanish folklore, intensively pondered adjectives for the color and form of
natural things, the exact word for a mule's cry—'maimed noises'—the
difference between the sound of ripe figs dropping and the patter of olives
shaken down by the wind; single lines of verse imprisoning these things"
(228). Although Austin's use of the word *imprison* to describe how her language manages to capture, embody, or represent the reality of the desert
might strike the poststructuralist critic as evidencing too great a faith in the
accuracy of linguistic representation, it does suggest a second recognition
about language that accords with poststructural theory: the power of language to colonize.

As poststructuralists and postcolonial theorists have thoroughly demonstrated, conquest, whether over people or nature, begins with the act of
naming or linguistically "claiming" the "other." The act of naming, especially
in one's own native tongue or after oneself, establishes a proprietary relationship over the thing being named, assumes the ability to "know" the thing
named, and, whether violence follows the naming or not, exacts a kind of
ideological violence over the "other's" identity. The first act of explorers in
the New World, for example, regardless of their country of origin, was to
name the (already occupied) lands they encountered in their native language
and claim that place in the name of their king or country.

Austin recognizes this colonizing power of language in much of her
work, writing in *Lands of the Sun*: "The name *Sequoia* is one of the few
cheering notes among our habitual botanical stupidities; an attempt to
express quality as it is humanly measured in a name" (1927, 203). Austin then
proceeds to relate the history behind the name: that it was taken from a
Cherokee chief, Sequoyah, who invented an alphabet, migrated west, and
settled in the Upper Kern River area. She also notes the importance of
attempting, in poststructuralist terms, to match the expression of the
signifier (the tree's and chief's names) with the quality of the signified (the

idea of the tree and the story of the chief) and the quality of the referent (the tree and the chief themselves). Austin observes reproachfully of the name: "At least no botanist with his nose in a book has usurped it" (204).

In *The Land of Little Rain*, Austin once again discusses the power and quality of naming, opening her preface by writing, "I confess to a great liking for the Indian fashion of name-giving: every man known by that phrase which best expresses him to whoso [*sic*] names him." Interestingly, this form of name giving embodies another tenet of poststructuralism that posits a kind of multiple subjectivity to describe the fact that we all experience the world—the same objects, events, people, and places—differently based upon our own individual subject position, or perspective. Austin asserts: "No other fashion [of name giving], I think, sets so well with the various natures that inhabit us, and if you agree with me you will understand why so few names are written here as they appear in the geography" (1997, xv). Here, of course, she is alluding to the fact that the majority of the names found in "geography" are the imported and imposed names of colonization, exploitation, and domination rather than the native names of habitation.

In "Lost Borders," Austin offers a second justification for her use of native names, arguing, in a manner that unites poststructuralist and postcolonial theories, that there is less distance among the signifier, signified, and referent in native names than in foreign ones: "[Y]ou can always trust Indian names to express to you the largest truth about any district in the shortest phrases" (1987, 156). Rather than offering a racist or culturally biased remark, Austin is simply referring here to the native practice of naming places with descriptive phrases. Although there are a number of exceptions in both Euro-American and Native American languages, as a general rule we tend to find fewer places named after people and more based upon descriptions of the physical landscape or a particular event that occurred there in indigenous cultures than in colonizing ones. Recognizing these tendencies exposes both an anthropocentric bias and a greater detachment from the natural world in colonizing cultures and their naming practices.

Austin resists this tradition on the grounds that it is both more exploitative of nature and less accurate in its representations of the natural world. She asserts that this "is a country where names mean something. Ubehebe, Pharanagat, Resting Springs, Dead Man's Gulch, Funeral Mountains. . . . There is always a tang of reality about them like the smart of wood smoke to the eyes, that warns of neighboring fires" (156). Austin adopts the traditional ecocritical position that names (at least some of them) can "mean something," or can adequately refer to or represent the natural world, yet she maintains a protopoststructuralist position that recognizes that they do not directly re-present or re-create that reality but point to it suggestively, just as surely as smoke points to fire.

AUSTIN, REPRESENTATION, AND FIELD EXPERIENCE

The particular strength of Austin's recognitions about the limits of literary representation is that they were founded on her own experiences living in the region while simultaneously writing about it for audiences who had never been there. Although Austin's first encounters left her grasping for the ideas and language necessary to express herself in a "wordless wilderness," her thirst for experiencing the region and learning from its inhabitants eventually led her to find a language so suitable, so fitted to the terrain, that her work still stands among the best desert literature in the English language.

As she records in her autobiography and many scholars have noted, Austin spent an extraordinary amount of time exploring the rugged and sparsely populated deserts of southern California and Nevada. She went on extensive camping trips with her husband, angled the snow-fed streams dropping down out of the Sierra Nevada, spent a great deal of time out on the Beale Ranch in the Tejon Region, and enjoyed riding atop the Mojave stage, swapping stories with the driver and perusing the landscape. In addition, she collected stories, information, insights, perceptions, ideas, and language from almost everyone she came into contact with, including the Paiute and Shoshone still living in the area, Mexican and Basque sheepherders, miners, stagecoach drivers, faro dealers, "bawdy girls," and children. Austin's experiences in the region form the foundation of her work, informing its literary style, prose rhythms, visual imagery, and ethical stance, as well as animating it with colorful characters, rugged landscapes, and interesting events. In short, both the form and content of Austin's fiction are derived directly from the southern California bioregions.

Melody Graulich notes the significance of Austin's personal experiences on her work: "Austin's Tejon notebooks show that she had been collecting stories and experimenting with form and style since arriving in California. . . . But it would take almost ten years for her stylistic experiments to pay off and for her understanding of her subject matter to mature" (1987, 10). Nowhere is this evidenced more clearly than in a comparison of Austin's literary representations of the region in "One Hundred Miles on Horseback" (1889) and *The Land of Little Rain* (1903). During the fourteen years separating these works, Austin's perceptions of the desert changed as her knowledge and experience grew, until the land dictated not only *what* she wrote about but also *how* she wrote about it.

In order to see clearly how Austin's perceptions evolved between the two works, I will examine her representations of the region's weather, landscape, native species, and local inhabitants. In "One Hundred Miles on Horseback," Austin describes "the pleasure of a journey on horseback through the most picturesque part of California," yet she evidences a variety of culturally determined notions that distance her from appreciating, experiencing, and accurately describing the region. She confesses, "A drizzling rain, forerunner of the rainy season, compelled me to abandon my equestrian ambitions and make an inglorious retreat to the canvas shelter of the wagon" for the rest of "the afternoon journey" (1996a, 25).

Fourteen years later, in *The Land of Little Rain,* she praises the pocket hunter because "he had gotten to that point where he knew no bad weather, and all places were equally happy so long as they were out of doors." Although Austin herself has not developed the "kind of weather shell" of the pocket hunter and the indigenes of the region, her attitude toward inclement weather has changed: "I do not know just how long it takes to become saturated with the elements so that one takes no account of them. Myself can never get past the glow and exhilaration of a storm, the wrestle of long dust-heavy winds, the play of live thunder on the rocks, nor past the keen fret of fatigue when the storm outlasts physical endurance" (1997, 47).

After ten years of living and traveling in the deserts and mountains of the Owens Valley area, Austin has developed a much more favorable view of the region's weather and an ability to distinguish between the characteristics of different types of storms. Whereas rain "drizzles" in her early representations, in the latter text storms "glow," "wrestle," and "play." In addition, she no longer alienates herself physically from such storms but has experienced at least some of them without mediation. The final line implies that Austin has actually felt "the keen fret of fatigue" caused by remaining out in such weather until the body reaches its physical limits.

Austin's perceptions of the desert itself have also changed, evolving from her preconceived and culturally biased notions of environmental aesthetics to a perspective that allows her to appreciate the region for its own inherent beauty and character. On her first journey into the region's arid lands she laments, "An autumn landscape in California is strangely devoid of color, and this silent succumbing to a process of nature made us homesick for the glory of the October hills of Illinois" (1996a, 25). Here, Austin imports culturally determined notions of fall "color" from a completely different bioregion and thus is incapable of "seeing" the desert as it truly is.

After having lived in the desert for more than a decade, however, she lauds its beauty, stating that "[n]one other than this long brown land lays such a hold on the affections. The rainbow hills, the tender bluish mists, the luminous radiance of spring, have the lotus charm" (1997, 11). By this point in her life Austin is able to recognize, and represent in literature, the desert's own colors, its own beauty and charm. Austin no longer has to mediate her representations through the filter of transplanted culture but is capable of representing the desert's inherent aesthetic value as it is. She has also recognized that her earlier aesthetic revulsion was not due to any quality inherent in the desert itself but was imposed upon it by the expectations of culture. "And yet—and yet—is it not perhaps to satisfy expectation that one falls into the tragic key in writing of desertness?" she asks her readers in an effort to make them aware of the same tendency in themselves (12).

Austin's love for the southwestern landscape extended to its inhabitants as well, as she demonstrates in her evolving representations of the region's wildlife and local residents. She complains, for example, in "One Hundred Miles on Horseback": "During that night coyotes came close up to the camp and howled, and growled, and barked, and shrieked like so many demons. There seems to be no limit to the hideous noises the animals can produce" (1996a, 28). The demonization of predators and the desert are traditional biblical themes, just as Austin's description of the "Mexican shepherds with their flocks and faithful dogs recalled vividly well-known scriptural scenes" (26). In addition, Austin applies such adjectives as *hideous* and descriptive verbs like *shrieked* to the yipping and howling of the coyotes, exhibiting a stark contrast to her later representation of them in *The Land of Little Rain*, where she describes a lone coyote signaling his pack "in a long-drawn, dolorous whine" (1997, 19).

Like Austin, I can recall the first time I heard the cacophony of yips, barks, and howls of a pack of coyotes close by camp in the darkness of night. I was about ten at the time and camping alone, and I did, indeed, find it an unnerving experience. However, as soon as I recognized that they were no threat to me and began to listen to the quality of their voices, without allowing any culturally induced nightmares of werewolves to distort the experience, the rising symphonic, multivoiced sound of their chorus was both haunting and beautiful. I sat up in the darkness listening to their singing for quite some time. And as the last of their voices dropped off and faded into the night, I found myself wishing fervently that they might come back and serenade me once again.

Similarly, as soon as we divest ourselves of our culturally induced prejudices against such predators—formed primarily by an ill-informed livestock industry—the intelligent nature and beneficial ecosystemic role of the coyote becomes apparent. As Austin notes in *The Land of Little Rain,* the coyote is intelligent, resourceful, and can actually aid other creatures in their survival: "The coyote is your true water-witch, one who snuffs and paws, snuffs and paws again at the smallest spot of moisture-scented earth until he has freed the blind water from the soil. Many water-holes are no more than this detected by the lean hobo of the hills where not even an Indian would look for it" (18). Although her description does anthropomorphize the coyote, calling it both witch and hobo, it is also extremely accurate about coyote behavior, recognizes their inherent intelligence, and is based upon personal experience.

As she admits later, she has often trailed a coyote "and found his track such as a man, a very intelligent man accustomed to hill-country, and a little cautious, would make to the same point. . . . [I]t is usually the best way,—and making his point with the greatest economy" (20). Here, Austin relates the coyote's intelligence in navigation not only to that of men, but also to that of a "very intelligent man" who is "accustomed to hill-country." As she states later in *The Land of Little Rain,* "The coyote is your real lord of the mesa" (96). In the intervening years between the composition of her first serious nature essay about the region and *The Land of Little Rain,* Austin has been able to observe, learn about, and come to appreciate the coyote on its own terms, in its own land.

Finally, Austin's representations of the human inhabitants of the country of lost borders change as well. Her first impressions of the Mexican shepherds of the region is that they are "outlandish," their houses "overflowing with dogs and children in dirty but picturesque confusion" (1996a, 26, 28). "Occasionally," she continues, "somewhat back from the house a little white wooden cross gleaming over a mound of earth made pathetically human a scene that might otherwise have been disgusting or merely amusing" (28). Here Austin's own ethnocentric prejudices are evident as she, the white colonizer, views the "disgusting," "dirty," and "amusing" colonized other who is only made "pathetically human" by the presence of death, signified by the cross, another sign of the dominant, colonizing hegemony.

By the time Austin wrote *The Land of Little Rain*, however, she had lived among both the Paiute and the Mexican inhabitants of the Owens Valley, made lasting friendships, and successfully dropped her culturally inherited prejudices so that she could finally see them as they were. She opens "The Little Town of the Grapevines" by saying, "There are still some places in the west where the quails cry '*cuidado*'; where all the speech is soft, all the manners gentle; where all the dishes have *chile* in them, and they make more of the Sixteenth of September than they do of the Fourth of July" (1997, 163). Though this representation does smack of romanticism, in many ways it is the representation of an insider to the culture, rather than that of a colonizer with cultural blinders on. The term *cuidado* needs no explanation, nor does the "Sixteenth of September," just as throughout the chapter the town is called by its Spanish name, El Pueblo de Las Uvas.

Austin's descriptions of the residents of the pueblo contrast markedly from her earlier descriptions of the "outlandish" or "pathetically human" occupants; in fact, while noting some of the town's problems, she elevates most of its inhabitants to an admirable level of humanity, decency, and compassion. She ends the chapter and the book by addressing her readers directly: "Come away, you who are obsessed with your own importance in the scheme of things, and have got nothing you did not sweat for, come away by the brown valleys and full bosomed hills to the even-breathing days, to the kindliness, earthiness, ease of El Pueblo de Las Uvas" (171).

Austin's ability to see and appreciate the desert and its inhabitants on their own terms evolved over the years due to her own experiences on the land and with its residents. By describing the land and its inhabitants accurately and sympathetically, Austin hopes to offer readers a vicarious experience similar to the physical and imaginative experiences that she enjoyed in the region.

READING AUSTIN IN THE FIELD

As many scholars have noted, Austin's fiction contains a fair amount of auto-biography; it is primarily derived from her own experiences or those of others she met in the rugged deserts and mountains of the Southwest. In "Mary Austin's Nature: Refiguring Tradition Through the Voices of Identity," Anna Carew-Miller notes that Austin's "narrative voice reflects her experience of nonhuman nature" and that this experience is the primary factor informing her fiction (1998, 79). Comparing the development of Austin's narrative voices in her fiction and her partly fictional autobiography, *Earth Horizon,* with those of her rooted female characters, such as Seyavi and Walking Woman, Carew-Miller contends that as an author, Austin strove to become so connected to the land that she could "write through her body, not her mind. Only then will experience supersede analysis in her understanding and representation of the natural" (88).

Unlike Austin, however, many Austin scholars have had little opportunity to study and explore the lands she writes about in a sustained manner and thus lack the experience Austin advocates. As John P. O'Grady notes in *Pilgrims to the Wild,* one of the consistent themes in Austin's work is "her insistence on the *experiential quality* of the wild. Although she knew that words were not up to the task of conveying such experience, she nevertheless continued to attempt its articulation" (1993, 127). Yet this attempt at articu-lating physical experiences in the natural landscape has been largely ignored by ecocritics. Because of our methodological constraints, we seem to be vol-untarily ignoring one of the most salient features of Austin's work and, by extension, one of the most important elements affecting all environmental texts, namely, their environment.

Such omissions may necessarily limit our knowledge of environmental texts and their relationships with American ecocultural regions simply by delimiting what we can include within our field of inquiry. Likewise, they also threaten us with critical and interpretive inaccuracy, as we remain largely ignorant of the very real physical, historical, and environmental influences operating in a given text.

Austin recognizes that many of her readers, lacking their own experience of the desert, may have difficulty understanding and appreciating it as she has. Therefore, she consistently adopts the second person, addressing her readers directly in order to encourage them to experience the arid Southwest themselves. In "Jimville"—a town Austin likens to a desert tortoise—she explicitly informs her readers that, like her, they will have to drop their culturally received ideas of the desert if they wish to truly see it. "You could never get into any proper relation to Jimville unless you could slough off and swallow your acquired prejudices as a lizard does his skin" (1997, 73). The best way to shed such prejudices, according to Austin, is through direct experience of the land. However, for those readers who are unable to gain these experiences physically, Austin at least provides them imaginatively by placing readers in the country of lost borders through the use of second-person prose.

Austin uses the second person to emphasize the importance of direct experience as well as to resist the mediated nature of linguistic representation. Writing in the second person also functions rhetorically to minimize the distance between the reader and the referent. For Austin, it is a conscious and deliberate strategy to overcome the inevitable mediation of language— the representative distance that exists among the signifier, signified, and referent. Placing the reader in the desert rhetorically through the use of second-person prose is the closest Austin can come to placing the reader there physically. She advises readers, "[F]or seeing and understanding [the land], the best time is when you have the longest leave to stay. And here is a hint if you would attempt the stateliest approaches; travel light, and as much as possible live off the land" (117). She encourages readers to gain as intimate an experience with the land as possible, not only traveling through the region but also living off whatever it provides, foraging for edible plants and hunting wild game. This type of interaction places one in much closer contact with the landscape and forces one to study its native species and their characteristics and habits very closely.

Direct experience of the land was exceedingly important to Austin, not only for understanding it, but also for understanding the literature written about it. In her notable work on American literature, *The American Rhythm*, Austin details a theory of "geographic determinism," arguing that the most important influence on American literature is the natural and geographical region from which it is produced. She argues that as American literary culture matures, we will find an increasing correspondence between its rhythms and those of the regional landscapes that produce that culture. Thomas W. Ford notes in "*The American Rhythm:* Mary Austin's Poetic Principle," "Mrs. Austin argues that rhythm is an *experience,* and as such is distinct from our intellectual perception of that experience. . . . The stimuli come from the environment, from the land, and a sense of well-being occurs in the human organism when the rhythms are coordinated" (1970, 4). Without our own experience in that land and with its rhythms, it will be difficult for us to fully understand or recognize the rhythms of its literature. Similarly, James Ruppert observes, "Austin saw movement, both the movements of necessary social labor in the environment and the movements of personal response, as playing an important role in the transmission of the rhythms of the land into the rhythms of the dance-drama and, ultimately song/poetry" (1983, 379). If we accept Austin's assertions about her own writing, we must be able to study both the rhythms of the landscapes she wrote about as well as the rhythms of her prose; thus, we must incorporate some manner of direct experience of, and movement in, those landscapes into our scholarly practice.

In "Lost Borders," for example, Austin asserts, "Every story of that country is colored by the fashion of life there, breaking up in swift, passionate intervals between long, dun stretches, like the land that out of hot sinks of desolation heaves up great bulks of granite ranges with opal shadows playing in their shining, snow-piled curves" (1987, 157). In addition to explicitly arguing that the land shapes the story, Austin illustrates her concept of geographic determinism in the long, slow, jumbled rhythm of her prose that mirrors the vast spaces and long silences of the broken and rugged basin and range. As is often the case in her work, Austin's prose is subtly onomatopoeic here. Instead of merely describing the elements of her southwestern landscape, she attempts to embody the rhythms and characteristics of the land in her prose, thereby resisting the mediated nature and distancing effects of linguistic representation. This careful attention to rhythm—this attempt to close the gap in signification between word and world—represents a conscious and concerted effort on Austin's part. In her autobiography Austin explains this correspondence between text and terrain in the third person, stating, "She had been trying to hit upon the key for it [*The Land of Little Rain*] for a year or more, and found it at last in the rhythm of the twenty-mule teams that creaked in and out of the borax works, the rhythm of the lonely lives blown across the trails" (1932, 296).

For Austin, the land not only informs the content of her work but shapes its formal structures as well. As William Scheick points out, "Austin particularly appreciates the minimalism of the desert" (1992, 38). One of the region's greatest values, and most distinguishing characteristics, for Austin, is its sparsely populated nature. Whether one is talking about the desert's native flora and fauna or native and immigrant human populations, a clear pattern emerges: space, silence, and scarcity dominate the landscape and define its inhabitants. In *The Land of Little Rain*, Austin celebrates this quality of desert flora: "There is neither poverty of soil nor species to account for the sparseness of desert growth, but simply that each plant requires more room. So much earth must be preempted to extract so much moisture" (1997, 8).

In her prose, Austin attempts to embody these minimalistic qualities of the desert by populating her stories with very few characters, allowing them very little speech, and spacing out both descriptions of their actions and instances of dialogue with long narrative sections of philosophical reflection, commentary, or descriptions of the surrounding landscape. In addition, she often attempts to infuse her prose with silence by leaving much unsaid and suggesting or merely hinting at her central point. She describes the ever present danger of dehydration, death, and mummification, for example, by euphemistically stating, "To underestimate one's thirst, to pass a given landmark to the right or left, to find a dry spring where one looked for running water—there is no help for any of these things" (6). The result of not finding water in the desert, in Austin's linguistic representation, is a nonaction, a nonevent. Instead of describing a flurry of frenzied activity, trying to find or obtain water, or detailing the slow, painful process of dying of thirst, Austin silences her prose. Instead of describing a presence—in this case death or the actions to prevent it—she posits an absence: the absence of help. As Austin asserts in "Regionalism in American Fiction" and embodies in this example, "The regionally interpretive book must not only be about the country, it must be of it, flower of its stalk and root" (Ellis 1996, 139).

AUSTIN'S MULTIPLE PERSPECTIVES

A final strategy Austin adopts for confronting problems of representation and authority is to adopt a number of different subject positions from which to observe the world. Rather than assuming the traditional stance of objective observer who holds authority over whatever he or she describes, Austin writes from a variety of perspectives. In *Earth Horizon*, Austin's autobiography, this practice of developing multiple personae or perspectives is significantly foregrounded. She writes of "I-Mary" in the first person and "Mary-by-herself" in the third person, alternating between describing her own actions and thoughts as those of one or the other of the two personae.

These two personae are quite different. As Linda K. Karrell observes, the "self-confident 'I-Mary' . . . is associated with writing, creativity, and . . . requires little emotional nurturance." On the other hand, "Mary-by-herself" is "much more uncertain, lonely, and achingly vulnerable to rejection" (1997, 269). Austin illustrates the poststructural recognition that pure objectivity is never possible because we are always already perceiving the world from within a particular perspective—a perspective that varies from person to person, as well as varying within the same individual from time to time or place to place.

In her fiction Austin extends her use of multiple-subject perspectives to adopt ecocentric points of view that stand in direct opposition to the traditional authority of the human observer. They provide readers with a variety of perspectives from which to view the desert country, and by adopting the point of view of particular animal species, places, and processes Austin encourages readers to drop their inherent anthropocentric perspectives. In *The Land of Little Rain,* for example, she adopts an explicitly coyote-centric point of view and forces readers not only to see the world, but also to see themselves from the coyote's perspective. Addressing readers in the second person, Austin observes, "[H]e makes sure you are armed with no long black instrument to spit your teeth into his vitals at a thousand yards" (1997, 96). In this passage Austin describes a rifle as she imagines a coyote might perceive it—a "long black instrument" for spitting "teeth" at prey. Although Austin must anthropomorphize a bit here, this description represents a concerted effort to make readers aware of the subjective positions of other desert inhabitants. Simultaneously, she encourages readers to recognize that their own way of seeing the world is not objective, or authoritative, but merely one of an infinite number of subjective perceptions. This destroys the transparency and assumed authority of the human observer's gaze and successfully resists its colonizing nature.

In addition to the artistic implications of these passages, they also introduce an element of realism (always a concern for Austin). As a longtime hunter, wildlife observer, and outdoor recreationalist, I support Austin's claim that animals like coyotes are intelligent enough to distinguish between a hunter and a hiker and even to tell the difference between the same person engaged in each activity. I have often known coyotes and rabbits to allow me to approach them very closely, and to even demonstrate curiosity toward me when I have been empty-handed, but to avoid my approach and run at first clear sight of me when I have had either my bow or rifle in hand. I can even recall one curious coyote who, after we watched each other for quite some time, disappeared in a flash as soon as I picked up my bow. Many hunters and hikers have had the uncanny experience of seeing a multitude of different wild creatures when hiking for pleasure or scouting terrain without a gun but not seeing a single animal in the same area when carrying their hunting tools.

As Austin describes in her chapter "The Scavengers," the desert dwellers in her country observe each other's behavior, listen to the calls and warning signals of other species, and demonstrate an intelligent awareness of the habits of others and what they signify. "Probably we never fully credit the interdependence of wild creatures, and their cognizance of the affairs of their own kind" (36). By adopting the perspective of these wild creatures, Austin is better able to demonstrate this "cognizance" and aids readers in dropping their culturally limited perceptions of the desert and its non-human inhabitants.

Austin pushes her experiments with perspective even further in the chapter "My Neighbor's Field," explaining, "Naboth expects to make town lots of it and his fortune in one and the same day; but when I take the trail to talk with old Seyavi at the campoodie, it occurs to me that though the field may serve good turn in those days it will hardly be the happier. No, certainly not the happier" (88). The "happiness" or "unhappiness" of the field implies a kind of sentience on its part. In this final passage of the chapter, Austin asks readers to adopt the perspective of Naboth's field, a place that up until now she has so far been observing, describing, and representing from the human point of view. She nudges readers subtly toward this "field-centric" perspective by admitting that it "occurs to me" that the field "will hardly be the happier." Then she repeats this idea in a short sentence fragment that acts as the final word of the chapter on the subject of Naboth's field: "No, certainly not the happier." The brevity of the sentence, its grammatical division from the preceding sentences, its repetition of the earlier field-centric recognition, and its placement at the end of the chapter all serve to emphasize the significance of the field's subjective experience and perception.

As Austin asserts in "The Friend in the Wood," "Even stick and stone, as well as bush and weed, are discovered to be charged with an intense secret life of their own; the sap courses, the stones vibrate with ion-shaking rhythms of energy, as I too shake inwardly to the reverberating tread of life and time; they are each in its sphere as important to themselves as I to me" (1990, 196). Austin not only posits that plants, animals, and inanimate natural objects have a type of sentience, but also that they have, and are aware of, their own inherent value, a value equal to that which we assign to ourselves.

By adopting these varied perspectives, or subject positions, Austin is able to resist the distancing effects of language while encouraging readers to see the natural world from an ecocentric perspective. In addition, by embodying these multiple-subject positions, she is able to more accurately describe the various features, details, and experiences of the deserts and mountains of the southern California ecoregion. The Owens Valley area Austin writes about covers a number of distinct ecosystems and ecotones, ranging from desert lakes to playas and mesquite-covered basins, from arroyos and sagebrush steppes to the pinyon and juniper forests of the desert ranges and the Jeffrey and ponderosa pine of the southern Sierra Nevada.

This wide variety of both ecosystems and experiences was emphasized to me on the last day of an early spring backpacking trip my wife and I took on the Pacific Crest Trail just west of Austin's home in Independence, California. After camping on the Kern and spending several crisp spring days exploring the "Streets of the Mountains," as Austin calls them, we began climbing over a high pass in order to leave the trail and drop down the eastern face of the Sierra Nevada, ultimately coming out at Naboth's field and Austin's home. As we climbed toward the pass, we soon found ourselves confronted by six-foot-deep drifts of snow. A blanket of hard, crusty snow covered the entire area, leaving no way to circle the drifts and forcing us to hike over. In some areas the surface of the snowpack had melted and refrozen enough times to support our weight; in others we broke through, postholing with each step. With forty-pound packs on and no snowshoes, we struggled forward, thinking light thoughts and stepping as gingerly as possible across the icy drifts, only to break through with every few steps. The icy edges of the hard crust cut and clawed at our bare calves and shins, punishing us severely for each misplaced step. Within a few hours we were dropping rapidly down the face of what Austin called "the Sierra Wall" and could see the Owens Valley below us. We followed an old cattle trail down through the pines and into the lower elevation oaks and finally out into the sagebrush scrub. As we hiked through the now palpitating desert heat, the blood on my shins and calves dried and crusted over with absorbed layers of dust and sand. We wiped our sweaty brows, drained the last drops from our water bottles, and moved on through the sage, bitterbrush, and mesquite. Once again, I was reminded of the wonderful variety of landscapes in this region, a country of lost borders to be sure, but a country full of amazing diversity and starkly contrasting places.

In "Regionalism in American Fiction," Austin explains what is required to get to know her beloved land of little rain:

Time is the essence of the undertaking, time to live into the land and absorb it; still more time to cure the reading public of its preference for something less than the proverbial bird's-eye view of the American scene, what you might call an automobile eye view, something slithering and blurred, nothing so sharply discriminated that it arrests the speed-numbed mind to understand. (1996b, 140)

....

CHAPTER FOUR

Protecting Arid Lands
with Austin's Aesthetics

The earth is no wanton to give up all her best to every comer, but keeps a sweet, separate intimacy for each.

MARY AUSTIN,
The Land of Little Rain

As the dusky shadows of night rise out of canyons and creep out of caves, we climb a steep butte, moving between two cliff arms toward the darkening night sky. My students and I are deep in the heart of Austin's land of little rain, a country of lost borders and blurred boundaries. We have been exploring dry desert washes, wind-carved canyons, and cave-ridden cliffs all day. The land is so pocked and punctured, so brightly bathed in sunlight and shadow, that we feel as if we have been witnessing a sermon in form and color, a song in shape and stone. But now darkness is climbing like a tide out of the narrow canyons, and the stars are just starting to appear as tiny pinholes in the falling curtain of night.

As we move through the sage and mesquite, an erratic fluttering of small black shapes stops us in our tracks. "Bats," I whisper, as the blurring black shapes whiz by our heads and wheel up into the star-studded sky. We stand watching, still as stones, mesmerized by their movement. They flutter about from one cliff face to another, disappearing for a moment in shadow and then pausing for an instant, bat-shaped against the last faint glowing of the sky. We cannot move, we are so filled with wonder. At times they swoop in close, with a whirring of wings and a breath of wind. Smiles erupt on our faces; our eyes sparkle and flash in the night. In the exchange of shared glances, eyes and hearts say what words could never express: "This moment, this thing we are doing, this memory we will share, is somehow more valuable to me than I can even express or understand."

It is curious, I think, that the flight and feeding of bats have done this to us. These are supposed to be dangerous, ugly, rabies-infested harbingers of evil, yet tonight they fill us with nothing but awe and wonder. The graceful dance of their intricate and swarming flight plays out a silent symphony over our heads. A thousand near misses and abruptly avoided head-on collisions become, as we watch, a graceful dance of skill and sophistication, the purposeful pursuit of insect prey.

When our stunned and reverent silence finally passes, we begin to talk about the experience. How strange, we observe, that one of the most beautiful things any of us has ever seen was this flight of thousands of bats, creatures most people consider ugly, dirty, and dangerous. It is also interesting, we note, that it occurred here, in the middle of a high-elevation desert, a landscape most people see as inhospitable and barren.

Although the deserts and mountains of southern California held a powerful and unique beauty for Austin, she recognized that this view was not commonly held by her readers and those who had recently emigrated to the arid Southwest. Throughout her work, Austin attempts to alter these preconceived notions of beauty by moving from the traditional, culturally received aesthetic tastes of her readers to her own highly developed environmental aesthetics. She also encourages readers to experience the desert directly in order to come to an appreciation of its unique beauty, and she utilizes both scientific information and imaginative speculation to inform and shape readers' aesthetic tastes.

Austin recognized that one of the reasons for our failure to appreciate the beauty of desert lands is that they do not conform to our traditional notions of the beautiful and the good. Because the desert does not readily support human life, it is often associated with death, ugliness, and waste. Austin confronts our traditional associations of the "useful" with the "good" and the "good" with the "beautiful" in order to develop an alternative paradigm that is capable of seeing the desert's value in nonutilitarian ways. She writes, "Desert is a loose term to indicate land that supports no man; whether the land can be bitted [*sic*] and broken to that purpose is not proven. Void of life it never is, however dry and villainous the soil" (1997, 3). In this opening passage of *The Land of Little Rain*, Austin exposes the desert's relative lack of utilitarian value and then defends it against our most common criticism of such arid regions: that they are devoid of life. Throughout *The Land of Little Rain* she continues to demonstrate that the desert has inherent value, a rich diversity of life, and a unique charm and stunning beauty, all of which establish its value independent of the uses to which humans can put it.

This emphasis on the nonutilitarian values of arid regions demonstrates one of the great advantages of incorporating Austin's work into a scientifically focused environmental education curriculum. As Stan Godlovitch observes in "Evaluating Nature Aesthetically," we typically hand over

> the preservation and protection of nature to "nature critics" much as the protection and preservation of cultural heritage are left in the able hands of our cultural experts. These nature critics belong to a varied circle including conservation biologists, restoration ecologists, parks and wildlife managers, not to mention natural resource managers and environmental policy planners. (1998a, 113)

Unless these "nature critics" are trained to recognize the nonutilitarian values of natural landscapes, Godlovitch argues, "the aesthetic dimension will simply be cancelled out as an effective factor in nature conservation policy, leaving the field considerably more under sway of seductively operational and measurable resource values" (113). By incorporating Mary Austin's work into environmental education curricula, we can include the aesthetic and nonutilitarian values of desert landscapes with the variety of economic values and uses that must be considered when making decisions about the management of our arid lands. Without such explorations, our environmental studies students will be incapable of assessing the recreational, spiritual, and aesthetic worth of such landscapes and will necessarily consider only the economic value of resource development and the ecological value of ecosystem protection when making management or policy decisions.

Considering that recreation has rapidly risen to become the number-one source of income on our public lands, future public land managers and policy makers must be capable of taking into account the host of values, most of which are very difficult to quantify, that are associated with nonutilitarian uses of natural landscapes. Godlovitch notes that in determining conservation priorities, extensive consideration of the natural values of the site is undertaken, and "[g]enerally, these values are divided into resource and nonresource categories. This reflects not only economic and non-economic value, but often expresses the difference between easily quantifiable and not so easily quantifiable (or unquantifiable) values" (121). Unless future land managers are trained to be aware of, and sensitive to, these "unquantifiable" values, they will probably be omitted from the analysis, and a disproportionate level of importance will be accorded to resource-based uses that can be quantified. Ultimately, this will result in a dangerous marginalization of recreational and ecological values in favor of resource extraction and development.

One of the best ways to train young scientists and resource managers to assess the unquantifiable values of natural landscapes is to expose them to the field of environmental aesthetics and literature. The aesthetic appreciation that we derive from natural landscapes stands as one of the least-quantifiable elements of recreational value, yet it can be tremendously important. In 1991, the Environmental Improvement Program (EIP) was established in the Lake Tahoe Basin to improve the clarity of the lake's water. Millions of dollars in federal and state funding were allocated to the program, and numerous federal and local agencies, nonprofit organizations, and local businesses were marshaled for its support. Long known for its clear-blue waters and associated recreational activities, Lake Tahoe had been losing water clarity and its characteristic brilliant-blue hues. The simple recognition was made, by local businesses and governmental agencies alike, that the aesthetic appeal of the lake's clear-blue waters translated directly into hundreds of millions of dollars in tourism-based income. Although the EIP program thus seeks to improve lake-water clarity through ecological restoration and ecosystem protection, the original impetus for the program stemmed from a recognition of the economic importance of environmental aesthetics. Without the ability of land managers and policy planners to recognize and assess the nonutilitarian values of the lake's clear waters, local communities would have suffered economically and the basin's ecosystems and wildlife would have suffered ecologically.

Training in environmental aesthetics, then, can have enormous practical consequences for future public land managers and policy makers. Austin's work provides fertile ground for exploring issues of environmental aesthetics as they relate to arid environments, exposing students to both the unique beauty of desert regions and the common cultural preconditioning that limits our ability to recognize those aesthetic values.

ENVIRONMENTAL AESTHETICS

The term *aesthetic* comes from the Greek *aesthetikos* (having to do with perception) and *aesthesis* (having to do with the sensuous). Environmental aesthetics, then, is concerned with both how we perceive or represent particular environments and how we experience them physically. Because of this dual focus, field-based explorations in environmental literature offer a useful manner in which to approach issues in environmental aesthetics, giving students the opportunity to study both artistic representations of the natural world and their own sensual experiences in that world.

Environmental aestheticians commonly divide experience into the instrumental and the noninstrumental, placing aesthetic experiences firmly in the second category. As Paul J. Olscamp explains, "The instrumental kind of experience involves aiming at some end or goal, and its *raison d'etre* is that end goal. The non-instrumental does not seem to be goal directed" (1965, 251). The vast majority of our relationships with the natural world fall into the instrumental category, their reason for existing resting upon some goal external to the environment itself: the collection of food, resources, data, and the like. This end goal directs how we relate to the natural world, most often distancing us from intimate connection and understanding because the goal, rather than the environment itself, is the focal point of our attention and action.

Aesthetic appreciation, on the other hand, is much like play; it has purposiveness without being directed by a purpose. As Norman Fischer explains, "[P]urposiveness without purpose means that, although art frees us from a sense of purpose associated with our pragmatic relation to the world, it nevertheless has its own purposiveness" (1996, 368). The purposiveness in environmental aesthetics is to appreciate a particular environment for its own inherent aesthetic qualities and values, and thus our attention is directed to the landscape itself. This can be contrasted with such purpose-oriented forms of relating to the natural world as logging, mining, ranching, and many types of industrial recreation in which the ultimate purpose directing one's interaction with the environment is paramount to the environment itself.

Many forms of environmental science actually fall into this noninstrumental category. Whereas they most assuredly evidence purposiveness in the collection of data, design of experiments, and so on, they often have no purpose external to the environment itself, their ultimate goal being to increase our understanding of a particular aspect of that ecosystem. Additionally, the usefulness of preserving particular environments for scientific study is often as hard to quantify as the benefit of preserving those same areas for their aesthetic value. Both scientific study and aesthetic appreciation, though they can be applied in purposeful ways to understand, restore, or protect particular places, are more closely associated in their noninstrumental values than we commonly assume. Both approaches to the natural world focus directly on nature itself, its inhabitants, features, and processes, rather than on any human use to which it may be put.

Therefore, aesthetic appreciation and many forms of scientific study bring us into a much closer relation with the natural world than other forms of experience that fall into the instrumental category. Instrumental approaches to the natural world tend to involve a mediating effect between the observer and the observed, distancing us from the natural world itself. Austin notes this tendency in her description of Naboth's field, explaining that the townspeople's instrumental perspective prohibits them from appreciating the field itself and its role in the surrounding ecosystem: "The field is not greatly esteemed of the town, not being put to the plough nor affording firewood, but breeding all manner of wild seeds that go down in the irrigating ditches to come up as weeds in the gardens and grass plots." From an aesthetic and scientific perspective, on the other hand, Austin is able to value and appreciate the field as it is, as well as how it benefits the local ecosystem, without placing any anthropocentrically utilitarian judgments upon it. She confesses, "[W]hen I had no more than seen it in the charm of its spring smiling, I knew I should have no peace until I had bought ground and built me a house beside it, with a little wicket to go in and out at all hours, as afterward came about" (1997, 81). As Austin notes in this passage, and as the rest of the chapter illustrates, her aesthetic appreciation eventually led to a much more intimate relationship with and understanding of the field than was possible for the townspeople locked into their instrumental view of the natural world.

Though concern for the resource or instrumental value of natural landscapes tends to distance us from those environments, it also places us in a position of control over them. As Paul J. Olscamp observes, "In the instrumental experience, I must identify the present object as something which can be so manipulated that it will lead to a certain result. I must be able to *control* the means." The aesthetic experience, on the other hand, establishes a much more egalitarian relationship between the observer and the observed and recognizes the values inherent in natural environments that stand outside of human control and manipulation. According to Olscamp, "[B]oth the object and the observer are contributors to the value realized in the aesthetic experience. But this is not a controller-controlled relationship" (1965, 254).

Giving students trained within the sciences some experience with this form of "control-free" observation and interaction can serve as a much needed corrective to the positions of dominion often necessitated by manipulative field studies. By virtue of its methodology, the scientific method often entails that practitioners control and manipulate species and systems in order to improve experimental design, gather conclusive data, and test conclusions. If our students, however, are never trained in nonmanipulative methods of observation, analysis, and appreciation and never gain experience with the less quantifiable values of natural environments, such as their aesthetic, cultural, and spiritual values, they will be incapable of determining the most appropriate uses for particular places. As Stan Godlovitch notes, "The overall value of a site is determined by taking into account a range of resource and non-resource values including economic, recreational, ecological, aesthetic, scientific, religious, and other dimensions of value. Conservation priority attaches to sites with the highest overall value" (1998a, 121).

Incorporating the exploration of environmental aesthetics into environmental studies curricula, then, has a number of theoretical and practical benefits. In addition to offering pragmatic guidance in distinguishing between the various forms of value found in a particular environment, such an approach may also bring us into more intimate relationships with the natural world, relationships that are not predicated upon human use and manipulation. This becomes especially important when we turn our attention toward arid landscapes, which do not readily offer significant aesthetic or resource values. In the United States we have too often been incapable of recognizing the ecological and aesthetic significance of our arid lands, most often using them as locations for weapons training, toxic waste dumps, and other exploitative activities.

AUSTIN AND THE AESTHETICS OF "UGLINESS"

Because arid environments are not easily exploitable and do not readily support nonadaptive peoples, they have traditionally been represented in our culture as barren wastelands, devoid of life, and promising the possibility of death for all who enter. Austin asserts that we have commonly failed to see the aesthetic value of arid lands because "there is something incomprehensible to the man-mind in the concurrence of death and beauty." The ever present possibility of death in Austin's land of little rain overshadows the tender play of light, the splashes of varied colors, the symphonic compositions of sound and shape that, in other more hospitable landscapes, are commonly noticed and valued. In her characteristically rhythmic and lyrical prose, Austin asks her readers: "Shall the tender opal mists betray you? The airy depth of mountain blueness, the blazonry of painted wind-scoured buttes, the far peaks molten with the alpen glow, cooled by the rising of the velvet violet twilight tide, and the leagues and leagues of stars? As easy for a man to believe that a beautiful woman can be cruel" (1987, 43). In this passage from "Lost Borders," Austin openly confronts our common inability to appreciate the beauty of desert landscapes, addressing readers directly in the second person while composing lyrical descriptions of the "unlovable" desert. In addition, she notes that those who see the desert as beautiful are often unable to recognize its dangerous qualities. We seem incapable, she asserts, of recognizing that the desert simultaneously and unproblematically embodies both death and beauty.

By confronting the problem that our fear of death poses for our ability to aesthetically appreciate rugged environments, Austin makes her readers conscious of the anthropocentric and culturally received notions of beauty that direct how they perceive the natural world. As Yuriko Saito notes in "The Aesthetics of Unscenic Nature," there are a variety of animals and landscapes that we commonly view as ugly—such as snakes, insects, and deserts—because of the fear that has been associated with them in our culture.

Children, for example, often demonstrate intense interest in and fascination with snakes, admiring their sinuous movements, their intricate patterns of coloration, and the supple yet rough texture of their scaly skin. Such aesthetic appreciation, however, is commonly lost by adulthood, after one has been exposed to a series of culturally influenced representations of snakes as dangerous and evil. Saito argues, "[I]f we can bracket our concern for our safety, we can attain enough composure to observe and appreciate the aesthetic value of these dangerous creatures" or, in Austin's case, these dangerous landscapes (1998, 106). We have commonly "bracketed" concern for our own safety in the aesthetic appreciation of dangerous nature by distancing ourselves from it via a physical barrier (such as the use of bars and windows in zoos and fences and railings at scenic overlooks) or through representing it in some other form (through landscape photography, visual art, and environmental literature).

Although both of these forms of distancing necessarily distort nature and exercise a type of dominion over it, they also serve to resist and to readjust more common forms of cultural distortion and domination of the natural world as aesthetically worthless and dangerous. As Marcia Muelder Eaton notes in "Fact and Fiction in the Aesthetic Appreciation of Nature," we have often used fiction to respond to nature imaginatively and appreciate it aesthetically. "Fiction," she observes, "plays an enormous role in shaping the way a culture perceives and conceives the environment" (1998, 150). Through her fiction, Austin attempts to readjust common stereotypes of arid regions as dangerous wastelands by developing alternative representations and associations that recognize the desert's inherent beauty, complexity, resilience, and value. Saito accords with Austin's approach, asserting that "some of our negative responses toward these things can be overcome with unlearning or distancing ourselves from these associations and cultural suppositions" (1998, 106).

The difficulty for most Americans in coming to terms with the aesthetics of arid environments is related to the fact that the major ideological strains of our culture were developed in the much colder, moister, and greener environments of central and northern Europe. Austin is, of course, well aware of her readers' culturally biased aesthetic values. In order to change how they perceive the desert, she often begins her descriptions from within this culturally confined perspective and then reverses, or readjusts, it so that the desert's positive aesthetic values can be recognized. Austin begins the first chapter of *The Land of Little Rain*, for example, with the following description: "This is the nature of that country. There are hills, rounded, blunt, burned, squeezed up out of chaos, chrome and vermilion painted, aspiring to the snowline. Between the hills lie high level-looking plains full of intolerable sun glare, or narrow valleys drowned in a blue haze. The hill surface is streaked with ash drift and black, unweathered lava flows" (1997, 3). This initial description of the land contains many culturally influenced judgments of the desert as a "chaotic" wasteland full of "intolerable sun glare." Yet the passage is lyrically written. The rhythm of the prose echoes the forceful geologic history of the country, and the polychromatic descriptions of the desert hills represent well one of the most unique and beautiful features of arid regions. Because of their sparse vegetation, the arid regions of the Southwest often contain stunning displays of geology: exposed layers of multicolored stone, wind-carved ridges, and brightly hued sunbaked hillsides. Although starting from the traditional paradigm of the desert as wasteland, Austin is able to recognize these aesthetically pleasing aspects of the desert's coloration and topography.

In the paragraph immediately following this initial description of the country, Austin develops her aesthetic perspective further: "Here are the long heavy winds and breathless calms on the tilted mesas where dust devils dance, whirling up into a wide, pale sky. Here you have no rain when all the earth cries for it, or quick downpours called cloud-bursts for violence. A land of lost rivers, with little in it to love; yet a land that once visited must be come back to inevitably" (5). In this passage, Austin assumes her readers' aesthetic perspective, a land with "little in it to love," and reverses this judgment by concluding that once visited the land must be returned to "inevitably." She also adjusts readers' aesthetic appreciation of arid regions by shifting their focus from the visual, or scenic, to the auditory, sensual, and experiential.

Western culture has traditionally emphasized vision as the means by which to appreciate natural environments, focusing on the "scenic" or "picturesque" at the expense of those landscapes that do not fit neatly into our common conceptions of these terms. As Yuriko Saito notes, this focus on the visually picturesque "requires the reduction of the environment to a scene or view" (1998, 102). Austin attempts to expand this reductionist perspective by writing lyrically about the aesthetically pleasing aspects of desert environments that cannot be experienced visually: the sensual and auditory pleasure of the desert's "long heavy winds" and "breathless calms" and the invigorating experience of the region's occasional "cloud-bursts." In addition, she continues to rely on visually pleasing images and rhythmic prose to encourage her readers to perceive the desert's special beauty, describing the "dancing" and "whirling" of dust devils under "wide, pale" skies. Rather than imposing her culture's imported standards of aesthetic value on desert regions, Austin acknowledges and appreciates the diverse ways in which different landscapes express their own unique types of beauty.

AESTHETICS AND EXPERIENCE

A second strategy Austin adopts to readjust her readers' culturally constrained environmental aesthetics is to confront readers directly, encouraging them to experience the desert for themselves instead of relying on distorted cultural representations of the region. She admonishes readers in *The Land of Little Rain*, "You of the house habit can hardly understand the sense of the hills" (1997, 123). She recognizes that it is difficult to appreciate that which we do not know and encourages her readers to experience the desert directly before judging it.

Austin also, however, has very specific ideas about how one should "experience" the desert in order to truly understand and come to appreciate its diversity and beauty. She tells her readers that "the real heart and core of the country are not to be come at in a month's vacation. One must summer and winter with the land and wait its occasions" (xvi).

For Austin, it is not only the length of time one spends in the desert that will dictate how well he or she comes to know it, but also how that time is spent. "Mesa trails were meant to be traveled on horseback, at the jigging coyote trot that only western-bred horses learn successfully. . . . It takes days' journeys to give a note of variety to the country of the social shrubs" (91). Interaction with the desert's inhabitants and complete immersion in the region are necessary if one is to come to an understanding of its inherent beauty and unique aesthetic value.

In her study of the relationships between environmental aesthetics and aesthetics relating to culturally produced works of art, Marcia Muelder Eaton observes, "[O]ne is more immersed in nature than in art, for one literally moves through it. . . . And the ways in which people move deserve serious attention" (1998, 151). Like Eaton, Austin recognizes that *how* we move through or experience a particular natural environment can have lasting effects on how we perceive or come to value that environment.

Because our aesthetic values are tied so closely to our own experiences, we often find that anything that is unfamiliar, or *strange,* is often considered ugly. Austin recognizes the difficulties inherent in trying to encourage her primarily eastern audience to develop an appreciation for the sights, sounds, and smells of the arid Southwest. She confronts these problems directly, noting that it is only after long association with the rugged and wild lands of the arid Southwest that one comes to appreciate them deeply: "There are some odors, too, that get into the blood." She then proceeds to catalog a series of these natural aromas and the pleasant associations they bring to mind for one who has come to understand and appreciate the country. She writes longingly, for example, of "the smell of sage at sundown, burning sage from campoodies and sheep camps, that travels on the thin blue wraiths of smoke; the kind of smell that gets into the hair and garments, is not much liked except on long acquaintance, and every Paiute and shepherd smells of it indubitably" (1997, 100).

Austin recognizes, as have many aestheticians, that our ability to appreciate certain phenomena aesthetically often depends upon the length of our association with that particular phenomena. Whereas the incenselike aroma of burning sage brings up pleasant and nostalgic associations with the comfort of home and camp for westerners who have spent a good deal of their lives in the wild, it may be nothing more than irritating and stifling smoke to the urban easterner with no experience of such things. Instead of simply describing the aesthetic pleasure she finds in the smell of sage smoke, Austin explains to her readers that a certain background, or personal history, is often necessary for appreciating it, that it is an acquired taste of western rural lands.

Austin intuitively recognizes that our aesthetic appreciation of a particular place or thing will depend upon the sum total of our past experiences. As Mary Carman Rose explains in "Nature As an Aesthetic Object," "[H]ow [a person] sees any aspect of nature depends upon his scientific training or lack of it, his technological interests and ecological commitments, and his personal experiences with nature. Thus even though they may all take delight in the colour, grace and form of trees, these are not seen in the same way by botanist, forester, lumberman, builder and artist" (1976, 4). Exposing our students to the aesthetic perspectives offered in Austin's fiction will aid them in better assessing the holistic value of natural environments and prevent them from being confined to a particular disciplinary or professional perspective.

AESTHETICS AND SCIENTIFIC INFORMATION

Most scholars, such as Cheryl Foster, Yuriko Saito, and Marcia Muelder Eaton, divide aesthetic experiences into two categories or types. The first category, most closely allied with the environmental sciences, has been variously termed by these scholars as *scientific, narrative,* or *cognitive aesthetic experience.* In short, this form of aesthetic appreciation relies upon an informational background or narrative that gives greater depth and meaning to the aesthetic object. The second category, often called *imaginative, ambient, experiential,* or *sensual aesthetic appreciation,* is tied more closely to the immediate imaginative or sensual experience of the object than any knowledge about it. However, as Cheryl Foster asserts, "Neither approach in isolation can fully articulate the experience of nature as it gives rise to what we might know of aesthetic value" (1998, 127). In order to fully understand and appreciate the aesthetics of natural environments, then, we must utilize both narrative and ambient approaches.

In her fiction, Austin makes use of both forms of aesthetic appreciation, alternately offering scientific information and imaginative musings to round out her observations. She often employs the narrative aesthetic strategy by supplying natural history information to provide a context for understanding and appreciating a particular species, feature, or process. She also utilizes the ambient aesthetic perception to develop imaginative associations based upon her phenomenological experience to ground readers in the aesthetically pleasing present. These two strategies combine to give readers a much more complete appreciation of the desert's aesthetic values.

Austin's use of natural history information is evidenced in her description of the adaptations of desert species to their harsh environment. "Very fertile are the desert plants in their expedients to prevent evaporation, turning their foliage edgewise toward the sun, growing silky hairs, exuding viscid gum" (1997, 6). She purposefully uses the word *fertile*, an adjective not commonly associated with desert environments, to describe the plants' adaptations and subvert our traditional association of deserts with infertility and barrenness. She then describes the plants' adaptations with active verbs, stating that the plants "turn" their leaves to the sun rather than using a more passive construction such as "the leaves are turned toward the sun." The use of active verbs implies a type of sentience and agency on the part of the plants. This coupled with the background information regarding the plants' unique abilities to adapt to the harsh environment encourages readers to understand and appreciate qualities of desert plants that are normally not considered aesthetically pleasing: their thorniness, stickiness, and sparse leaf cover.

As Saito notes, "[J]ust as proper appreciation of art must begin with the correct art-historical understanding of the object, the appropriate appreciation of nature must also be based upon correct information regarding it" (1998, 104). From this perspective, Austin's descriptions serve to replace inaccurate perceptions of desert plants as ugly and unpleasant with more ecologically appropriate evaluations of these plants as adaptive and resilient. This natural history information promotes perception not only of the sensuous surface of the natural world, but also of its deeper origins, functions, and mechanisms and enables us to better appreciate the unique aesthetic qualities of desert environs.

Similarly, students can gain a greater appreciation for Austin's aesthetic perceptions of desert inhabitants by deepening their own understanding of the biology, evolution, and life history of each species. Austin describes the Joshua trees of her beloved home, saying, "Nothing the desert produces expresses it better than the unhappy growth of tree yuccas. Tormented thin forests of it stalk drearily in the high mesas. . . . The yucca bristles with bayonet-pointed leaves, dull green, growing shaggy with age, tipped with panicles of fetid, greenish bloom" (1997, 8). Although on the one hand Austin's descriptions of Joshua trees seem to emphasize the negative, the passage itself is lyrically written and is followed by words of praise and respect for the hardiness of the desert's native flora:

> There is neither poverty of soil nor species to account for the sparseness
> of desert growth, but simply that each plant requires more room. So

much earth must be preempted to extract so much moisture. The real struggle for existence, the real brain of the plant, is underground; above there is room for a rounded perfect growth. In Death Valley, reputed the very core of desolation, are nearly two hundred identified species. (8)

During one particular class I led through Austin's land of little rain, our own field studies and interdisciplinary research brought us to a much deeper understanding of the awe she holds for these "Tree yucca." The Joshua tree, now classified as *Yucca brevifolia*, is a wonderful example of adaptation and symbiosis. It cannot propagate without the aid of the pronuba moth, which lays its eggs on the yucca flower. What is so interesting about this relationship is that the pronuba moth's actions fertilize the yucca flower and enable it to form seedpods. The larvae later bore their way out of the seedpods, leaving small holes in them. Because neither species can survive without the aid of the other, this relationship represents a remarkable case of symbiosis. As we explored Joshua tree forests, we could not find a single seedpod without the associated larvae holes. Understanding this relationship gave us an important narrative context for appreciating the relationship among Joshua tree forests, pronuba moth populations, and the history of human settlement in the region. As Austin notes, "Before the yucca has come to flower, while yet its bloom is a creamy cone-shaped bud of the size of a small cabbage, full of sugary sap, the Indians twist it deftly out of its fence of daggers and roast it for their own delectation. So it is that in those parts where man inhabits one sees young plants of *Yucca arborensis* infrequently" (8). Such explorations and added knowledge aided us in gaining a greater respect for both desert ecosystems and Austin's eloquent writing about them.

The practical significance of this type of ecologically informed aesthetic appreciation cannot be overemphasized. As Marcia Muelder Eaton points out, "[I]t is precisely a failure to understand the proper function of certain kinds of trees or forest soils, for instance, within their specific biosystems (i.e., context) that has led to mismanagement of forests even when providing aesthetic value has been one goal" (1998, 151). Austin's ecologically informed aesthetic appreciations of southern California's desert regions promise to aid students in seeing the beauty inherent in such landscapes, as well as understanding the ecological processes that must be preserved in order for that beauty to survive.

AESTHETICS AND LITERARY IMAGINATION

We should recognize, though, that the narrative, or scientifically informed, aesthetic perception is not, by itself, sufficient. In "Valuing Nature and the Autonomy of Natural Aesthetics," Stan Godlovitch offers this cautionary note: "If, on the other hand, we must properly appeal to ecological features like stability, endemism, representativeness, integrity, functional centrality, equilibrium, health, and the like, one wonders why the aesthetic perspective needs to be invoked at all" (1998b, 196). The danger in using the ecologically informed aesthetic approach alone is twofold: First, ecological values are much easier to quantify than aesthetic values and thus tend to be represented more effectively in land-management decisions. And second, there are some aesthetic values that exist apart from ecological values that should still play a significant role in the decision-making process. Austin's solution to this problem is to augment her ecologically informed descriptions with a variety of aesthetically pleasing representations of the desert that are not based upon scientific information, but rather are founded upon her own felt experience and imagination.

Austin, always a strong believer in the power of intuition and imagination to reveal the world to us, compares imaginative appreciation of the natural world to direct visual observation in *Lands of the Sun*. Describing the generationally shifting ecotone between the desert's sagebrush steppe and the mountain's higher-elevation forests, Austin writes: "All along the back of the Sierra Madre wall, the desert laps like a slow tide, rolling up and receding with the drouths [*sic*] and rains. The eye takes it in no less slowly than the imagination" (1927, 50). Here Austin seems to assert that the imagination is just as capable as the eye of perceiving the reality of the natural world. In this case, her comparison is especially appropriate because the generational succession of desert plants takes place slowly, over decades, and cannot be witnessed or understood without an act of the imagination. Similarly, Austin uses the metaphor of the ocean's tide to describe this generational rise and fall of vegetation, an apt metaphor but still an act of imagination.

Austin's imagination comes alive once again in "The Friend in the Wood" in which she has an aesthetic experience of the sublime—that which is both beautiful and terrifying. She writes, "Slowly at first, and then menacingly, the mountains came alive, they swelled with unappeasable insistence that filled the canon like a tide" (1990, 191). Her personification of the mountains here as "alive," "menacing," and "swelling" is obviously an act of her imagination. However, she is still describing her felt experience accurately.

My students and I have often witnessed this same strange effect. As the sun descends on the other side of the Sierra Nevada, the eastern-facing walls do seem to come alive and grow, shrouded in a climbing mantle of darkness until they occupy the entire field of vision and attention. Cheryl Foster explains, "Via the senses we can encounter that which stretches *beyond* text-book propositions into a full knowledge by acquaintance" (1998, 132). Whereas our ambient aesthetic perceptions may not accord with our intellectual understanding of mountains as inanimate, they do accord with our phenomenological experience of the mountains as exerting a felt presence, appearing to move as light and shadow play upon them.

In addition to using her imagination to develop metaphors and descriptions that can accurately reflect her felt experience in the land, Austin also uses it to consider how other inhabitants of the deserts and mountains experience their home region. In a manner similar to her personification of the mountains in "The Friend in the Wood," Austin imagines a sort of "mountain consciousness," or awareness, in the still lakes of the high Sierra Nevada. "The lake is the eye of the mountain, jade green, placid, unwinking, also unfathomable. Whatever goes on under the high stony brow is guessed at" (1997, 128). First Austin imagines facial features in the mountain's natural topography and then likens the water's reflective ability—its continual representation of all that occurs around it—to the mountain's consciousness through the use of metaphor. She imbues the mountain with consciousness so that her readers might be able to imaginatively perceive the land and its inhabitants from this geologic perspective. To paraphrase Gary Snyder, from the mountain's perspective, the trees are just passing through.

Imaginative perception is a key ability in appreciating nonhuman nature and distancing ourselves from our traditional anthropocentric and egocentric perspectives. Water—literally the source of life in the desert—is often perceived imaginatively by Austin, anthropomorphized, and imbued with both life and consciousness. She describes the changing attitude and behavior of a mountain stream as it cascades from the high country to find mellower channels in the foothills and on the valley floor, writing, "[T]he high note of babble and laughter falls off to the steadier mellow tone of a stream that knows its purpose and reflects the sky" (135). Austin is able to appreciate the changing moods of the stream by comparing its growth to that of any other creature. In its early stages it is full of energy, "babbling" and "laughing" like a child, but in its later stages it is "mellower" and full of "purpose" like an adult. This act of imagination helps Austin, and by extension her readers, to appreciate the stream on a much deeper level than as a mere topographic feature for channeling runoff according to the laws of gravity.

Emily Brady notes this ability of imaginative perception, explaining, "Imagination encourages a variety of possible perceptual perspectives on a single natural object or a set of objects, thereby expanding and enriching appreciation" (1998, 142). Through the use of her own imagination, Austin attempts to show readers that the deserts and mountains of her home are filled with a wide variety of hidden beauties, many of which cannot be seen from traditional anthropocentric and utilitarian perspectives.

Austin consistently refers to the wildlife of the region as "little people" and "hill folk" and discusses their behavior with a mixture of scientific objectivity and imaginative personification. In her description of the comings and goings of the "little people" to the isolated springs in the Ceriso, Austin first nudges readers out of their traditional anthropocentric perspective, asserting, "It seems that man-height is the least fortunate of all heights from which to study trails" (17). She then encourages readers to consider the animals not as unconscious automatons of instinct but as intelligent, thinking, and discriminating beings. Of the predators who stealthily visit the springs in the early evenings, she states, they "are not there from any mechanical promptings of instinct, but because they know of old experience that the small fry are about to take to seed gathering and the water trails" (21).

After Austin has given her readers the proper background and perspective from which to see the "little people" of the Ceriso, she provides a beautiful and lyrical description of them and their movements. She likens the flocks of quail that come down to the spring to the life-giving water they seek, recognizing both the flowing nature of their movements and the life they represent to the predators of the region: "[G]reat flocks pour down the trails with that peculiar melting motion of moving quail, twittering, shoving, and shouldering. They splatter into the shallows, drink daintily, shake out small showers over their perfect coats, and melt away again into the scrub, preening and pranking, with soft contented noises" (25). Austin's metaphorical description of the quail as water offers readers one of many possible perspectives for appreciating their unique beauty. The rhythm of her lyrical prose mimics the movements of the quail. As they approach the spring and come closer together, increasingly bumping into one another, the frequency of grammatical stops and pauses increases as well. As readers, we are directed by both the form and the content of Austin's prose to appreciate the graceful movements of the flock as a whole and to imagine what their presence means to the other inhabitants of the region.

AESTHETIC APPRECIATION AND ENVIRONMENTAL PROTECTION

Although Austin's imaginative flights of fancy might at first glance appear far removed from direct conservation priorities, how we perceive a particular landscape, in many ways, dictates how we will behave toward it. Marcia Muelder Eaton contends, "Our attitudes toward nature are largely determined by the metaphors with which we conceptualize it; many of these have come to us from literature" (1998, 154). By providing her readers with new metaphors and new manners of perceiving the inherent beauty, diversity, and value of desert landscapes, Austin supplies them with powerful tools for readjusting their attitudes and actions toward arid environments. Her use of both narrative (or scientific) and ambient (or imaginative) aesthetic perspectives is recognized by Eaton as being the most effective strategy we have for changing deep-seated environmental values and attitudes: "The task for all of us is to develop ways of using the delight that human beings take in flights of imagination, connect it to solid cognitive understanding of what makes for sustainable environments, and thus produce the kind of attitudes and preferences that will generate the kind of care we hope for" (155).

In agreement with Eaton, Norman Fischer and a number of other ecocritics have noted that environmental literature is extremely adept at synthesizing factual information and imaginative speculation—or, in literary terms, realism and fantasy—to create intellectually and emotionally powerful images. This combined approach has proved quite effective in readjusting basic environmental values and beliefs.

Whereas environmental studies curricula tend to rely upon transmitting scientific information, in the hope that increased knowledge and awareness will lead to greater appreciation, without a similar transformation in students' imaginative and emotional responses to natural environments we will see little change in their basic environmental values and attitudes. Cheryl Foster compares the effectiveness of these two modes of knowing and appreciating the natural world and concludes that the more imaginative and sensual modes of perception embodied in ambient aesthetic experiences have tended to be more effective in developing ecologically sensitive attitudes and values. "The ambient dimension of aesthetic value can act as a catalyst for the inculcation of a sensibility toward the environment: ecological, political, economic, or recreational kinds of concern often grow out of this more isolated yet fundamental kind of environmental experience" (1998, 134). For environmental studies students, who are already receiving instruction in objective assessments of environmental value, exposure to the more subjective values people find in the natural environment is both beneficial and necessary.

A wide variety of conservation decisions are in fact based upon such subjective criteria rather than scientific or economic data. The Wilderness Act, for example, establishes "outstanding opportunities for solitude" as one of several criteria for determining whether a particular area qualifies for designation as wilderness. The Bureau of Land Management's initial surveys in Austin's country—the Mojave and Great Basin regions of southern California and Nevada—excluded a host of wildlands from consideration for designation because they lack the vegetative or topographic screening necessary to supply "outstanding opportunities for solitude."

Because you can take a weeklong backpacking trip through these areas and never see another person, or if you *can* see someone off in the distance the rugged nature of the country often means that they are at least a full day's travel away, many wilderness advocates have recently challenged the BLM's assessments. In fact, with the passage of the Black Rock High Rock Emigrant Trail National Conservation Area Act in 1999 and the Clark County Lands Act of 2002, a number of these "unqualified" areas have in fact received wilderness designation.

This shift in policy suggests a similar shift in public perception of desert environments. Thanks to the work of writers like Mary Austin and Edward Abbey, and the tireless work of wilderness advocates in the arid Southwest, the American public and its land-management agencies have begun to recognize the aesthetic, recreational, and ecological value of desert regions. These areas, once considered too ugly for designation, have become a haven for outdoor enthusiasts who have learned to appreciate the unique beauty, immense space, and awesome stillness of our southwestern deserts.

Marcia Muelder Eaton notes the power of fiction to direct how we perceive, value, and act toward the natural environment, arguing that our behavior is more often directed by our subjective experiences, emotional attitudes, and values than by objective information and received knowledge or statistics. When presented with objective information that contradicts the emotional thrust of fiction, she observes, "[w]e tend to respond as the fictional account directs us to respond" (1998, 152). Though our rational minds argue otherwise, our behavior indicates that most often our actions toward the natural environment are dictated by subjective responses and emotions, rather than by objective information and knowledge. This highlights the need for incorporating some exploration of environmental aesthetics and values into environmental studies curricula so that we may engender in our students a deep love of, and care for, the earth.

These environmental values, then, can act as a guide to direct our students' actions and the application of their ecological and scientific knowledge. As Norman Fischer reminds us, this "emotion does not work against realism, but can enhance it. Play, then, can develop self-identification with an imagined, constructed, or preserved environment—an identification which makes humans more sensitive to real environmental characteristics, such as nature's integrity" (1996, 384). Forming strong links among our students' environmental awareness, ecological knowledge, personal values, and actions is vital if we are to be successful in preparing them to meet the current environmental crisis. Unless our students begin to identify emotionally with the natural environment, they will be content to witness and record its destruction on graphs and in reports while doing nothing to slow, stop, or reverse that destruction.

Austin describes her own emotional and spiritual connection to the wild, confessing, "It was the Friend-in-the-Wood and answered to no other name. Always it could be found anywhere beyond the house infested places; sometimes it called from these insistently and had no appeasement until I left my work and all, and went apart where it could find me" (1990, 189).

Whereas Austin's "Friend-in-the-Wood" was usually a disembodied presence, mine came to me in fur and flesh, in the form of a small sleek-bodied weasel on a bright desert morning. I was sitting on a sun-drenched stone, writing, sipping coffee, and soaking up the day's first gentle rays of sunshine. A small noise at my feet announced the arrival of a furtive and furry visitor: a small weasel, long and lean, with a black-tipped tail, a cream-colored patch on his chest, and a tan coat that shone like wet gold in the early morning light. He was of course a long-tailed weasel, *Mustela frenata,* a common native to the region but one seldom seen by human visitors. Although weighing less than eight ounces, he came straight up to me with a directness that could only be born of some undeniable courage and placed his two front paws atop my dust-covered hiking boot. He looked up at me for a few long-drawn-out seconds, holding me still with a pair of unblinking black beads for eyes. His feet gripped my Vibram-soled boot steadily, like a pair of small hands, while his nose and whiskers twitched, carefully reading my purpose on the scent-ridden air. Then, having said all he had come to say, he moved off through the rocks and sand, unhurried and without fear.

To this day, I still feel that his visit, that strange and silent encounter, was some form of gift. Even here, writing at my computer, or in the middle of a heated public hearing or land-management meeting, I think of him as my Friend-in-the-Wood, as one of Austin's hill folk, and this memory renews my resolve to do what I can to preserve his home and repay his gift.

CHAPTER FIVE

John Muir on the Range of Light

> Whether these picture-sheets are to vanish like fallen leaves or go to friends like
> letters, matters not much; for little can they tell to those who have not themselves
> seen similar wildness, and like a language have learned it.
>
> JOHN MUIR,
> *My First Summer in the Sierra*

I am sitting on the thick trunk of a fallen incense cedar spanning Yosemite Creek. As the sound of the creek water trickles up from below, the roar of Yosemite Falls washes over me from above. I am amid a thick forest of ponderosa pine, incense cedar, alder, black oak, willow, and fern, all growing from the jumbled layers of round river-stone and rich sediment deposited by the ever changing courses of the creek's many channels. The creek begins just to the north, at the foot of Yosemite Falls, and then cascades through boulders to wind its way in braided channels to this secluded spot. As I write in my journal, a mule deer, *Odocoileus hemionus,* silently materializes out of the thick underbrush, stares at me for a few minutes with dark, blinking eyes and, with a flick of the tail, walks daintily off through the woods.

Sitting above the creek like this reminds me of what John Muir's cabin must have been like with its miniature hand-dug stream flowing under and through the middle of the "shanty made of Sugar Pine shingles." Muir describes this unique feature of his hand-built home in his unfinished memoirs, explaining, "From the Yosemite Creek, near where it first gathers its beaten waters at the foot of the fall, I dug a small ditch and brought a stream into the cabin, entering at one end and flowing out the other with just current enough to allow it to sing and warble in low, sweet tones, delightful at night while I lay in bed" (1923, 1:208). Nearby, a plaque placed by the Sierra Club commemorates Muir's cabin site. Much debate exists about whether its placement is accurate, but in this area of multiply braided and constantly moving stream channels, precise accuracy is impossible. On the banks of the small stream meandering beneath my perch, I have found several masonry abutments. Perhaps they are from the sawmill where Muir worked, perhaps from his cabin itself, or more likely from a bridge built quite some time after Muir's departure.

Regardless of whether I sit on the exact cabin site or not, I am surely within fifty feet of Muir's front doorstep. I cannot help but imagine what his life must have been like here, especially as I envy his choice of location. On the northern side of the valley, this area gets the most sun, enjoys the ever changing tones of the Yosemite cataracts, and is located in the dappled shadows of the thick forest's edge, near a wide, grassy meadow. Not only was Muir's cabin surrounded by natural beauty, but the house was also pervaded by it. He describes this porous connection to the natural world in detail:

> In the spring the common pteris ferns pushed up between the joints of the [floor] slabs, two of which, growing slender like climbing ferns on account of the subdued light, I trained on threads up the sides and over my window in front of my writing desk in an ornamental arch. Dainty little tree frogs occasionally climbed the ferns and made fine music in the night, and common frogs came in with the stream and helped to sing with the Hylas and the warbling, tinkling water. (208)

As I sit, writing and thinking about Muir's life here, I am forced to keep up a constant drumming of mad slaps and smacks as voracious and innumerable mosquitoes descend upon me like a pack of ravenous wolves. Why did these feisty little vampires escape Muir's usually precise attention to detail? I wonder. Perhaps it was because he seldom spent time here in the summer or the longer and thicker clothes worn during that time than now. Or perhaps he was just too damn tough to notice them, I think, recalling how one of my field classes complained about his use of words like *saunter* and *ramble* to describe difficult and strenuous mountaineering ascents.

After cresting a particularly high pass with a brutally steep ascent, these students had all collapsed in the rock and dust beside the trail to breathe, pant, wheeze, and whine. Rubbing their burning thighs, blistered feet, and bent backs, they complained that Muir never mentioned the difficulties of mountain travel, that he wrote of the most challenging ascents as if they were pleasurable strolls though the meadows and woods. Reminding them that he did not even have the luxury of such well-built trails as the PCT and that he rarely had a pack on, and in fact does mention, in a few places, his physical exhaustion from the day's adventures, did little to assuage their feelings. But the discussion did cause me to think about the kinds of details that are left out of Muir's work, as well as the kind that are kept in.

A month later, I am here at Muir's cabin site, thinking again about his process of composition and revision. When I read Muir's descriptions of particular places or species and then compare them with my own experiences and observations, I find them extremely accurate, precise, and informative. He even seems to capture well the subjective experiences and feelings that arise in me when camping in wild and rugged country. I wonder, though, as I write and sketch in my own field journal, about the difficulties inherent in preparing such material for publication. Which passages does one select, omit, elaborate, or change? Should one follow the original chronological order or restructure events and reflections thematically or narratively? What were Muir's guiding intentions as he wrote and as he revised?

MUIR ON WRITING

Writing did not come easily, nor was it enjoyable, for John Muir. Compared with the physical hardship and tremendous exertion of his mountaineering expeditions through the Sierra Nevada, writing was a demanding and difficult chore that never seemed to fulfill its promise. Muir writes in an 1872 letter to his friend Jeanne Carr, "Book-making frightens me, because it demands so much artificialness and retrograding. . . . These mountain fires that glow in one's blood are free to all, but I cannot find the chemistry that may press them unimpaired into booksellers' bricks" (2:7).

Muir's primary concern about writing, apart from the effort and time required, was that it never seemed to effectively capture the life, beauty, and grandeur of the natural world. In another letter to Mrs. Carr, written in 1873,

Muir again laments his dissatisfaction with the ability of the written word to represent the natural world: "The few hard words make but a skeleton, fleshless, heartless, and when you read, the dead bony words rattle in one's teeth. Yet I will not the less endeavor to do my poor best, believing that even these dead bone-heaps called articles will occasionally contain hints to some living souls who know how to find them" (1:382).

Although Muir disliked the task of writing and was never completely satisfied with it as a medium for expressing truths about the natural world, he remained committed to describing and defending wild areas in the written word throughout his life. As the above passage testifies, Muir maintained an optimistic hope that his writing, despite its shortcomings, could be an effective tool for teaching people about the natural world and engendering action on its behalf. As Ronald H. Limbaugh notes in "John Muir and Modern Environmental Education," Muir's "best teaching medium was the written word" (1992, 176). Muir's effectiveness as an author and activist rested upon his ability to translate powerful experiences into meaningful prose. Although it was an unpleasant chore for Muir, writing was an effective and useful tool, one that this Scottish taskmaster refused to shy away from.

Many scholars have noted Muir's dislike for the writing process, citing his numerous criticisms of the written word in both his published works and his private letters. Laboring away in the confines of his second-story "scribble den" in his home in Martinez, California, must have been a frustrating distraction from his great love: experiencing and studying the natural world directly. Yet, despite his many complaints, Muir kept up voluminous correspondence with friends and family members and incessantly filled his own private field journals and sketchbooks with observations and reflections throughout his life. Michael P. Cohen makes note of this distinction in Muir's attitudes toward writing, asserting, "Writing for the public did not come easy for him because he suspected the understanding of a general audience was limited" (1984, 128). Cohen's claim is corroborated by Muir himself. In an 1872 letter to Mrs. Carr, he writes,

> I can proclaim to you that moonshine is glorious, and sunshine more glorious, that winds rage, and waters roar, and that in "terrible times" glaciers guttered the mountains with their cold hard snouts. This is about the limit of what I feel capable of doing for the public—the

moiling, squirming, fog-breathing public. But for my few friends I can do more because they already know the mountain harmonies. (1923, 2:7)

As Muir hints at the end of this passage, one must experience the mountains themselves in order to understand his literary representations of them. In *My First Summer in the Sierra,* Muir explicitly states that his writing can tell little to "those who have not themselves seen similar wildness, and like a language have learned it" (1916c, 121).

MUIR AND FIELD EXPERIENCE

Muir consistently urged his readers to drink from nature's "fountains" and study the divine natural world directly. Like Austin, Muir clearly recognized the limits of linguistic representation and sought to overcome them by coupling physical experience with literary imagination. Ronald H. Limbaugh points out, "Muir also used personal experience as a check on book learning" and encouraged his readers to do the same (1992, 175). Muir's insistence on direct experience of the natural world as a means to interpret his writing stems from the fact that the majority of his works were initially composed in the field. John P. O'Grady notes in *Pilgrims to the Wild* that "[t]he bulk of Muir's published work in the last twenty years of his life—the books upon which his literary and environmental reputation rests—is derived substantially from revision of sketches, essays, letters, and journal entries originally composed between 1867 and 1877" (1993, 48).

The decade described by O'Grady as producing the foundation for Muir's later work was also the period in which Muir explored, climbed, and studied the Sierra Nevada the most. It was only two years later, in 1879, that John Muir became engaged to Louie Strentzel and took his first trip to Alaska. In the following years, Muir spent less time exploring the Range of Light, while increasing time and attention was taken up with family, running the orchards in Martinez, revising his field journals for publication, and joining expeditions to Alaska. It is no surprise, then, that because Muir's compositional method relied so heavily on direct field experience, he would recommend the same practice to his readers.

Because of its experiential and referential basis, Muir's work represents, in microcosm, many of the problems associated with the ecocritical study of nonfiction nature writing as a whole. John Elder discusses the writing process as it relates to what he calls "the literature of Wilderness," observing that all nature writing contains the same three elements: "close observation of nature, within an awareness of the modern science of ecology; a journal of the author's own growth, by means of that intense relation to nature; and speculation about larger religious and political issues connected with the cause of wilderness-preservation" (1981, 375). In short, when we read similar works of environmental literature we are retracing that author's process of close observation of nature, reflection of self-growth, and increasing ethical awareness of the natural world. Our own process, however, as it is contained within the methodologies of traditional literary criticism, usually entails only the close observation of that author's words, seldom includes reflection of our own self-growth, and involves an ethical awareness of the natural world that is derived completely from books rather than from direct contact with that world. Such a process stands in opposition to Muir's methods, his recommendations for readers, and much of what we know about the limits of linguistic representation.

One possible alternative to the traditional textually confined approach is to engage our students (and ourselves) in the same process of observation, reflection, and awareness that authors themselves practice, using their texts both as subjects of study and as models for how to engage in the process of investigation. Such an approach is supported by Muir himself, who writes, "I would fain ask my readers to linger awhile in this fertile wilderness, to trace its history from its earliest glacial beginnings, and learn what we may of its wild inhabitants and visitors" (1916b, 150). In both his published works and his unpublished letters, Muir consistently calls for his friends and readers to witness and experience the wonders of his beloved Range of Light directly.

In addition to these explicit admonishments, Muir developed a literary persona that emphasized his own field studies in natural history and mountaineering experiences. Christine Oravec comments on this common quality of Muir's work: "The story of his discovery thus presented as a sequence of events became a training guide or manual for readers" (1981, 250). In recognizing that one function of Muir's work extends beyond the representation of the natural world to include didactic instruction on how to study and experience it, Oravec illuminates one of Muir's central authorial concerns: how to get readers to know, understand, value, and protect wildlands and

natural ecosystems. Oravec also notes that Muir's inclusion of daring mountaineering exploits served to "involve the reader in the active mountaineering life, not only as passive observers but as vicarious participants" as well
(251). If he could not convince readers to "climb the mountains and get their
good tidings," Muir would attempt to give them an imaginative experience
through literature that was as similar to the real thing as possible.

Many scholars have noted the experiential foundations of Muir's work,
but few have attempted to re-create them in their own work. However, *The
Pathless Way,* by Michael P. Cohen, recognized as one of the most authoritative studies of Muir's life and work, stands as a notable exception to this rule.
In Muir-like fashion, Cohen admits:

> I, for instance, have had to put on my pack and spend several days in
> the Grand Canyon of the Tuolumne to remind myself of what I am
> talking about. Even late in the season, when the oaks are flaming and
> the aspens are dropping their yellow leaves, one needs to sit by a camp-
> fire and remind oneself that the real research library of Yosemite lives
> in its canyons, rivers, lakes, meadows, forests, and mountains. (1984, 275)

Like Cohen and Muir, I have found that one of the best means for providing
the proper perspective in which to study works of environmental literature
is to visit the particular places represented in a text and use the author's
methods as a model for my own studies. Muir's work, for example, serves as
a useful model for understanding both the common methodologies employed by nature writers and some of the possible methodologies ecocritics
might develop and use themselves.

MUIR'S RHETORICAL STRATEGIES

Much of Muir's writing demonstrates a consistent use of three particular
rhetorical strategies for representing and responding to the natural world:
first, close, objective observation and description of natural phenomena; second, subjective, emotional, and self-reflective responses to those phenomena;
and third, the development of a literary persona—the mountaineer–natural
historian—who acts as a model for readers to follow either physically or
imaginatively. By studying how Muir utilizes these three strategies and then
applying them in the field with our own writing and scholarly experiences,

or those of our students, we can gain new insight into his literary work and the natural world in which we live.

Muir's reliance on field journals and sketchbooks as sources of material for his published work supports using just such an approach. By engaging in a similar process of direct observation, self-reflection, and physical experience, we can come to a better understanding of Muir's writing process and the mechanics of translating field journals into published works of environmental literature.

We can witness Muir's first rhetorical strategy, for example, in an 1875 field journal where he models the manner in which one must use detailed observation as a foundation for the study of the natural world. In one section of the journal, Muir sketches and dissects cones and seeds from the red fir, or *Abies magnifica,* noting that each cone has approximately 280 scales with 2 seeds in each. He then includes, with his sketch, careful measurements of the cones, scales, and seeds along with a verbal description of their distinguishing characteristics. Similarly, in his studies of "The Big Tree," *Sequioadendron giganteum,* Muir performed meticulous calculations to determine how many seeds a mature sequoia would produce in a season. By counting the number of seeds in each cone, the number of cones on an average-size branch, and the number of branches on a tree, then multiplying these figures together, Muir concluded, "No other Sierra conifer produces nearly so many seeds. Millions are ripened annually by a single tree, and in a fruitful year the product of one of the northern groves would be enough to plant all the mountain ranges of the world" (1916b, 205). Through such careful observation, Muir not only teaches his readers about the unique characteristics of his mountain friends, but also demonstrates the value of the scientific study of wild nature and the manner in which it should be performed.

According to Michael P. Cohen, Muir "inherited a disciplined approach to the creation from Louis Agassiz, who had introduced the method of close inspection and comparison to American schools" (1984, 41). Although Muir most often used words like *saunter, wander,* and *prowl* to describe his physically grueling explorations of the Sierra Nevada, and although he thought of his studies in natural history as "pleasure" rather than "work," his disciplined approach rivaled that of many of the scientists of his day and often yielded, as in the case of his glacial studies, groundbreaking insights. In "Exploration of the Great Tuolumne Canyon," Muir describes his methodology in characteristically humble terms yet evidences a very careful, disciplined, and patient approach to environmental studies:

> I drifted about from rock to rock, from stream to stream, from grove to grove. Where night found me there I camped. When I discovered a new plant, I sat down beside it for a minute or a day, to make its acquaintance and hear what it had to tell. When I came to moraines, or ice-scratches upon the rocks, I traced them back, learning what I could of the glacier that made them. I asked bowlders [*sic*] I met, whence they came and whither they were going. (qtd. in Cohen 1984, 41)

In addition to engaging in disciplined scientific studies of the natural world, Muir used his own imagination, religious philosophy, and emotional responses to the grandeur and diversity of the Sierra Nevada to convey the subjective qualities of wilderness experience that escape quantification and explanation by science alone. Describing in lyrical prose the beauty of Sierran sunlight or the sublime vistas offered by thousand-foot precipices represents Muir's second rhetorical strategy. He used value-laden images, metaphors, and reflections to connect readers emotionally and viscerally to the intellectual insights offered by his objective descriptions.

Of the Jeffrey and ponderosa pines, for example, he writes that there is nothing more impressive than "the fall of light upon these silver pines. It seems beaten to the finest dust, and is shed off in myriads of minute sparkles that seem to come from the very heart of the trees, as if, like rain falling upon fertile soil, it had been absorbed, to reappear in flowers of light" (1916b, 185). Such eloquent and emotional descriptions of the inherent beauty of the natural world serve to both translate the quality of Muir's experiences for his readers and advance his preservationist cause. Steven J. Holmes describes the effect such descriptions have on readers: "Muir's selective, interpretive representation of the landscape begins as well to evoke more specific, value- and emotion-laden responses" (1998, 399). By supplementing readers' newfound knowledge of the natural world with moving descriptions of its beauty and worth, Muir is able to more effectively engage them on its behalf.

Although Muir's method of study was primarily "scientific," he was not a professionally trained scientist. He believed that science alone—objective observation, analysis, and quantification—could not convey the reality and significance of the natural world. According to Michael P. Cohen, Muir believed "that a scientist's duty went beyond 'angular factiness'" (1984, 44). He attempted to unify poetry and science in his work, to synthesize lyrical and emotionally laden descriptions of nature's beauty and diversity with scientifically informed observations and research. His synthesis of objective and subjective approaches has long been known to be the most rhetorically and pedagogically effective method for persuasion. As Ronald H. Limbaugh observes, "Environmental educators must be prepared as well as persuasive. Muir was both" (1992, 174). As the great "Sage of the Sierra," Muir was committed to both environmental education and activism. Through the use of objective and subjective rhetorical strategies, he was capable of working toward both of these goals simultaneously.

In addition to appealing to readers' emotion and reason, Muir also attempted to bring them into the wild physically. Or, at least, he attempted to give them the closest substitute for real physical experience he could devise with the written word by developing a bold mountaineer's persona with whom readers could identify. Ronald Limbaugh points out, as have many scholars and readers over the years, that one of the keys to Muir's success as a teacher was his "fascinating stories" of mountaineering adventures, physical hardships, and near escapes from the jaws of death (173). All of these, however, are endured, or in fact enjoyed, with the same humble, curious, and awe-filled attitudes that have come to characterize the literary John Muir. Cohen describes Muir's attempts to offer readers vicarious and imaginative experiences of mountain living and travel, stating that Muir "would provide through art the immediate pleasures [readers] had not received through their lives, so that they might be converted to a belief that wilderness was important" (1984, 240).

Because Muir's intense and prolonged studies in the Sierra Nevada were central to the development of his own environmental ethics and attitudes, he recognized that readers needed similar experiences to draw from. If they could not follow his advice and come to "read this mountain manuscript" of the Sierra directly, they could at least gain a similar experience imaginatively and vicariously through identifying with Muir's character as he explores the range and the region.

"We are now in the mountains and they are in us, kindling enthusiasm, making every nerve quiver, filling every pore and cell of us," Muir proclaims in *My First Summer in the Sierra* (1916c, 16). Here Muir uses the inclusive "we," perhaps referring to his human companion, Billy, dog Carlo, the horses, and the sheep. However, because there is no direct mention of these companions prior to the exclamation, the inclusive "we" also serves to bring the readers into the book's field of description and experience. While "we" (Muir and his companions) are in the mountains physically, "we" (Muir's readers and Muir-the-author) are in the mountains imaginatively. Muir uses the inclusive "we" to aid readers in their identification with him and to develop further the vicarious experience of mountaineering adventure. In the same way that Mary Austin uses second-person narration to situate her readers imaginatively in the desert landscape, Muir adopts an inclusive first-person narrative to place readers beside him in the high Sierra.

Because Muir's literary persona was so closely based upon his own experiences and personality, these mountaineering stories also serve to develop the author's ethos and lend the credibility of firsthand experience to the accounts. Christine Oravec contends, "Muir discovered that developing a portrait of himself as both a learned expert on mountains and an experienced guide would establish human perspective upon the complexity of nature and ground his descriptions in scientific fact" (1981, 250).

Two of the problems associated with criticizing Muir's representations of the Sierra Nevada stem from the authority he successfully lent to this authorial ethos. The accuracy of his observations was made difficult to assail because of his own vast personal experience in the region, whereas the sentimentality and effusiveness of his emotional and religious reflections were offset by the physical rigor and daring of his mountaineering exploits. H. Lewis Ulman concludes of these aspects of Muir's literary persona: "[T]he rhetorical power of much nonfiction nature writing stems from the construction of an ethos that compellingly represents ways of seeing and believing that promise to show us how to be and act at home in the natural world, even when the author's circumstances, perceptions, and values seem far removed from our own" (1998, 227). Even for Muir's eastern and contemporary audiences, many of whom would never have any direct experience of similar wildlands, Muir's literary persona and the imaginative experiences it provided were powerful guides in developing their own environmentally appropriate ethics and attitudes.

Muir's literary representations of the Sierra Nevada, then, can be seen to function much like his activist work to preserve the region. Through his writing and activism, Muir succeeded in giving Americans the opportunity to experience the beauty and grandeur of the Sierra, first through literary and imaginative experiences by reading his work and second through physical experiences by visiting the parks and places he helped preserve.

MUIR AND THE PROCESS OF REVISION

In order to better understand how Muir used his personal experiences in the Sierra Nevada, the record of them as captured in his field journals and the revised publications to inform and affect his readers, we can engage in a similar process ourselves while using Muir as a methodological model. By engaging in similar experiences, keeping our own field journals, and studying the types of changes made by Muir to revise his journals for publication, we can learn much about his process, intentions, and concerns. By extension, this process will also illuminate the practices common to most nature writers.

Through the use of a variety of specific journal assignments, all based upon types of entries found in Muir's journals themselves, I have students gain some experience with the process of field journaling. We note the types of things that attract one's attention, the problematics of composing in the field, the limitations of space, the complication of revising at home and not having recorded all the necessary details in the field, and so on. After gaining a baseline of experience to fall back on, we then compare Muir's field journals and notebooks to his published works to observe the kinds of changes he made, the types of things he was concerned with as evidenced by the revision process itself, and the solutions he found to the common problems we experienced.

From such examinations we have noted that objective descriptions and observed details are rarely changed or modified by Muir. Subjective reflection and effusive emotional responses are not, as some might expect, added for literary effect during the revision process but are, just like the objective observations, composed in the field. As a general rule, we find more revision of these passages than the observational ones. However, the changes are primarily cosmetic and deal with issues of style, diction, syntax, rhythm of language, and the sounds of particular words. The mountaineering passages, similarly, are composed in the field and evidence changes in linguistic form rather than in content. Michael P. Cohen notes that Muir "seemed to pay painfully close attention to the key terms of other writers, and was equally attentive to his own diction" (1984, 132). The most significant modifications we see between the field journals and published works actually come in the form of omission, addition, and the restructuring of events. From his own studies Cohen agrees: "Before a choice of diction or rhetorical strategy, however, came a selection of material" (133).

Because Muir often mined his field notes for particular descriptions, phrases, metaphors, and events, his published works often do not follow the chronological sequence of events he experienced in the field and sometimes synthesize observations and reflections made on different expeditions as if they occurred at the same time or in the same place. With these general observations in mind, a closer look at Muir's journals will reveal just how extensive, and intensive, his process of revision was.

My First Summer in the Sierra

My First Summer in the Sierra was not actually published until 1911 but was based on Muir's first two summers in the Yosemite region and excerpted heavily from the field journals he kept during that time. Although a forty-year gap exists between the composition of the field journals and the publication of the revised work, *My First Summer* is a good place to begin studying Muir's compositional process for two key reasons. First, though many scholars and students study *My First Summer in the Sierra,* one of Muir's most canonized works, few study how it came into being. The standard assumption of most readers seems to be that it is a fairly accurate account of his first season in the Sierra high country. Such an assumption is supported no doubt by the journalistic quality of the text—complete with separate dated entries—and the level of detail and direct observation. However, as Steven Holmes asserts, "the published *First Summer* is based not upon an original journal but upon three handwritten notebooks that date from 1887; whatever journal he actually kept during the summer of 1869 is now lost" (1999, 3). This presents the scholar interested in Muir's process of field composition and revision with some difficulty, as we can be reasonably sure that the 1887 notebooks were already heavily revised and there is no way of checking them against the journals upon which they were based. However, the revisions made to the notebooks for the 1911 publication were all made toward the end of Muir's literary career, after he had perfected his techniques and developed to its fullest his compositional process. Second, as Muir's field journals and sketchbooks are often very difficult to read, smudged, torn, and cut up to remove sketches and passages, beginning our study of his original materials with the much clearer 1887 notebooks gives students and scholars some training in working with archival materials before tackling the difficulties presented by the field journals themselves.

From a careful study of these notebooks, one can see that a narrative structure is already being formed through revisions that were not existent in the original journal. Like Thoreau in *Walden* and later Edward Abbey in *Desert Solitaire,* Muir has collapsed the events, observations, and reflections of two seasons in the Sierra into a single summer. Obviously, such a condensed narrative structure is going to entail omitting passages and transposing others in order to create a unified narrative that will cohere chronologically and thematically.

In his study of the 1887 notebooks, Holmes concludes that the recorded account of Muir's "first summer" "can probably be trusted only in a very limited way: the sheer record of the places and objects that Muir encountered in his travels is in large part reliable, but much of the narrative structure and interpretive language of the 1887 notebooks is the product of an extensive process of revision that was undertaken at some as-yet-unknown time(s) between 1869 and 1887" (4). From our own study of the notebooks as well as our own experiences with field journaling, we can fairly confidently come to a similar conclusion.

However, if the notebooks are any indication of the type of revision Muir performed, we can assume that many of the changes made in moving from the field journals to the notebooks were similar to the changes made in turning the notebooks into the published work. As we shall see, although the modifications are often extensive, they are usually stylistic changes that leave the content—the accuracy of the observation or the facticity of the event— intact.

For example, on a single page of Muir's 1887 notebooks, we can see that although the original thought is most often left, the language used to convey it goes through extensive revision until almost no word is left untouched. In the original we find this passage, "Oh, these glorious old mountain days. Ripe and sweet and luscious, like fruit to be eaten," which is crossed out and replaced with "O, these great," and "great" is crossed out and replaced with "vast," so that the revised passage reads "O, these vast, calm, measureless mountain days, so peaceful, workful, indef[atig]ably fine." And a few lines later we can see the original "So rocky and substantial, yet so infinitely spiritual, exciting at once to work and rest. Bestowing substance in its grandest forms, yet throwing open a thousand windows to show us heaven" is also crossed out and replaced with a slightly revised version: "Exciting at once to work and rest. Days in which light, everything seems equally divine, opening as a thousand windows to show us God" (1986, 103).

As these passages indicate, one of Muir's major preoccupations as he revised his field journals for publication was literary style. He works and reworks his diction and syntax to produce a rhythmic and lyrical prose that, although the content remains the same as in the original, better embodies the nuances of feeling he hopes to communicate. One particularly famous scene in *My First Summer* has Muir clinging to a vertical cliff face, sliding out over a thousand-foot abyss with only his heels on a three-inch-wide ledge in order to see the plummeting waters of Yosemite Falls. He even admits to having to chew a mouthful of bitter *Artemisia,* or sagebrush, leaves to prevent giddiness. These autobiographical details remain unchanged from the 1887 notebooks to the published work. However, Muir extensively revises the diction and syntax of the account in order to provide more suspense through the rhythm of the prose and to create a greater correspondence between the sounds of the words and the images they describe.

The first change one notes between the two accounts is that the rhythm and pace of the language in the revised version much more closely correspond with the rhythm and movement of the water as it drops through a series of pools to the great fall. In the 1887 account, Muir writes:

> Emerging from its last canon Yosemite Creek glides in wide flattened lace-like rapids down a smooth-polished incline and into a small pool where it seems to rest and compose its gray agitated waters before taking the grand plunge. Here its waters become blue and calm, nearly every foam bubble vanishes, then slowly gliding over the lip of the pool it descends a glossy incline with rapidly accelerated speed and plunges out in a magnificent curve into the free air. (60)

The final version of this passage is composed as a single sentence, moves much more rapidly, and evidences much greater care with diction. In fact, many of the changes between the original and the published version are observable in the notebooks themselves, as words and phrases are commonly crossed out with alternative constructions penciled in as insertions or marginalia. In the version published in *My First Summer,* Muir writes:

> Emerging from its last gorge, it glides in wide lace-like rapids down a smooth incline into a pool where it seems to rest and compose its gray, agitated waters before taking the grand plunge, then slowly slipping over the lip of the pool basin, it descends another glossy slope with rapidly accelerated speed to the brink of the tremendous cliff, and with sublime, fateful confidence springs out free in the air. (1916c, 118)

By combining the two sentences into one, Muir is able to keep a continuous, flowing rhythm that mimics the flowing nature of the water he is describing. The pace of the sentence slows in the middle as the water pools; then, just as the water slips over the lip of the pool and begins to accelerate, the prose likewise accelerates until both are left floating in the free air and space at the end of the paragraph.

Although no evidence has surfaced to prove it, this type of revision seems to indicate that Muir read his work aloud as he revised and paid careful attention to sound and rhythm as he wrote. Ronald H. Limbaugh agrees: "I am convinced that, like many authors, he read everything he wrote aloud to himself before releasing it for publication. His words are too finely tuned for silent contemplation. They are composed for the ears, not just for the eyes" (1992, 176).

In addition to being supported by Muir's process of revision, such a supposition seems to accord with how Muir perceived the natural world. Although he often uses picturesque language and visual images to describe the Sierra Nevada, his writing is also full of winds that "chant," trees that "preach," flowers and boulders that "speak," and rivers and streams that "sing." Early on in *My First Summer,* he describes the Sierra Nevada as "a glorious wilderness that seemed to be calling with a thousand songful voices" (1916c, 13). If the sounds of the natural world were of such importance to Muir in the field, then it stands to reason that the sounds of his words were also important to him in his published work.

In another famous passage, Muir describes his only human companion, the shepherd Billy, and likens him to a natural (but dirty) feature of the landscape. Comparing the notebooks to the published version reveals the same care with diction demonstrated earlier, a great deal of omission, and the transposition of entire passages, sentences, and phrases. As is often the case, Muir synthesized observations and descriptions of a single species even if they were made on different occasions with different members of the same species. In this case, it appears that Muir's observations of and reflections about Billy's appearance and demeanor took place over a number of days. Even after being revised and transcribed into the 1887 notebooks, many of these distinct passages are transposed and synthesized again to make a coherent whole for the published work.

In the original version, Muir introduces Billy by saying, "Our shepherd's name was Ba or Bawsly properly enough" (1986, 40). "Was" is cancelled and replaced with "is Billy," and "Bawsly" is cancelled and replaced with "nearly so." Muir then launches directly into a description of Billy's six-shooter and greasy overalls. The published version, however, is quite different. Muir begins by stating, "Our shepherd is a queer character and hard to place in this wilderness," omitting mention of his name because it has already been given earlier in the text (1916c, 129).

In addition, Muir adds two long, detailed sentences describing Billy's habit of sleeping on the ground in the sheep corral to set up the following description of his overalls, descriptions that will comically emphasize their dirtiness. Before describing Billy's greasy pants, however, Muir transposes a description of the lunch rag Billy carries on his six-shooter belt from a later portion of the journal in order to better explain and set up the detailed and humorous description of Billy's greasy overalls. The original reads, "He wore a heavy six shooter on his hip swung by a belt that partly held up and held together a pair of overalls, very greasy, though he made his way through the world with much friction nevertheless" and then proceeds directly to describe the overalls in detail (1986, 40). The revised passage, on the other hand, begins, "Following the sheep he carries a heavy six-shooter swung from his belt on one side and his luncheon on the other" and then describes in detail the luncheon cloth hanging from Billy's belt and the fatty gravy juices dripping down from it to cover the overalls and give them their peculiar sticky nature (1916c, 129).

Although the differences between the accounts are considerable, they relate more to literary style and rhetorical effect than to the accuracy of the representation or the facts of the tale. Some conspicuous additions also demonstrate this concern with rhetorical effect. Muir emphasizes the comic nature of the passage by adding, "Man is a microcosm, or at least our shepherd is, or rather his trousers." And the connection between the layers of accreted grease and dirt on Billy's pants and the geological strata Muir studies is made tighter and more obvious by the final sentence of the paragraph, which is also an addition. Giving us the final word on Billy's pants, Muir writes, "Instead of wearing thin they wear thick, and in their stratification have no small geological significance" (130). An additional effect of this final passage is to shift the emphasis of the description from the human to the natural. Although the primary subject of the paragraph is human—the shepherd Billy—he is ultimately subsumed by the natural world, shifting the emphasis from the anthropocentric to the ecocentric. As Christine Oravec notes, "Whenever Muir introduced a human presence into his descriptions, he consistently subordinated it to the surrounding elements" (1981, 249). Though one can come to this recognition by studying Muir's published works alone, by comparing them with his journals we can see that this is a conscious rhetorical strategy that is often added in revision for the effect it will have on the audience.

Recognizing that Muir engaged in a process of extensive revision and organization of his original field notes does not necessarily mean that the published version of *My First Summer* is an inaccurate or untruthful account of Muir's experiences. Especially when we consider the kinds of revisions Muir commonly made, we can see that the facticity of events, observations, and even emotional responses remains intact. Muir's concerns in revision are primarily stylistic, rhetorical, thematic, and structural. The overarching intention of Muir's process of revision seems to be to remain faithful to the veracity of experience while using the rhetorical strategies available to him to increase the effectiveness of his writing in conveying the beauty and value of wilderness.

Noting these aspects of the revision process teaches us that *My First Summer* is indeed a literary text, a product of both close observation of nature in the field and the imagination and intellect. Such a realization allows us to look again at the craft involved in the creation of *My First Summer* and aids us in improving our own process of crafting literary representation out of personal experience.

The Mountains of California

Field scholars can engage profitably in the same manner of study with any of Muir's works. Muir's first book, *The Mountains of California,* published in 1894, serves as another excellent work to focus on for two reasons. First, it covers much of the ground that the Pacific Crest Trail passes through, and second, the original field journals upon which it was based are extant. In addition, although Muir had been publishing articles and essays for years, *Mountains* was his first book-length project. Many of the chapters and sections, in fact, were taken from previously published work. *Mountains,* therefore, demonstrates well the concerns preoccupying Muir's mind as he worked to bring his studies and experiences in the Sierra Nevada to the reading public. Michael P. Cohen points out that "Muir felt the necessity of craft in this book perhaps more than in any other he wrote" (1984, 285). *Mountains* was published only two years after the establishment of the Sierra Club and thus became not just an entertaining and informative foray into the California wilds, but also a political book with explicitly preservationist goals.

Muir's political and rhetorical concerns can be seen in his additions to the famous and often-quoted "Range of Light" passage. The fact that Muir's term *Range of Light* has been taken by a number of environmental organizations and the frequency with which this passage is quoted and referred to in activist publications, commercials, brochures, billboards, and films demonstrate its political effectiveness. The changes between Muir's original version and the published one are minor but telling. In the published passage Muir writes:

> Then it seemed to me the Sierra should be called, not the Nevada, or Snowy Range, but the Range of Light. And after ten years spent in the heart of it, rejoicing and wondering, bathing in its glorious floods of light, seeing the sunbursts of morning among the icy peaks, the noonday radiance on the trees and rocks and snow, the flush of the alpenglow, and a thousand dashing waterfalls with their marvelous irised spray, it still seems to me above all others the Range of Light, the most divinely beautiful of all the mountain chains I have ever seen. (1916b, 5)

The only changes from the original are that "bathing in its glorious floods of light" originally read "seeing its glorious floods of light," and the last phrase, "the most divinely beautiful of all the mountain chains I have ever seen," is a completely new addition.

Although minor, these changes demonstrate two things. First, the change from "seeing" to "bathing" demonstrates Muir's concern with diction, a calculated change to emphasize the waterlike nature of the "floods" of light, while shifting the perceptual focus from the passive and visual to the active and tactile. This change demonstrates Muir's concern with immersing readers in the experiential, a process readily available to field-studies students and scholars and advocated by Muir. Second, the addition of the final phrase evidences Muir's political agenda, emphasizing that the unique and magnificent qualities of the Sierra Nevada deserve protection.

Muir continues to make careful changes in diction throughout *The Mountains of California,* attending to the rhythm of his prose while ensuring that his descriptions are both accurate and lyrically effective. In his journal, Muir writes, "This sunny openness and accessibility of the Sierra forests is one of their most marked and charming characteristics" (1986, 2). He then moves into the second person and addresses readers directly, telling them what they will see and how easy it is to "saunter" through the "magnificent colonnades" of forests. In the revised version, Muir writes, "The inviting openness of the Sierra woods is one of their most distinguishing characteristics."

The next sentence describes the forest's "sunny colonnades" but uses the general third person ("one") rather than the specific second-person construction ("you"). He returns to the second-person form, however, adding, "Now you cross a wild garden, now a meadow, now a ferny, willowy stream" (1916b, 163). The minor changes made to the first sentence—replacing "sunny" and "accessibility" with "inviting" and "marked and charming" with "distinguishing"—demonstrate Muir's continual concern with precision and concision in his use of language. The result of the other changes is twofold: First, the reader is moved more slowly and smoothly from the descriptions of the forest to the second-person prose. And second, the paragraph ends in the revised version with the second-person construction, thereby emphasizing the reader's vicarious experience of the forest.

Muir's concern with language is evident again in his description of the sugar pine, *Pinus lambertiana.* In addition, in this section we find entire passages—excerpts from David Douglas's journal—that have been added during the revision process. In his journal, Muir opens the section with the following lines: "This noblest pine ever yet discovered in the forests of the world is the Sierra Sugar Pine, *Pinus lambertiana*. It surpasses all others not merely in size but in beauty and impressiveness. I wish I could carry a specimen from its mountain home to compel the tribute of praise that I am sure every human being would gladly accord to it" (1986, 20). Following this introduction, in the journal, Muir proceeds to describe the pine's stature, pattern of growth, and natural history. In revision, however, he makes a few key changes to increase the rhetorical effectiveness of the opening. He begins the passage similarly: "This is the noblest pine yet discovered, surpassing all others not merely in size but also in kingly beauty and majesty" (1986b, 171). After this tightened introduction, Muir omits the passage about taking the sugar pine from its home and launches directly into his description of the species. The shortened sentence and changes in diction serve to emphasize the noble "beauty and majesty" of the tree—the central point Muir wishes to convey. Similarly, because Muir cannot physically take the tree and show it to the world, he does the next best thing and shares the sugar pine with his wide readership in a virtual manner, thereby enacting through his description the wishes voiced in the sentence that was cut during the revision process.

The published version also contains substantive additions. Muir includes historical information regarding David Douglas's "discovery" of the noble pine, and an entire page is quoted from the botanist's journal describing the event. This background information, though not included in the original journals, does not detract from the immediacy or accuracy of the descriptions but instead supplies readers with useful contextual information. This information was researched by Muir after the expedition in which the journal pages were first completed and added during the revision process. This represents one of the most substantial types of changes Muir made during his process of revision. Although Muir often followed his journals quite faithfully, major additions often came as a result of subsequent research and observation. Often he added information to a description or related a particular ecological insight that was not known at the time of composition but was applicable to the subject at hand. His inclusion of his own already developed theories of glaciation in *My First Summer in the Sierra* represents one example of this. During the historical first summer in the Sierra Nevada, Muir had not yet developed his glacial theories, but by the time he published the literary *My First Summer* his glacial theories had been fully developed, published, and corroborated by the scientific community.

Another example of this type of informative addition is seen in Muir's description of *Pinus tuberculata,* or the "hickory" pine. A fairly uncommon pine, often unnoticed and restricted to growing in specific localities, the hickory pine was probably not a species Muir had the opportunity to study often. In both his journal and the published versions of *The Mountains of California,* Muir describes the species, but his account is shorter than that of many of the other species treated in the same work. *Mountains,* however, contains a key passage relating to the tree's reliance on ground fires for propagation that appears to have been absent from the original journal. I say "appears" because in one journal these observations can be found; however, they are written in a thinner ink and a slightly different hand than that used in the rest of the journal, indicating that they may have been added at a later date than the original entries. Additionally, both the kinds of observations they make and their placement at the end of a page suggest that they were made over a long period of time and added at a later date.

Muir, in fact, seems to imply just such a process when he introduces the observations: "In my studies of this species I found a very interesting and significant group of facts, whose relations will be seen almost as soon as stated" (170). He then relates three distinct facts he has observed about all of the *tuberculata:* One, all the trees examined are of the same age; two, groves are always found on hillsides prone to fire; and three, there are no seedlings or saplings in living *tuberculata* groves, but they spring up profusely in groves destroyed by fires. This type of information can be gained only over a series of separate field studies so that one can compare various groves with others and look for connections among different sites of growth.

Because of the nature of the observations and the form in which they appear in the journal, we can reasonably assume that they were added years after the initial observations of the species were recorded in the journal. Like the historical information relating to David Douglas's first meeting with the sugar pine, the insights into the fire ecology of the hickory pine seem to have been added later to offer readers a greater depth of understanding about the species.

Muir's concern for his audience's complete understanding is demonstrated in many other places as well. Whether it is in the form of added research or greater detail in description, Muir was always conscious of the limits in his readers' experience, knowledge, and understanding. In his description of the Douglas squirrel, *Sciurus douglassii,* for example, Muir's additions, although minor, show this concern very well. In the original version, Muir writes, "Go where you may through the Sierra forests in all the zones you find this interesting little squirrel the master of existence" (1986, 2). In the revised version, however, he replaces the general descriptive phrase "all the zones" with much more detailed descriptions of the zones themselves: "Go where you will throughout the noble woods of the Sierra Nevada, among the giant pines and spruces of the lower zones, up through the towering silver firs to the storm-bent thickets of the summit peaks, you everywhere find this little squirrel the master of existence" (1916b, 252). Although the phrase "all the zones" is sufficiently detailed for Muir, who has experienced each of them intimately, it does not convey enough information for readers who may have no idea what each of these different zones is like or where they are located. The additional detail enables readers to understand the wide variety of forests and elevations in which the Douglas squirrel comfortably makes its home. Without such additions, the reader's understanding would necessarily be limited.

A final type of addition that is often encountered in comparing the journals to the revised works relates to the development of Muir's literary persona as a means of establishing authority. The authority of Muir's literary persona, as well as that of the historical Muir himself, rested primarily upon the quality, intensity, and extensiveness of his experiences in the regions he wrote about. His theory that glaciers had carved the Sierra Nevada was originally scoffed at by Josiah Whitney and other contemporary scientists. However, because it was founded upon evidence gained directly from the field, it could be easily confirmed by others and was soon adopted by the general scientific community.

In a similar fashion, Muir occasionally inserts first-person references to himself in the published works that were nonexistent in the original journals. He does not, however, dramatize himself as the central protagonist of the action. Rather, as in his description of Billy, Muir subordinates the human to the surrounding natural world. The first-person insertions are not meant to aggrandize Muir or make him a more central figure driving the action or capturing the focus of the narrative. Instead, they serve to subtly remind readers of his extensive experience in the Sierra Nevada as support for his authority to speak for the region.

One of Muir's most famous mountaineering exploits captured in a narrative, one often anthologized and mythologized, concerns his climbing of a Douglas spruce to experience the power of a massive Sierran windstorm. Before this dangerous, yet exciting, experience is related, Muir describes the storm as a "high festival" and the swaying, windblown trees as a chorus of rejoicing vocalists. In his journal, Muir writes, "Each was expressing itself in its own way and the amount of individuality manifested was far greater than would be anticipated by those who had never seen these woods" (1986, 15). Although Muir also makes a number of changes in diction and adds some new descriptors, the most substantive revision comes in the form of changing the general third person to the specific first person. In *The Mountains of California,* Muir writes, "Each was expressing itself in its own way,—singing its own song, and making its own peculiar gestures—manifesting a richness of variety to be found in no other forest I have yet seen" (1916b, 279). Here Muir avoids distancing his audience from the event by reminding them that they have "never seen these woods" and reinforces his own authority by reminding readers of his vast amount of experience studying similar forests, by stating, "found in no other forest I have yet seen."

Taken as a whole, these changes demonstrate several key features of Muir's work. First, his published works exhibit a much greater deal of craft and manipulation than is generally accepted, yet they are also extremely accurate with regard to the experiences Muir had and the observations he made. Second, we are able to observe Muir's intensive concern for literary style and rhetorical effect and note how carefully the diction, rhythm, and sound of particular passages are wrought. Finally, we are able to appreciate the self-conscious intention with which Muir constructed his published work, adding in parts of himself (which he was reluctant to do) when it was necessary for persuasive effect and relying upon lyrical language and scientific information to affect his readers on a variety of levels. Noting these aspects of Muir's revision process leads one to conclude that Muir's driving purpose in composition was activist oriented. He wanted, through his writing, to make readers know, understand, experience (vicariously or otherwise), love, and defend his beloved Range of Light.

In order to achieve this goal, Muir recognized that his observations and reflections had to be reliable and accurate, as well as beautiful and interest-ing, and that the narrator himself had to be credible and exciting. This syn-thesis of characteristics corresponds directly to the three modes of classical rhetoric—logos, pathos, and ethos—a triad that the exceedingly well-read Muir was sure to be familiar with. In a telling letter to Robert Underwood Johnson, Muir's editor, he openly discusses his concern with rhetorical effect in the composition of *Mountains:* "In it I have ventured to drop in the poetry that I like but have taken good care to place it between bluffs and buttresses of bold geological facts" (qtd. in Cohen 1984, 285). As is demonstrated by the reception of Muir's work and the manner in which it was produced, Muir should be considered not only a master of mountains but also an accom-plished rhetorician, not just a scientist but a poet as well.

CHAPTER SIX

Field Journaling with Muir in Mind

I tremble with excitement in the dawn of these glorious mountain sublimities, but I can only gaze and wonder, and, like a child, gather here and there a lily, half hoping I may be able to study and learn in years to come.

JOHN MUIR,
My First Summer in the Sierra

The angular rays of late afternoon sunlight cut through a pocket of Sierra old growth in shimmering beams of yellow and gold. Light sparkles and falls in drops and streams from the glittering canopy of ponderosa and red fir, towering hundreds of feet above us. Littered throughout the forest—on a fallen log here, at the base of a fir there, on a jutting granite outcrop above— my students write in their field journals and rest their weary feet and sore backs from the toil of the trail. One student sits on a polished boulder next to a small cascading stream, her bare pink feet soaking in the frigid water as it tumbles down from snowfields in the high country above us; another stands mesmerized by an ancient red cedar, attempting to capture its gnarled branches and massive form on the pages of his field journal. They are each participating in a weeklong backpacking trip, the field component of an off-campus interdisciplinary field-study course. These young scholars, having enrolled in English 499/790, "The Literature and Natural History of the Pacific Crest Trail," now find themselves amid a pocket of old-growth conifers in the middle of the John Muir Wilderness. Over the past week, they have been reading *My First Summer in the Sierra* and have been re-creating many of Muir's techniques in their field journals, while also gaining insight into the sheer physical reality of living in and traveling through the high Sierra Nevada, a reality that is usually obscured or ignored during traditional classroom-based approaches to Muir's work.

We hiked all morning through the charred remains of a mixed conifer forest, the tall fire-scarred and blackened snags standing ominously about us like tombstones. We noted the thick, impassable understory that had filled in between the boles of the blackened snags since the fire's passing: several species of currants, whitethorn, and manzanita, and in the riparian areas willow and alder were already coming back. As we moved through the scorched remnants of red fir and ponderosa pine we were treated to a hands-on lesson in Sierra Nevada fire ecology. The natural fire regime here, before Euro-American interference, promised a low-intensity ground fire, on average, every seven to eleven years. These frequent low-intensity fires crawled along the ground of Sierran forests, removing the dead and downed fuel, taking out small seedlings, and in general thinning the forest so that it maintained a more open appearance than it now has.

As Muir noted in the late 1800s, "The inviting openness of the Sierra woods is one of their most distinguishing characteristics. The trees of all the species stand more or less apart in groves, or in small, irregular groups, enabling one to find a way nearly everywhere, along sunny colonnades and through openings that have a smooth, parklike surface, strewn with brown needles and burs" (1916b, 163). Unfortunately for us, the "inviting openness" Muir spoke of was now absent from these forests. Only a carefully maintained trail, with a thick, sandy tread, allowed us to pass through that woody graveyard.

As we examined the charred snags and fought our way through the nearly impassable understory, we began to understand what had occurred here on more than an intellectual level. As we moved through that landscape, history became visceral, palpable, and real. We witnessed the legacy of clear-cutting during the Comstock era, which left this range with only 5 percent of its original forests intact, as well as the devastating results of one hundred years of fire suppression, leaving today's Sierran forests with higher fuel loads, thicker understories, and dangerous ladder fuels. The fires that move through this landscape now burn at a higher intensity and are more likely to climb mature trees and turn into canopy or stand-replacing fires. The haunting blackened pillars surrounding us stood as a silent testament to this history of human degradation.

As we made our way from one burned snag to another, we contrasted our bracken-beaten path through the choked understory with Muir's description of these forests before they were ravaged by years of overzealous logging and fire suppression. Muir writes, "One would experience little difficulty in riding on horseback through the successive belts [of trees] all the way up to the storm-beaten fringes of the icy peaks" (163). Yet today our way is so choked with the first generation of successional plants that it is difficult to move ten feet through the layers of scrub. We fight, push, and claw our way through the dense, thorn-clad bushes, collecting an array of barbs, pokes, and scratches, writing one part of this place's history on our skin, just as our studies have indelibly etched it into our minds.

Without Muir's dated descriptions of this area, and our own field experiences in it, these drastic changes in forest composition and natural fire regimes would easily have been lost to us. In order to know what this place is today, we must also know what it has been and how it has changed. Likewise, in order to understand what the Range of Light was to John Muir, we must begin to experience and reflect on what it is to us. Without such a dualistic approach—one that includes both texts and places, both past and present within the field of inquiry—our understanding of the Sierra Nevada, as well as its literature, will necessarily become simplified and static. We run the risk of losing, based on the exclusivity of our approach, some part of the complex and dynamic history—geological, biological, and cultural—that has made the Sierra Nevada all they are today and all that they have been in the past.

MUIR AS METHODOLOGICAL MODEL

Like John Muir, we have come to the Sierra Nevada to meet the mountains and talk to the trees and to learn what they have to teach us. Unlike Muir, however, we have two important guides from the human community to help us in our natural history studies: Both Muir's detailed observations of the stunning Sierra Nevada and the Pacific Crest Trail's carefully constructed route aid us in navigating this interesting and difficult terrain. When Muir first began his studies of the Sierra, however, he did not have the comfort of such guides. He had to develop much of his methodology himself.

Despite his lack of formal training in the sciences, Muir was a particularly careful observer of the natural world, a voracious reader, a prolific writer, and a disciplined field scientist. He approached his studies of the natural world with a formal discipline inherited from Louis Agassiz and benefited greatly from his correspondence with Asa Gray. He read works on geology and botany when he could get his hands on them, often carried plant presses with him into the field, and consistently sent specimens to and discussed his observations with professional colleagues. As noted Muir scholar William F. Badé records, "In the absence of authoritative treatises on the plants, insects, and wild life of the region he had to send specimens to classifying specialists for identification" (Muir 1923, 1:265).

Despite his lack of formal training, Muir came to be recognized, even by his contemporaries, as an accomplished natural historian. Nowhere is this more evident than in the advances in scientific understanding attributed to Muir. He was responsible for developing theories of glaciation in the Sierra Nevada that literally revolutionized the geological field and for a host of newly discovered plant and animal species. In 1871, for example, amateur entomologist Henry Edwards wrote to Muir: "In the small box you sent me are *four species new to my collection*, and *two of these are new to science*. I cannot, if I wrote for a week, tell you how interesting they are to me" (264; emphasis in original). Ten years later, Edwards would name the butterfly *Thecla muiri* after his old friend and colleague.

The secret to Muir's success as a scientist rested upon his painstaking attention to detail and the vast amount of direct experience he gained in the field. As an environmental author and activist, Muir's success rested upon this scientific authority and his ability to translate his own experiences, reflections, and emotions into words that gave his natural history studies human interest, perspective, and emotional power. In fact, Muir's journals themselves formed the foundation upon which all of his later scientific and literary work would be based. Because he was so effective at composing field journals and translating his field experiences and observations into useful insights for readers, Muir serves as an excellent guide for directing our own studies in natural history. As Michael P. Cohen notes, "[H]e becomes himself an example. We watch him and learn" (1975, 185).

One of the most useful things we can learn from Muir is to follow his example and develop useful and varied strategies for studying and responding to the natural world. In this way, his published work can do much more than teach us about the Sierra Nevada or give us a vicarious mountaineering thrill. It can also serve as a methodological model, one that we can follow as we develop our own techniques for keeping field journals and studying the natural world directly.

Using Muir's work in this manner accords well with his authorial intentions and is particularly beneficial because of the wide variety of journal entries he compiled. Muir used his journals for more than merely compiling scientific information. He also recorded his mountaineering exploits, philosophical ruminations, emotional responses, and aesthetic evaluations of the Sierra Nevada. Christine Oravec contends, "He unified aesthetic, rational, and ethical response to nature in an effort to lessen the degree of alienation between humanity and the natural world" (1981, 258). Studying Muir's techniques for keeping field journals illuminates how he synthesized these various modes of perceiving the natural world and teaches us more about the places in which we study or recreate.

Using Muir's journals and published works as a model, I have developed a series of exercises for composing field journals that can help environmental studies students to understand the natural world from a variety of perspectives. I have included below a sample of the types of approaches that can be found in Muir's work and that I have found beneficial for my own use and for that of my students. Each exercise is designed to give the practitioner experience with a different disciplinary approach, or way of understanding and responding, to the natural world.

Although these perspectives can later be unified, as Muir did in his own writing, it is often easier for the novice field student to try out each perspective individually. The seven field journaling exercises detailed below take the following disciplinary approaches: ecological, historical, sensual, autobiographical, psychospiritual, philosophical-ethical, and literary. By incorporating such assignments into our environmental studies pedagogy, we can ensure that an interdisciplinary and comprehensive understanding of the place being studied is gained. This is especially important for environmental studies students who will primarily receive a scientific or ecological viewpoint of the natural world, as well as for students of environmental literature who need to augment their textual studies with direct observations and experience.

The Ecological Perspective

The first journaling exercise I use with students directs them to pick a particular species of plant or animal and study it in detail. Muir relied heavily on this approach, and, in fact, it was his most common field journaling method. Muir admits, "When I discovered a new plant, I sat down beside it for a minute or a day, to make its acquaintance and hear what it had to tell" (qtd. in Cohen 1984, 41). For this particular approach, I encourage students to do the same. After reading works like *My First Summer in the Sierra* and *The Mountains of California*, students have seen Muir model this approach repeatedly and are quite capable of employing it themselves.

One may also choose to take the same approach to a particular topographic, geologic, or hydrologic feature of the landscape, taking as one's subject the erosive action of a stream, glacially polished granite, or the volcanic formation of cinder cones and fumaroles. Muir also used this approach: "When I came to moraines, or ice-scratches upon the rocks, I traced them back, learning what I could of the glacier that made them. I asked bowlders I met, whence they came and whither they were going" (qtd. in Cohen 1984, 41). Regardless of the particular subject, much can be learned about it, and its relationship to other members of the region, through such field journaling exercises.

I usually begin by having the students sketch the particular species they have chosen as a means for focusing their observational study. We use Muir's own sketches both as subjects of study and as models, for as Steven Holmes observes, after Muir came to Yosemite, "sketching became one of his major activities and even preoccupations, as a way to begin to grasp and to take in the new landscape" (1999, 206). Although Muir's contemporary readers are familiar with the many published examples of his completed sketches, his journals and notebooks contain hundreds of field sketches that are less complete or artistic but demonstrate careful attention to detail and an attempt to visually represent past geologic and hydrologic forces. Muir often used his sketches as a means to identify species and to explore how particular topographic features were formed. For students, the process of sketching and visually studying their subject forces them to slow down, focus, and analyze distinguishing features and characteristics while engaging in a process of representation that is related to but different from literary and linguistic representation.

After they have completed their sketches, the students begin the compositional process by describing their species objectively, recording its distinguishing characteristics, size, shape, pattern of growth, and location. Then they use field guides to supplement their observations with accurate information regarding the species' history and life cycle. From this exercise, students become familiar with taxonomic classification, botanical and anatomical terminology, major plant associations, and a host of other ecologically oriented concepts.

Finally, they record their own subjective responses, generated by reflecting on the value and unique characteristics of the particular species they have been studying. Again we use Muir's own writing as a model, noting how he fuses emotional response with scientific information in order to give readers a comprehensive picture of his subject and his relationship to it. Such a process engages students on a variety of intellectual and emotional levels, increases their knowledge of and appreciation for the natural world, and gives them experience with synthesizing different rhetorical modes and perspectives.

For a model, I commonly use Muir's description of the sugar pine, *Pinus lambertiana*, in *The Mountains of California*, because it exhibits all of the approaches described above. In this section Muir details the pine's range and distribution, pattern of growth, and the shape and color of its cones, seeds, and needles, and he even relates historical information concerning its use by Native Americans and lumbermen and its "discovery" by botanist David Douglas. Additionally, in characteristically Muir-like fashion, readers are treated to an especially rich series of emotional responses, lyrical descriptions, and philosophical reflections on *lambertiana*'s beauty, grandeur, and value. A microcosmic example of this synthesis of perspectives can be found in the sentence in which Muir writes, "Full grown specimens are commonly about two hundred and twenty feet high, and from six to eight feet in diameter near the ground, though some grand old patriarch is occasionally met that has enjoyed five or six centuries of storms, and attained a thickness of ten or even twelve feet, living on undecayed, sweet and fresh in every fiber" (1916b, 172). In this passage Muir not only describes the distinguishing features of the tree, but also emphasizes its longevity and responds evaluatively to its health and vibrancy as a form of subtle argument in favor of its preservation.

The Historical Perspective

A second approach to field journaling is to take a historical approach to one's particular subject. In this form of field study, students are directed to pick a particular feature of the landscape that evidences some form of change, either human induced or natural. Students might decide to focus on forest succession, fire ecology, erosion, glaciation, indigenous uses of local species, trail construction, recreational impacts, or a host of other forces that change the landscape.

For the observational portion of this exercise, students may choose to sketch or simply describe what they see, answering such questions as: What evidence of change exists? What might have caused this change? What are its effects? Because this exercise focuses on a historical perspective, students are then required to conduct textual research to discover what historical events might account for the change they have witnessed and described. Because the bulk of Muir's published work is almost a century old, it can often be used as a historical document. Our earlier observations regarding forest composition and fire ecology benefited in precisely this manner. By comparing our experiences in dense forests where fire had been absent for too long and recently burned stands had suffered from canopy fires to Muir's descriptions of the healthy Sierran forests that were thinned periodically by ground fires, we were able to learn much about forest composition, fire ecology, and historic fire suppression in the Sierra Nevada region. It was precisely because of such comparisons that prescribed fire was introduced into Yosemite National Park in 1971 as an attempt to correct the effects of harmful fire suppression that had been practiced in the past.

Muir also exemplifies this approach in his treatment of the sugar pine, lamenting, "Unfortunately it is greatly prized by the lumbermen, and in accessible places is always the first tree in the woods to feel their steel. . . . [T]he havoc they make is most deplorable" (1916b, 177). Because it was selected by early lumbermen as a choice species for harvest, the sugar pine's range and numbers have been severely limited. To this day, the sugar pine is seen much less often, and in fewer places, than it was in Muir's time.

The historical approach is extremely beneficial for helping students to explore and understand human relationships with natural landscapes, especially how those relationships and landscapes have changed over time.

The Sensual Perspective

A third approach to journaling in the field that I have found of benefit directs the practitioner to study the natural world with the four senses that are usually marginalized by the visual gaze. We tend to rely so heavily on visual observation and knowledge of the world that we often miss many of the subtler and more important qualities of the natural world that are available only through our other senses. For this exercise students may be directed to choose one of their nonvisual senses or all four—hearing, touch, smell, and taste—and to record how they perceive the world through that particular perspective.

If a student chooses to study the sounds of the natural world, for example, I direct them to sneak quietly to a secluded and comfortable spot, sit down where they will be unobtrusive, and close their eyes for at least twenty minutes. The longer the students sit with their eyes closed, the more successful the exercise tends to be. It often takes those of us living in the modern world quite some time to slow down, turn off our inner monologue, and truly listen to the world around us. After the initial period of auditory observation is completed, the students open their eyes and record in their journals all of the sounds they heard, what they think might have made them, what they sounded like, their proximity to the listener, and anything else that seems relevant. Periodically, the student might close his or her eyes again for a few minutes to listen some more and then record further observations. At the end of the exercise, students are directed to reflect upon the differences between what they noticed through their sense of hearing and what they noticed with their sense of sight.

Muir often notes the auditory delights of the Sierran wilderness, rejoicing in the "preaching of trees" and the "singing of streams." He even asserts that he can distinguish between the different species of Sierran trees by the varied tones with which they give voice to the wind. In his description of a raging Sierran windstorm, he writes, "Even when the grand anthem had swelled to its highest pitch, I could distinctly hear the varying tones of individual trees,—spruce, and fir, and pine, and leafless oak,—and even the infinitely gentle rustle of the withered grasses at my feet" (1916b, 279).

Regardless of the sense they choose to focus on, this exercise aids students in perceiving the richness of the natural world on a variety of levels, rather than merely relegating it to the purely visual. Such a process is psychologically important for those of us living in a world that privileges the visual and desensitizes us to the subtleties of the natural world, but it is also beneficial on a practical level. We can, for example, use our nonvisual senses to aid in the identification of native plant species. The Jeffrey and ponderosa pine, *Pinus jeffreyi* and *P. ponderosa*, for example, both have long needles grouped in threes, similar-looking bark, and similarly sized cones. They do differ markedly, however, in smell and texture. The bark of the Jeffrey pine, for example, emits a strong vanilla or pineapple odor when you press your nose into its deep furrows. The cones of each species, likewise, help to distinguish them. Each bract on the cone of both species ends in a sharp, prickly growth that curves inward on the Jeffrey and outward, pricking the hand, on the ponderosa. Thus, students learn to distinguish by feel between the "gentle Jeffrey and prickly ponderosa."

Many other species can be similarly identified using nonvisual clues, such as the incense cedar, *Calocedrus decurrens,* which can easily be identified by the pungent incenselike aroma emitted when its needles are crushed between the fingers, or the antelope bitterbrush, *Purshia tridentata,* which can be distinguished by the sharp, bitter taste of its leaves when chewed and tasted with the tip of the tongue.

The Autobiographical Perspective

A fourth approach that can be particularly useful for the field-studies student or scholar is to practice composing journal entries from an autobiographical perspective. This method of journaling in the field generally comes easiest for students, as many have kept some sort of journal, diary, or logbook of their activities in the past. For this particular exercise, I direct students to pick a particularly memorable event, activity, experience, or day of their field-studies expedition and to compose a short narrative about it.

First, we look to Muir to find particularly interesting and effective examples to use as models. We make note of the rhetorical effectiveness of engaging audiences through intriguing, exciting, and suspenseful narratives in order to relay other types of ecological or ethical information and insight. Christine Oravec points out that Muir often did just this: "Muir often transformed the narrative line of scientific exposition into the narrative adventure, thereby involving the reader in the active life of the mountaineer-guide" (1981, 250). Muir's famous tale of climbing a Douglas spruce in the middle of a Sierran windstorm in order to feel the full effect of the "grand anthem" demonstrates this technique.

Muir describes the ferocity and power of the wind as a means to create suspense and danger in the story, while also demonstrating the amazing resilience of the region's great conifers.

> Colossal spires two hundred feet in height waved like supple goldenrods chanting and bowing low as if in worship, while the whole mass of their long, tremulous foliage was kindled into one continuous blaze of white sun-fire. The force of the gale was such that the most steadfast monarch of them all rocked down to its roots with a motion plainly perceptible when one leaned against it. (1916b, 278)

Muir then proceeds to inform readers that he wanted to climb a tree to witness the windstorm for himself but that the choice of which tree to climb was a "serious matter"—a means for introducing more suspense in the passage. Finally, Muir is atop his perch, and the danger and suspense have resolved in pure exhilaration and exultation in the grandeur of nature. Muir exclaims:

> The slender tops fairly flapped and swished in the passionate torrent, bending and swirling backward and forward, round and round, tracing indescribable combinations of vertical and horizontal curves, while I clung with muscles firm braced, like a bobolink on a reed. In its widest sweeps my tree-top described an arc of from twenty to thirty degrees, but I felt sure of its elastic temper, having seen others of the same species still more severely tried—bent almost to the ground indeed, in heavy snows—without breaking a fiber. I was therefore safe, and free to take the wind into my pulses and enjoy the excited forest from my superb outlook. (281)

Whether students have such adventurous subject matter to work with or not, understanding the rhetorical effectiveness of including similar autobiographical adventure stories in their work is paramount if they wish to understand, and make use of, literature's effectiveness in connecting readers to wilderness experiences. As Muir had clearly discovered by 1911, when *My First Summer in the Sierra* was published, developing a narrative structure to support his ecological studies and preservationist philosophy not only was extremely effective, but was, in fact, required by his audience.

The Psychospiritual Perspective

A fifth approach to exploring the natural world and our place in it entails studying not the natural landscape itself but our emotional responses to it. For this exercise, I encourage students to find a particular location that seems to affect them in some dramatic way. They may choose the comfortable quiet of a mountain meadow ringed by trees, the dizzying heights of a granite precipice, the roar of a waterfall, or the sigh of the wind in the trees (or even a busy downtown street corner). Regardless of the students' choices, I direct them to sit still for fifteen to twenty minutes and to observe both the characteristics and features of the place they are in and their associated mental states, their feelings and thoughts. I also encourage students to contrast their present feelings with how they feel at home, at work, and in other settings that are quite different from the one they are presently in. In their journals the students record these observations and attempt to find connections between their inner feelings and the outer landscape. As Muir exclaims in *My First Summer:*

> We are now in the mountains and they are in us, kindling enthusiasm, making every nerve quiver, filling every pore and cell of us. Our flesh-and-bone tabernacle seems transparent as glass to the beauty about us, as if truly an inseparable part of it, thrilling with the air and trees, streams and rocks, in the waves of the sun,—a part of all nature, neither old nor young, sick nor well, but immortal. (1916c, 16)

Muir was very conscious of the interpenetrating character of wilderness experience and human psychology, the correspondences of inner and outer worlds.

For Muir, however, these psychological revelations often took religious, or spiritual, form. In a letter to his friend Mrs. Carr, Muir proclaims:

> I'm in the woods woods woods, and they are in *me-ee-ee*. The King tree and me have sworn eternal love—sworn it without swearing and I've

taken the sacrament with Douglas Squirrel, drank Sequoia wine, Sequoia blood, and with its rosy purple drops I am writing this woody gospel letter. . . . I wish I was so drunk and Sequoical that I could preach the green brown woods to all the juiceless world, descending from this divine wilderness like a John Baptist eating Douglas Squirrels and wild honey or wild anything, crying, Repent for the Kingdom of Sequoia is at hand. (1923, 1:271)

Interestingly, this letter was written in ink prepared from Sequoia cones. It demonstrates not only Muir's ecstatic religious vision and belief in inner and outer correspondences, but also his attempt to convey the immediacy and quality of this experience as closely as possible to his friend by writing in the "blood" of the "King tree."

For environmental studies practitioners who are primarily absorbed in the scientific and objective study of the natural world, engaging in such a process of subjective experience and evaluation can offer an important corrective. Students will gain insight into the less quantifiable values people find in natural landscapes and will, perhaps, develop a greater appreciation for sites considered sacred by Native Americans and other pantheistically oriented people.

The Philosophical-Ethical Perspective

A sixth perspective by which to view particular natural landscapes, or features of them, is to explore what they have to teach us with regard to how we should live in, rely on, and interact with them. For this field journaling exercise, students are encouraged to reflect upon some facet of the landscape or their experience in it and to discuss the values, ethics, and ideas it generates or that seem associated with it. Reflecting upon the movements of a mountain stream, for example, might lead one to notice the manner in which our actions affect others, our mutual interdependence with all beings, and the fact that we all, literally, live downstream. Likewise, consideration of the slow geological process of mountain making and erosion might encourage one to consider contemporary problems from a longer temporal perspective.

Regardless of one's approach, or where one's musings lead, natural landscapes can, and do, lead to deeper philosophical reflection and aid in the development of environmental ethics and actions. Aldo Leopold's famous "Land Ethic" was developed in just such a way. After years of working as a wildlife manager and attempting to restore his family's degraded farm, Leopold formulated an ethical principle for guiding human interactions with natural landscapes. He wrote: "A thing is right when it tends to preserve the integrity, stability, and beauty of the biotic community. It is wrong when it tends otherwise" (1949, 225). Our students should be encouraged to explore their own attitudes toward the natural world and to try to develop ethical and philosophical positions based upon their interactions with it.

Muir often augmented his scientific observations with philosophical reflections engendered by the species he was studying. His discussion of poison oak, *Rhus diversiloba*, for example, leads him to contemplate the anthropocentric nature of humankind. "Like most other things not apparently useful to man, it has few friends and the blind question, 'Why was it made?' goes on and on with never a guess that first of all it might have been made for itself" (1916c, 26). From such philosophical ruminations on the value of such anthropocentrically "worthless" species as poison oak, mosquitoes, and alligators, Muir was able to develop the beginnings of an ecocentric philosophy.

Similarly, in *Our National Parks*, Muir contemplates the slow-growing nature and longevity of trees and develops an ethical stance toward them. After detailing the wanton destruction caused by turn-of-the-century logging practices, Muir notes, "Few that fell trees plant them; nor would planting avail much towards getting back anything like the noble primeval forests. During a man's life only saplings can be grown, in the place of old trees—tens of centuries old—that have been destroyed" (1916d, 393). From this recognition Muir develops a strong preservationist position that asserts that protection of existing wild places is paramount to the restoration of them after they have been degraded.

The practical effectiveness of this kind of exercise becomes readily apparent when we see how easily particular ethical insights translate into support for specific political policies. Muir concludes his ruminations on the preservation of our forests by stating, "Through all the wonderful, eventful centuries since Christ's time—and long before that—God has cared for these trees, saved them from drought, disease, avalanches, and a thousand straining, leveling tempests and floods; but he cannot save them from fools,—only Uncle Sam can do that" (393).

By encouraging our students to develop their own philosophical and ethical speculations from direct experience with the natural world, we can help them to understand the important linkages among their own personal environmental ethics, the landscape in which they live, and the policies of their government. The fact that students often discover that there is little correspondence among these three things merely serves to emphasize the need for and value of this type of activity. If more Americans understood these relationships better and had developed environmental attitudes appropriate to the places in which they live, our public policies would surely be much different from what they are today.

The Literary Perspective

A final approach to field journaling about the natural world and our responses to it involves exploring the connections between the texts we read and the landscapes we explore. For this approach, I direct students to pick a particular passage, theme, or idea in Muir's work and to compare it to what they find in the natural world. Students might look for correspondences between the text and the field, noting whether the descriptions are accurate and if Muir's experiences seem similar to theirs. Or they might explore his rhetorical choices and strategies, asking why he chose to represent a particular feature of the landscape, or experience, in a particular way. Such an approach asks us to compare literary representations of the natural world with the reality of that world as we directly observe it. Although the insights gained from such an exercise might tell us something about the natural world, they will surely teach us something about ourselves. We might, for example, note that our experience of wild animals through the medium of television and film is one of continual action, combat, predator-prey relationships, sexuality, and overpowering presence. On the other hand, our experience of native animals in the wild is usually one of absence, subtle signs, and perhaps a rare glimpse of one moving in a less than dramatic manner. Such a recognition teaches us much about our failing powers of perception and patience, our need to dramatize, and our insistent misunderstanding and misrepresentation of the nonhuman world.

Often Muir's work affords students wonderful opportunities to trace textual and environmental correspondences. The accuracy of his descriptions, when field checked, often leads students to praise the reliability of his texts.

At other times, however, it is the differences that students notice most. After one particularly tough ascent during a field-study course on the PCT, we plopped down as a group to rest in the trailside gravel. Our breath came in long-drawn-out wheezes at the top of the ten thousand–foot mountain pass. Our hearts were pounding in our ears after the dizzying ascent of several thousand feet, which took us up switchbacks layered on top of each other like stairs. Our mercilessly heavy packs lay strewn about us where they had randomly been dropped as we collapsed trailside to catch our breath and take in the expansive view. After a short respite, but before my students' breathing had returned to normal or their legs had stopped burning from the buildup of lactic acid, I thought it appropriate to share Muir's thoughts with them on the experience of ascending high mountain passes. Muir wrote, and I read, "Fear not, therefore, to try the mountain passes. They will kill care, save you from deadly apathy, set you free, and call forth every faculty into vigorous, enthusiastic action. Even the sick should try these so-called dangerous passes, because for every unfortunate they kill, they cure a thousand" (1916b, 91). The students responded with an appropriate series of grunts and groans of disapproval, which later, after further rest, gave way to a few insights about Muir's literary techniques and rhetorical choices.

We noted how, even in our own journals and the stories we told to friends after such trips, our perspectives unconsciously shifted. While climbing the steep switchbacking route, the only things most of us could focus on with our bent backs and bowed heads were the slow movements of our sore feet, the burning in our thighs, and a host of other aches and pains that seemed constantly to plague us. However, after a short rest, and especially after returning to the comforts of campus, these memories faded all too quickly. All we seemed to remember, and what we tended to focus on when telling stories about our expedition, were the exciting, exhilarating, and unique experiences that made the trip pleasurable. Through the lens of nostalgia the pain faded while the pleasure grew. This was especially true in the oral and written accounts of the adventure we gave to others, leading us to recognize how the mere context of the telling—the medium, audience, time, and location—all seemed to affect the message.

These explorations helped us recognize the effect that rhetorical context has on any form of communication about the natural world, whether it is a scientific report or a mountaineering adventure. Students are then able to see how even in the objective world of scientific discourse a particular researcher's institutional affiliation, funding stream, disciplinary background, and even childhood experiences can have a tremendous effect on how he or she interprets or communicates data.

: : :

Although an infinite number of field journaling exercises could be developed from Muir's writing, or the work of other environmental authors, these are some of the approaches I have found to be the most successful. Utilizing the techniques modeled by Muir gives us insight into his method of study and his effectiveness as an activist. It also teaches us much about the bioregions in which we live and the ways in which we might develop closer and more committed relationships to them. As Michael P. Cohen observes, "In showing the reader how he has discovered the power of the wilderness he presents the strongest possible argument for wild National Parks as places where each man can seek, according to his ability, direct intercourse with the elemental forces of nature" (1975, 185). By engaging in our own process of study and exploring the many ways in which the natural world sustains us physically, intellectually, emotionally, and spiritually, we may develop a greater conviction to defend it from degradation. In so doing, we will also be defending future generations from this age's shortsightedness and greed. If we are successful, our children and grandchildren will one day be able to exclaim with enthusiasm, just as Muir did in his day, "Glorious days I'll have sketching, pressing plants, studying wonderful topography and the wild animals, our happy fellow mortals and neighbors" (1916c, 122).

CHAPTER SEVEN

Gary Snyder at Kitkitdizze

Lay down these words
Before your mind like rocks.

GARY SNYDER, *Riprap & Cold Mountain Poems*

Kneeling in the dust, I heave a large granite boulder up and into place atop a slowly growing rock wall. A slight wobble, however, indicates that the fit is not quite right. Even the most imperceptible movement now will cause it to loosen over the seasons of heavy snow, summer heat, and the incessant pounding of hiking boots and horses' hooves. Eventually, the weakened section will cause the entire wall to collapse, and it will have to be built again. I am working on a short retaining wall meant to hold one of the trail's switchbacks in place while also reducing weather- and human-induced erosion. Pulling the stone toward me, I flip it off the wall and onto the ground below. It lands with a heavy thud that I can feel vibrating up through the soles of my feet. With a rock hammer I chip at the underside, showering myself and the surrounding area with a barrage of sharp pieces of flying granite. Once the stone is shaped to fit the boulders on which it will rest, I grunt it back into place, being careful to keep my back straight and lift with my legs. A few hearty shoves fail to budge the heavy rock, and I head off, upslope to a large talus field, to find another stone for the wall.

Working above and below me on various sections of the trail are a number of members of the Nevada Conservation Corps. University students for the most part, they have been working on this section of the trail for weeks. Although this area is not on the PCT itself, we are rebuilding a badly eroded section of a spur trail that leads down into the Lake Tahoe Basin. Well-maintained trails reduce erosion, protect vital habitat, and improve the clarity of the lake's water. These trails will also enable other people to experience, enjoy, and appreciate the rugged beauty of this region while directing them away from sensitive species and minimizing their impacts on the area. For many of the young men and women building this trail, this represents the first time that they have ever given any thought to the trails on which they hike, backpack, mountain bike, and ride horses. This project offers them an opportunity to give back to the public lands and trail systems they have enjoyed and will continue to enjoy all their lives. For me, it is not only a chance to serve the public lands in my local watershed, but also an opportunity to meditate upon one of Gary Snyder's best-known poems: "Riprap."

During lunch, as we rest in the pine duff and decomposed granite beside the trail, munching sandwiches, drinking ice-cold water, and clearing our sinuses of the thick, black, sooty trail dirt that inevitably collects there as we work, I share Snyder's poem with them. Most express some amazement that anyone has actually written poetry about building trails, and I am reminded that Snyder once wrote, "The truly experienced person, the refined person, *delights in the ordinary*" (1990a, 153; emphasis in original).

Others share the new appreciation they have found for the trails they have so often hiked and taken for granted. They note that until now, they never really paid attention to how trails were routed, constructed, and maintained. They simply hiked them as if they were a given, a natural part of the landscape that had always been there, rather than a carefully planned and painstakingly constructed human artifact. We discuss the fact that many trails were first game trails, then travel and trade routes for indigenous populations, then eventually larger trails, wagon roads, and finally super-highways. Thinking of our modern cities, roads, and highways in this manner puts them in quite a different perspective.

After lunch, I find myself repeating sections of the poem as I work, noting the rhythm and the sound of the words. They seem to reflect the slow, repetitive rhythm of finding, hauling, and shaping rock, of working with the hands and the body, the rising and falling pace of ascending and descending mountains. Gary Snyder must have experienced these rhythms himself, as he worked on the Yosemite trail crew and explored the Sierra Nevada. These rhythms of the land, as well as the rhythm of working on it, clearly inform Snyder's poetry and affect both its form and content. In a 1976 interview, Snyder stated, "It's the use of the *body* and the involvement of all the senses that is important" (1980, 56; emphasis in original). I think about these ideas as I repeat the actions described in the poem, feeling my way through its rhythms and images with both my mind and my body.

How many critics have built backcountry trails as a means to interpret poems like "Riprap"? I wonder. Although it is difficult to pinpoint precisely, there does seem to be something illuminating about the experience. I feel that I understand better both the experiences that gave rise to Snyder's poem and the craft put into its laborious construction.

"Riprap" serves as an excellent example of how closely Snyder's work is based upon specific experiences in particular natural landscapes. In it he uses the practice of building trails with riprap as a metaphor for both the craft of writing poetry and the carefully designed, intricate interrelationships of all things in the universe. This general theme of the poem, as well as its foundation in Snyder's trail-building experiences, has often been commented on by critics who seem to have little experience with backcountry trail construction. Most critics, however, have avoided misreading the poem because Snyder includes, within his text, the key to interpretation. On the title page of *Riprap,* he writes, "riprap: a cobble of stone laid on steep slick rock to make a trail for horses in the mountains" (1990b, 3). By including the key to interpreting the poem in the text, Snyder is attempting to point critics to the referential and experiential sources influencing the poem. Few critics, however, have noted the manner in which the experience of riprapping trail informs the poem's rhythms, diction, textual spacing, and craft. For example, Snyder writes:

> Lay down these words
> Before your mind like rocks.
>   placed solid, by hands
> In choice of place, set. (32)

The slow, repetitive rhythm with the heavy end stops and pauses in the center of the lines recalls the physical experience of building backcountry trails. On such projects, one repeats an endless series of rhythmic tasks: searching talus fields for just the right shape and size of rock, crouching and lifting, carefully navigating one's way back to the trail over boulders and through bushes, dropping the heavy rock with a solid thud on the trail, chipping and shaping it to an exact fit, setting it heavily in place, and returning to the talus slopes again, again, and again. The care and craft, and repetition, involved in such a task are quite similar to the process of writing: choosing just the right word or image, lugging it around, searching for a place where it fits, shaping and molding it, and finally, hopefully, setting it down "In choice of place, set . . . each rock a word / a creek washed stone" (32). Without direct experience of the process and rhythms involved in such work, however, most literary critics are forced to rely upon the one-sentence definition provided by Snyder himself.

I cannot help but feel that my own understanding of the significance behind Snyder's metaphorical conflation of building trails and writing poems has been deepened by engaging in both practices myself. Likewise, my appreciation for the images and rhythms used in the poem itself has increased as I note, through direct experience, how closely they correspond to the physical experiences that originally inspired Snyder.

I am concerned that it might be a little irresponsible for literary critics to comment as authoritatively as they do on the poem, without any knowledge or experience of its informing practices. Snyder also laments the practice of writing about that which one has not experienced; formulating a dictum that could be applied to all ecocritical scholarship, he states, "If you haven't seen these things you shouldn't write about them" (1980, 156). Without some form of direct experience, it can be difficult, at times, for the scholar to provide a completely authoritative and accurate interpretation. Though Snyder has been generous enough to aid scholars with the key to interpreting "Riprap," we have assumed too often that such a textually based understanding of the intricate process of building backcountry trails is sufficient to understand the poem's experiential foundation completely. As readers and critics of Snyder's work, we will find that both our appreciation and our understanding of his poetry deepen when we engage in the practices, or visit the places, about which he writes.

In addition to gaining a deeper understanding of poems like "Riprap" through such forms of field-based scholarship, we may also find that direct experience works well to augment existing scholarly interpretations. While field-based scholarship has not generally been applied to Snyder's work, interdisciplinary ecocritics who engage in such practices will often find that they support and modify existing scholarship in interesting and useful ways.

Snyder's work has enjoyed a great deal of critical attention by notable literary scholars such as Charles Molesworth, Patrick D. Murphy, Sherman Paul, and Katsunori Yamazato. Few people would suggest that a serious student of Snyder's work ignore the scholarship produced by these and other critics. Likewise, I contend that Snyder scholars should also take advantage of the insights gained through direct experience and field studies. From my own experience, the best strategy for coming to understand Snyder's work is to make use of both of these vital resources: field experience and literary scholarship. As I hope to demonstrate, the two are often mutually informative; generally, the insights gained through one method support, rather than subvert, the conclusions attained via the other. By joining traditional literary scholarship with field-based studies, we can come to a deeper understanding of Snyder's work as well as that of other ecopoets and nature writers.

THE EXPERIENTIAL KEY

Gaining direct experience of the natural world is especially important when interpreting the work of an ecopoet like Gary Snyder, whose work is so strongly informed by and focused on the natural world itself. The first poem to appear in *Riprap & Cold Mountain Poems,* "Mid-August at Sourdough Mountain Lookout," demonstrates Snyder's consistent emphasis on the extratextual natural world. Based upon his experience as a lone fire lookout, the poem resists the classical romantic emphasis on the subjectivity of the speaker and instead places the focus on the external physical world. After describing the view looking down from atop Sourdough Mountain in the first stanza, Snyder writes:

> I cannot remember things I once read
> A few friends, but they are in cities.
> Drinking cold snow-water from a tin cup
> Looking down for miles
> Through high still air. (1990b, 3)

Most of the poem is descriptive of nature, often carefully noting minute details such as the fact that "Pitch glows on the fir-cones." However, Snyder refrains from making subjective evaluations of the landscape; his emotions are conspicuously absent from the poem. There are few adjectives, and things remembered but not truly present—such as friends in cities—are described in exceedingly general terms. The marginalization of textuality is emphasized by the line "I cannot remember things I once read," while the focus on the extratextual present is reaffirmed by the closing lines. Snyder ends the poem by launching readers off the peak he is sitting on and out into the "high still air." This emphasis on the reality of the natural world, on physicality over textuality, is a trademark of Snyder's work.

Similarly, most Snyder scholars agree that there are four major influences affecting his work: anthropological materials and the insights of indigenous cultures, Buddhist scripture and practice, ecological terms and concepts, and the physical experience of work and play in the mundane world. Because of the textual bias inherent in our field, however, many of these critics have tended to emphasize the first three influences while marginalizing or ignoring the latter. Even when several of these influences are clearly linked in Snyder's poetry, critics have tended to focus on those that are most readily interpretable through textually based methodologies rather than those that require some form of bodily experience or physical practice. By adding our own explorations into the experiential foundations of Snyder's work, we can fill in a few of the gaps left by text-based methodologies, as well as strengthen many existing critical interpretations with complementary evidence.

An example of the way in which field experiences can be used to augment traditional interpretations of Snyder's poetry can be seen by looking at two divergent but equally useful interpretations of Snyder's "Song of the Taste." He begins by describing, in biological terms, the act of eating other living organisms:

Eating the living germs of grasses
Eating the ova of large birds

  the fleshy sweetness packed
  around the sperm of swaying trees

The muscles of the flanks and thighs of
  soft-voiced cows . . .

Eating roots grown swoll
inside the soil.

Snyder then proceeds to describe this same act of eating in explicitly sensual terms:

Eating each other's seed
    eating
ah, each other.

Kissing the lover in the mouth of bread:
        lip to lip. (1992, 169)

In his approach to the poem, Robert I. McClintock notes, "Ecological concepts and language permeate Snyder's vision" and lists such renowned ecologists as Eugene Odum, Howard T. Odum, and Ramon Margalef as major influences on Snyder's thought and work (1994, 110). McClintock asserts that "Song of the Taste" is a poetic evocation of the ecological concept of energy transfer, as exemplified in the food chain. Snyder agrees, stating in an interview: "If you think of eating and killing plants or animals to eat as an unfortunate quirk in the nature of the universe, then you cut yourself from connecting with the sacramental energy-exchange, evolutionary mutual-sharing aspect of life" (1980, 89).

A second interesting interpretation is developed by Rod Phillips, who views the poem as eroticizing a "pre-existing sexuality inherent in nature." He argues that Snyder "imbues the natural world with an all encompassing sensuality, thereby creating an atmosphere in which all of nature—plants, animals, and entire food chains—resound with sexual energy." Again, Snyder's own comments accord with these critical interpretations, as he admits, "For me I guess nature is just naturally sexy" (Phillips 2000, 39).

Both of these approaches to "Song of the Taste" are valid and useful, and they clearly accord with both Snyder's intentions and the linguistic cues given in the text. Both critics are able to point readers toward the ecological and sexual concepts informing the poem. However, their critical practice itself still represents the type of intellectual exercise Snyder tends to question and attempts to replace with physical experience. Until we pluck "the fleshy sweetness packed / around the sperm of swaying trees" off the trees themselves, notice the striations of muscle on "the flanks and thighs of / soft-voiced cows" as we butcher them for consumption, and dig up "roots grown swoll / inside the soil," the significance of Snyder's realization remains purely intellectual. When we eat canned fruit, shrink-wrapped meat, and frozen vegetables, we are removed from the immediacy of the "communal" experience described by Snyder. The ecological, or sensual, nature of the experience he describes—in fact, the experience itself—is lost to us. That such a loss is important to Snyder is evidenced in *The Practice of the Wild,* in which he states, "It's not enough to be shown in school that we are kin to all the rest [of nature]: we have to feel it all the way through" (1990a, 68). By adding some form of direct experience (such as harvesting and eating natural whole foods) to the intellectual understanding provided by McClintock and Phillips, we will come to a richer understanding of Snyder's poem.

For Snyder, one of the key insights of the poem is the "felt experience" of "Kissing the lover in the mouth of bread: / lip to lip." My students and I have often found this poem to be much more powerful, and our understanding of it to be deepened, when we have reflected upon it in conjunction with the consumption of wild edibles. I commonly teach students how to make a mildly stimulating and pleasant-tasting tea out of ephedra. Also called Mormon, squaw, or joint tea, this easily distinguishable shrub of the Sierra Nevada—with its conspicuously evergreen and jointed leafless stems—can be steeped in hot water, or left in a water bottle in the sun, to make a refreshing tea. Because the plant contains small quantities of ephedrine, it also supplies one with a mild "pick-me-up," weaker than coffee but still nice after a long day's hike.

On one field-studies trip, we found a number of Sierra onions, *Allium campanulatum,* growing in an open pine forest near a wet meadow. After using the discovery as an opportunity to teach the students how to identify native plants and compose field journal entries, we harvested a few of the delicate flowering plants. We noted the pungent aroma of the tiny bulbs and remarked at their intensely strong onionlike flavor, which almost seemed to burn the tongue. Similarly, on another trip we were fortunate enough to find a patch of wild strawberry, *Fragaria platypetala,* and were soon crawling on our hands and knees beside the trail to find as many of the tiny sweet berries as we could. For many of these students, whose parents had never gardened, this was the first time that they had ever dug up, washed off, and eaten their food themselves.

Likewise, I can still recall leading two young women through their first ant-eating experience. After discussing native subsistence techniques and wilderness survival strategies, they expressed some amazement about the prevalence of insect-eating indigenous peoples. As an exercise in experiential education and to combat their culturally induced prejudices against such food, I suggested eating a few of the large carpenter ants, *Camponotus,* living in a downed log near our camp. They readily accepted the challenge, and in a few minutes we were each crouched by the log, closely examining a bright black ant as it crawled across our hands and over our fingers. After discussing the various manners in which to eat a live ant (crushing it between the fingers first, swallowing it whole, or chewing it up), I explained that my favorite way was to bite the ant with my front teeth so that the tip of the tongue, which is the most sensitive to their citruslike flavor, can get the entire effect. I ate a few, and then, amid nervous laughter, both women tried their first ant and broke into beaming smiles. They seemed to appreciate, and be moved by, this dining experience much more than by any of the freeze-dried meals I had served them back in camp. In each of these instances, we were, as Snyder says,

> Eating each other's seed
> > eating
> ah, each other.

We not only gained an experiential and visceral understanding of Snyder's point, but we also came to appreciate and feel closer to the region in which we were studying. Indeed, we were no longer merely in the wilderness; it was now inside us.

Gaining such an experiential understanding of Snyder's poetry is necessary because of its intensively experiential and referential basis. As Robert Kern notes, "[L]anguage and literature per se are less crucial in determining Snyder's imagination than direct experience of the world" (2002, 237). Though it is a given that literary critics must be well trained in analyzing texts, it is assumed that they do not need any direct knowledge of the experiential foundations of those texts. For some works that are more literarily allusive, such an assumption may not pose a significant problem. However, for an author like Gary Snyder, whose experiences direct both the form and the content of his poetry, it limits the range, depth, and accuracy of interpretation. As Snyder himself explicitly states, "[I]f I don't have a ground of actual physical experience I don't make reference to it" (1980, 20). Similarly, our experiences with wild edibles led us to accord with McClintock's and Phillips's interpretations while also engendering a deeper, more visceral, and immediate understanding of the sensual nature and ecological impact of eating.

Most ecocritics are quick to note Snyder's insistence on direct experience, but few engage in the practices he advocates, and fewer still use those methods to explicate his work. Even though some scholars of Snyder's work engage in "field experiences" as a means to gain a better personal understanding of his work, we have been discouraged from using these insights to explore and interpret his work professionally. Because the field of literary criticism has traditionally operated by way of a textually confined methodology, ecocritics are often reluctant to experiment in their scholarship with approaches that have been proven, on a personal level, to supply new insight or aid in interpretation. Instead it has been easier, and has posed less professional risk in the past, to focus on the ideological and structural aspects of Snyder's poetry while marginalizing or ignoring the experiential and referential. This has been true, I believe, not because Snyder scholars have failed to recognize the importance of physical experience in Snyder's work, but simply because the methodologies required to explore such experiences do not fit neatly into the conventional methodologies of literary criticism.

Snyder notes this tendency, among scholars, to ignore the experiential and marginalize the mundane world and also seems to find fault with our profession as a whole, rather than with individual critics. He states, "An education is only valuable if you're willing to give as much time to de-educating yourself as you gave to educating yourself." By "de-education" Snyder explains, "I mean get back in touch with people, with ordinary things: with your body, with the dirt, with the dust. . . . Get away from books" (64). A place-based and experiential approach to Snyder's work, then, seems to accord with his own ideas about what is necessary for understanding and interpreting it.

Because of the vital influence of physical experience in the natural world in Snyder's thought, I contend that an interdisciplinary field-based methodology is necessary for coming to a full and accurate understanding of his work. Such a methodology is not meant to replace or resist existing Snyder scholarship, or traditional textually based methods of literary analysis, but rather to enliven and supplement these practices. The following examples are offered to demonstrate how such forms of place-based experiential scholarship can aid us in understanding Snyder's thought and interpreting his poetry.

Kitkitdizze

Snyder's home place, Kitkitdizze, incorporates many of the same features that critics have so commonly noted in his poetry. The home itself is based on both Japanese farmhouses and Mandan earthen lodges, synthesizing, as Snyder does in his poetry, Asian and Native American philosophy and cultural practice. Likewise, both Snyder's home and his poetry are informed by ecological principles. As Katsunori Yamazato notes, the house "is surrounded by a workshop, a woodshed, a sauna bath, a barn, and an outdoor kitchen used mainly in summer. These outbuildings indicate that Snyder and the building crew designed and built a house that could naturally adapt to the climate of the foothills of the Sierra Nevadas" (1993, 53).

These aspects of Snyder's home life also infuse his written work. As he describes his home life in "The Porous World," "We came to live a permeable, porous life in our house set among stands of oak and pine. Our buildings are entirely opened up for the long Sierra summer" (1995, 195). Snyder goes on to describe the mud daubers who make nests in his house, cooking amid the evening's community of insects, and listening to deer and wild turkeys in the night. These experiences then find their way into Snyder's poetry and prose, instilling it with the insights and images gained from direct experience of and close contact with the natural world. Yamazato asserts, "The poems that Snyder wrote and included in *Turtle Island* (1974) and *Axe Handles* (1983) reflect his life as a reinhabitory person . . . [showing] how the residents at Kitkitdizze explore the land and create their sense of place out of direct contact with the land" (1993, 58).

This process of exploring the land directly—knowing it intimately without mediation—is a guiding principle in Snyder's life and work; unfortunately, however, the textually based methods of traditional literary criticism limit our ability to use such place-based knowledge in critical investigations of that work. Snyder's home place, Kitkitdizze, for example, has been referenced by a number of scholars who note that the name is taken from a Wintu word for a native shrub that grows abundantly on the property. Few critics, however, go beyond these textually based observations to describe the plant, list its scientific name so that it can be identified and researched, or note its important role in Sierra Nevada fire ecology (an important topic for Snyder). Distinguished Snyder scholar Katsunori Yamazato, however, moves beyond the text to relate that *Kitkitdizze* "was taken from the Wintu word for *Chamaebatia foliolosa,* a low-growing, spicy-odored shrub . . . also known as mountain misery, bearclover and tarweed" (51). Such a description recognizes the guiding principles behind Snyder's choice of a native name for his home place and begins to fulfill, through the scholar's practice, the goals of reinhabitation. From Yamazato's explanation one could reference the plant in a field guide and identify it in the field, as well as conduct further research into its role in the ecosystem and even its ethnobotanical uses, thus deepening one's understanding of Snyder's poetry and practice.

A more comprehensive ecocritical approach, however, would entail that the scholar conduct this interdisciplinary research him- or herself and use it to inform interpretations of Snyder's work. As scholars of Snyder's work, unless we engage in our own interdisciplinary field-based studies, we will never know, as Yamazato does, what kitkitdizze is, what it looks like, how it functions, or why Snyder named his home after it. Such forms of experiential knowledge often hold the key to unlocking Snyder's frequent, and often subtle, references to the physical world. In addition, this type of periodic grounding will do much to ensure that our interpretations remain responsible to the real world, that Kitkitdizze, the plant or the place, does not become replaced by our linguistic assertions about it.

"Manzanita"

The importance of gaining such reinhabitory knowledge when working with Snyder's poetry can be demonstrated by exploring "Manzanita," a poem about another native Sierra Nevada plant. In his discussion of "Manzanita," Charles Molesworth, despite an insightful understanding of the linguistic elements in Snyder's poetry, demonstrates the dangers of misinterpretation that often arise when exploring poems that are so pointedly referential. In discussing the poem's closing lines, he writes: "'The longer you look / The bigger they seem,' says the last stanza of the poem, describing the Manzanita bushes. This poem then concludes by citing the etymology of the plant's name, 'little apples'" (1991, 151). Molesworth correctly identifies the etymology of the poem's title, which comes from early Spanish explorers' travels in California. *Manzana,* meaning apple in Spanish, has the feminine *ita* or *small* added to it to form *Manzanita, or little apples.*

However, despite his etymological accuracy, Molesworth mistakenly claims that the "bush" itself is the subject of these lines. From our own field studies in Snyder's home country, we noted that the small berries of the manzanita, usually smaller than a blueberry, do indeed look like miniature apples. This observation brings us to recognize that the lines "The longer you look / The bigger they seem" do not, in fact, refer to the manzanita bushes but refer to the berries themselves. Seemingly an inconsequential detail, this interpretive discrepancy is not to be taken lightly. As Molesworth rightly notes, this poem is about, in part, "'ethnobotany,' the use of vegetative life in human culture" (151). If Snyder's poem is indeed about ethnobotany, which I agree it is, then we are remiss as critics not to have even the most rudimentary understanding of its subject, which is, in fact, our subject.

As a whole, Molesworth's treatment of "Manzanita" is accurate and useful, but the limitations of text-based interpretation, in this particular instance, have become readily apparent. As Molesworth demonstrates, without adding some form of interdisciplinary or field-based research to our text-based methodologies it is impossible to determine the correct subject of these lines, to distinguish the bushes from the berries.

From our interdisciplinary research in both texts and the field, my students and I discovered that the "little apples" of the manzanita do indeed grow in the mind's eye the longer you stare at them, were named by Spanish explorers as the etymology of the word describes, and were often used (despite their slightly bitter taste and mealy texture) by the Wintu, Maidu, Paiute, and other Native American tribes of the region to make a flavored drink and as an emergency food source. My own personal favorite use for manzanita berries is to smash them in water, make sun tea out of the mixture, strain the tea through a coffee filter, then drink and enjoy. Without engaging in our own field-based interdisciplinary studies, we run the risk of interpretive inaccuracy and missing much of the rich referentiality contained within Snyder's work. In addition, we also miss out on much of the wisdom contained within both his prose and his poetry for living a rooted and ecologically responsible life.

"Foxtail Pine" and "Kusiwoqqobi"

The limitations of language as a means of representing the world, or interpreting poetry, can be demonstrated by looking at further examples of referentiality in Snyder's work. Snyder himself often reflects upon and attempts to combat the limitations inherent in attempting to represent reality through language. Thomas J. Lyon asserts, "The first thing that strikes one about Snyder's poetry is the terse, phrase-light and article-light diction, the sense of direct *thing*-ness" (1991, 37). This sense of "direct *thing*-ness" is most often achieved through unmodified, unevaluative representations of things and experiences in the natural world. Lyon explains: "The solidity in Snyder's writing, which is often commented on, results from the fact that his ideas, like the verse rhythms, flow from close attention to wilderness, unmediated perception of grain and wave" (41). Snyder's emphasis on achieving unmediated knowledge of the natural world and conveying it through his poetry may also serve as a guiding principle for interpreting his work.

In the poem "Foxtail Pine," for example, Snyder emphasizes the natural history of the native pine and fir of the Sierra Nevada region, noting the evolution of and describing how to identify several different species.

> *bark smells like pineapple: Jeffries*
> *cones prick your hand: Ponderosa . . .*
>
> *"the true fir cone stands straight,*
> *the doug fir cone hangs down." (1992, 96)*

Yet, at the same time, he notes that such information is not enough. He reflects on our own ecological illiteracy and on the limitations of language for adequately representing the natural world. He writes, "nobody knows what they are, saying / 'needles three to a bunch,'" and after describing the foxtail pine questions the appropriateness of naming: "What am I doing, saying 'foxtail pine'?" Snyder continues with his critical questioning of the English names we use to identify these species, asking, "do whitebark and white pine seem the same?" (96). Soon, however, he seems to come to a sort of resolution as he describes the foxtail pine:

its leaves are needles
like a fox's brush
(I call him fox because he looks that way)
and call this other thing, a
        foxtail pine. (97)

Lyon correctly notes that this poem, in part, is about the "deceit of naming" and that it brings to the fore of the reader's attention the relationships among "Snyder and his poem and the tree" (1991, 37, 38). By engaging in field studies (one of Snyder's reinhabitory practices), one soon recognizes the difficulties inherent in identifying native plants by common and Latin names, remembering their distinct characteristics, and learning their potential human uses and roles in the ecosystem. Engaging in such a process, as an ecocritic, helps one to gain an understanding of the kinds of issues that preoccupy the reinhabitory Snyder, issues that make up, as Lyon notes, the subjects of Snyder's poetry.

The poet's concerns about "naming" are directly linked to an external reality and the difficulties of experiencing and representing it in an unmediated way. In "Kusiwoqqobi," for example, Snyder even questions the experiential associations we use to identify the distinctive smell of a Jeffrey pine:

Sweet smell of the pine.

Delicious! Like pineapple!
What did the Piute children think of,
Smelling Kusiwoqqobi,
What did they say? (1992, 363)

For Snyder, our estrangement from our own bioregions is evidenced by the fact that we have to use the smell of a nonnative tropical fruit to describe the aroma of a native tree in our local area. Similarly, even the words we use to name our local species are themselves imported from distant cultures and climates. Thus, Snyder uses the indigenous appellation *Kusiwoqqobi* rather than the colonizer's imported name, Jeffrey pine, or *Pinus jeffreyi*.

By questioning the very language itself through which he understands and represents the natural world, Snyder encourages us to question our own reliance upon language. He suggests that the "deceit of naming," noted by

Lyon, extends to literary criticism itself. He seems to imply that the inability of language to truly represent reality also problematizes literary criticism's ability to interpret texts solely through linguistic means.

"On Climbing the Sierra Matterhorn Again After Thirty-one Years"

Tim Dean asserts in *Gary Snyder and the American Unconscious* that "just as the reader has to work to understand and get meaning from the poetry of the landscape, so the reader has to work to situate him or herself within the landscape itself. This is one sense in which reading Snyder constitutes training in inhabiting the ground" (1991, 97). The problem, for ecocritics, however, is that the text-based methods of traditional literary scholarship are incapable of situating us in Snyder's landscape. Text-based interpretation can tell us much about Snyder's poetry, but it often leaves unanswered key questions regarding the referential and experiential basis of that poetry. By linking text- and field-based exploration, however, we will often find that the elusive answers to these questions are lying at our feet, waiting for discovery. In Patrick D. Murphy's discussion of Gary Snyder's famous Matterhorn poem, for example, we can see how these disciplinary limitations can be overcome through field-based methodologies so that through a combined approach we are left with a better understanding than through any single approach alone.

This short haikulike piece was composed atop the windswept, sawtoothed ridges of the Sierra Matterhorn, just west of Bridgeport, California. Reenacting a climb of the peak that occurred thirty-one years earlier with Jack Kerouac, which Kerouac immortalized in his 1958 novel *Dharma Bums,* Snyder found time to sit among the sharp, granitic spires of the peak and compose the following lines:

> *Range after range of mountains*
> *Year after year after year.*
> *I am still in love.* (1992, 362)

Murphy begins with a perceptive interpretation of the poem, based upon linguistic signs in the text, but soon hits upon a question that the textually based methods of his field are not suited to answer. He writes, "It expresses the value and power of cycles and repetition in human experience. Curiously enough, however, while the first two lines are quite explicit about their content, the final line leaves unstated what the primary object of Snyder's 'love' might be" (2000, 157). As Murphy rightly notes, we cannot satisfactorily answer this question by relying on the text alone. However, as my students and I discovered, field experiences can in this case be used to augment traditional textual analysis and provide the answer we are looking for.

I vividly recall a field-studies expedition that took us to the top of the Matterhorn to overlook the PCT as it traced a sinuous path across the landscape far, far below us. On the second day of our climb, we found ourselves in the middle of a great bowl-shaped snowfield. We trudged straight up the pockmarked snow, kicking in each step with care. If one of us slipped, a long, steep slide down to piles of rock and glacial detritus ominously awaited. The bright Sierran sunlight beamed back from below our feet in stabbing brilliance. The shafts of airy light blinded our eyes and forced us to avert our glance, as if we are walking up the face of a god.

A slow, scrambling rock climb, without ropes or harnesses, finally brought us from the top of the snowfield to a rocky, saw-toothed ridgeline. Constantly on guard against the gusting winds that seemed intent on blowing us off the mountain, we followed the ridgeline until it met the Matterhorn's peak. Standing atop the jutting, knife-edged, granitic peak, I was conscious of my exposure on every side to an immensity of space that was absolutely staggering. An endless series of mountain ranges marched off toward the horizon, stretching from our feet to fill distances that seemed to grow in immensity before our eyes. To the east I could see the Sweetwater Range and beyond into Nevada, while to the north and west lay the innumerable peaks and ridgelines of the Sierra Nevada.

As we sat on the windblown peak, I leafed through the summit ledger, read what others had written, and added a few lines of my own. Inside the steel canister, I found a laminated copy of Snyder's Matterhorn poem. Although I had read the poem many times before, as I read it there, atop that peak, I wondered whether I had ever truly understood Snyder's words. As I read the poem again, amid the roaring wind, thin air, and sunlight, all of which seemed to be stretching space and vision out to eternity, the words seemed to come alive in my hand. The poem was written in black calligraphy on brown paper, and although I could recite it from memory, I studied the words carefully, reading the short poem again, and again.

Finally I was shouting Snyder's words out for my companions to hear over the gusting winds:

> *Range after range of mountains*
> *Year after year after year*
> *I am still in love.*

Caught up in the moment and the power of the place, we stood facing into the wind and shouted the words. Then we turned and faced another series of ranges. We shouted the lines again. Another turn and the lines were torn, flying from our mouths on the whistling wind currents to disappear into the raucous sky.

I would be fortunate enough to hear Gary Snyder read that same poem in Sacramento, at a literary conference, a few months later. And although the poet's presence lent a new quality to the words, I felt as if the poem had lost some of its power, as if some portion of its life had been taken out of it. Like some animal ripped from the wild and put in a cage, it seemed as if in taking the words and ideas from their home, from the place that gave birth to them, some part of their being had been lost.

Such an experience—reading Snyder's poem in the place in which it was written—leads one to recognize that above all things and people, Snyder's "love" refers to the land beneath his feet, to the mountains and forests of Turtle Island's great western shores.

"Logging"

Whereas the textually based methods of traditional literary criticism are clearly useful for interpreting Snyder's work—and are, at times, completely adequate by themselves—they can misdirect our responses to Snyder's work if we are not careful. In Sherman Paul's discussion of the "Logging" section of *Myths & Texts*, for example, an extremely adept analysis is weakened, at one point, by the limitations of the textual method. Paul has produced a large body of scholarship that can arguably be considered required reading for anyone attempting to understand Snyder's work. He insightfully expli- cates dense passages of Snyder's poetry; traces literary, philosophical, and ecological allusions; and often provides a useful historical context for under- standing Snyder's work. However, without the critical framework required to include interdisciplinary experiential explorations of the places and issues

informing poems like "Logging," Paul occasionally runs the risk of misinter-
preting their referential basis.

Although the vast majority of Paul's discussion of "Logging" is both accurate and useful, the following comment can be used to demonstrate the dangers of misinterpretation that are inherent when dealing with such directly
referential forms of poetry without a field-based perspective. Paul argues,
"There is the incontestable truth of 'Creeks choked, trout killed, roads.' I
won't argue about what he says of 'suburbs,' but question *roads*. What is the
way to Kitkitdizze?" (1986, 233). In this particular comment, the textual primacy of traditional literary criticism encourages Paul to neglect two important facts, one textual and the other referential, and, instead, to focus on the
word *roads*. First, the poem in question is referring more specifically to logging than to the construction of suburbs. Though Snyder does mention that
the "sacred groves" are "Cut down to make room for the suburbs," he goes
on to write specifically about logging, rather than development.

> *Bulldozed by Luther and Weyerhaeuser*
> *Crosscut and chainsaw*
> > *Squareheads and finns*
> > *High-lead and cat-skidding*
> *Trees down*
> *Creeks choked, trout killed, roads.*
>
> *Sawmill temples of Jehovah.* (1992, 42)

These descriptions refer more specifically to timber companies, logging
practices, and the ecological damage that often ensues than to the secondary
subject of suburban sprawl (two sometimes related but completely distinct
issues).

The second problem Paul encounters is that the textually based methods
of literary criticism he is working with do not aid him in distinguishing
between the various meanings of the word *roads*. Traditional text-oriented
methods of literary criticism are unable to recognize the critical differences
between logging roads in our national forests and the engineered and
improved roads people use for transportation, physical and ecological
differences to which Snyder is specifically referring in the poem. It is only
through an interdisciplinary, and perhaps also experiential, approach that

we can come to understand these vital differences and thus recognize the different definitions of the word *roads* with which Snyder is working.

I recall hiking on the PCT through the Shasta National Forest in northern California and coming across a selective-logging operation. This particular section of the PCT runs through a small parcel of land owned by the American Land Company, and although the slopes below the trail were at a sixty-degree incline, or greater, they had recently cleared the primarily red fir forest of all of its old-growth and codominant trees. About 50 percent of the trees were gone. Slash lay piled everywhere, creating a severe wildfire hazard, and poorly constructed skid roads were bulldozed into the hillside every hundred feet or so. The steep hillside, now carved up and devoid of strong tree roots to hold the soil in place, was littered with newly formed and heavily eroding ravines. Such forms of logging-induced erosion represent one of the most serious environmental impacts caused by timber production on our public lands. According to the World Watch Institute, "Under natural conditions, each hectare of land loses somewhere between 0.004 and 0.05 tons of soil to erosion each year—which is more than replaced by natural soil-building processes. On lands that have been logged or converted to agriculture, however, erosion typically washes away 17 tons per hectare a year in the United States" (Abramovitz 1998, 13). This increased erosion damages terrestrial ecosystems and causes harmful sedimentation in aquatic systems, endangering commercial, game, and other fish populations. Additionally, such logging practices exact a high human cost, increasing the threat of wildfire and—as in the case of the town of Stafford, California, which was buried on New Year's Eve 1996—often cause destructive mud slides.

The logging roads Snyder specifically criticizes in this section of the poem are not engineered to last very long and thus wash out, ruin vital habitat, cause mud slides, and are subsidized by taxpayers so that large private industry can profit. Engineered roads like the one running to Kitkitdizze, on the other hand, though they do fragment habitat, do not cause the litany of ecological problems associated with logging roads. As Snyder explains in *A Place in Space*, "Necessary roads should be thoughtfully routed and of modest width, with the occasional fire-truck turnout. Fire protections should be provided by having the roads well brushed along the edges, with plenty of thinning back into the woods, rather than building an excessively wide roadbed. If roads are a bit rough, it will slow cars down, and that's not all bad" (1995, 197). The road to Kitkitdizze, in fact, fits Snyder's description quite well. It is an exceedingly narrow road, with trees growing within a foot of the travel way, and because it is not graded, it is crisscrossed in sections by thick roots from still-living trees, making the road bumpy, slowing traffic, and reducing its impact on the forest through which it passes. Although rough and narrow, it is well engineered and maintained and evidences little erosion, unlike the logging roads Snyder criticizes. Regardless of the scholar's ability, these critical differences cannot be explored within the textually based confines of conventional literary criticism. It is only through an inter-disciplinary field-based methodology that we can make these distinctions and accurately interpret the extratextual references informing poems like "Logging."

"Front Lines"

This ironic tendency, on the part of ecocritics, to dismiss or ignore the natural world is evidence of both methodological and theoretical biases that are explicitly textually based and anthropocentric. Regardless of the critic's intentions, it is often difficult to overcome these discipline-induced biases because they underlie so much of our theory and critical methodology. For example, although an impressively adept Snyder critic, Charles Molesworth demonstrates the strong influence these disciplinary biases can have in his treatment of "Front Lines," when he concludes, "Since Snyder has written this poem before, and generally better, the best reading of its inclusion here would argue that the problem of alienated labor has not gone away, and recognition of the problem is demanded even in a group of primarily cele-bratory poems" (1991, 151).

Despite Molesworth's claim that "Front Lines" is about "alienation of labor," the poem contains only one reference to the issue, when it describes a bulldozer working "In the pay of a man / From town" (1992, 218). The rest of the poem, however, is focused on environmental degradation and the con-version of local habitats, arguing the reinhabitory position that we must begin the work of defending the natural world at home, in our own local areas. In fact, the descriptions Snyder gives of the environmental damage caused by the bulldozer completely overshadow the line concerning alienation of labor.

> *A bulldozer grinding and slobbering*
> *Sideslipping and belching on top of*
> *The skinned-up bodies of still-live bushes.*

And in the final stanza he makes the subject of the poem explicitly clear when he writes,

> *Behind is a forest that goes to the Arctic*
> *And a desert that still belongs to the Piute*
> *And here we must draw*
> *Our line.* (218)

The "line" that Snyder would have us draw is no mere metaphor, but a literal and physical line drawn on the landscape that can be witnessed over much of California. One does not have to travel far off the major highways to see the square-shaped patchwork that selective clear-cutting has made of our wild forests. From a number of places along the PCT itself, one can look out and see miles of once forested ridges cut up like a chessboard, a gridiron of chain saw– and bulldozer-sculpted lines inscribed on the landscape.

For Snyder, or anyone who has witnessed such wanton destruction firsthand, what is of paramount importance are

> *The edge of the cancer*
> *Swells against the hill . . .*
>
> *Landseekers, lookers, they say*
> *To the land,*
> *Spread your legs.* (218)

These are the issues of the most ecological and political import to Snyder. Alienation of labor is only one small component of the larger problem that he wishes to focus on. However, the anthropocentric bias reinforced by literary criticism's focus on textual primacy forces insightful critics like Molesworth to ignore the more powerful ecocentric concerns informing the poem. Unless we successfully resist these conservative discipline-induced forces, we run the risk of interpretive inaccuracy and will fail to recognize what seems to be so obvious to someone, like Snyder, who is immersed in the environmental issues affecting the Sierra Nevada.

"Piute Creek"

A final example of how the textual bias of traditional literary criticism can impede the interpretation of Snyder's work can also be seen in Tim Dean's explication of "Piute Creek." Although the bulk of Dean's treatment of the poem is both accurate and useful, he is forced by his discipline to privilege the cultural over the natural and thus reverse the emphasis of the poem. In the first stanza Snyder describes the vast, sublime, and inhuman landscape of the Sierra Nevada and seems to be trying to find something smaller, something of human scale, upon which to focus.

> One granite ridge
> A tree, would be enough
> Or even a rock, a small creek,
> A bark shred in a pool.

Failing to find a human scale by which to judge the landscape, Snyder sets up the ecocentric perspective that will be the focus of the poem: "All the junk that goes with being human / Drops away, . . ." He further develops and emphasizes this perspective by ending the stanza with the following three lines:

> Words and books
> Like a small creek off a high ledge
> Gone in the dry air. (1990b, 8)

Here Snyder compares a cultural artifact—books—to a natural feature of the terrain in such a way that the human artifact disappears and only the natural world descriptively remains. Dean, on the other hand, compares Snyder's descriptions of the natural world to cultural artifacts in such a way that his descriptions of the natural are subsumed by the cultural. Dean writes, "The imagery of Snyder's poem also brings to mind some of Ansel Adams's photographic images" (1991, 168). He goes on to compare Snyder's imagery to that of Ansel Adams, Georgia O'Keeffe, and the British romantics'. These comparisons, however, unlike Snyder's, privilege the cultural, or the human, over the natural, or the inhuman. They miss the experiential basis of the poem, which argues that such cultural associations fall away in the face of wild nature and are literally "Gone in the dry air." In Dean's defense, however, these comparisons are both accurate and useful from within the anthropocentric perspective of the humanities. From a disciplinary perspective, his interpretation holds true; however, Snyder's poetry itself appears to be working in a different discipline or from within a different tradition, one that is less anthropocentric and more ecocentric.

The second stanza carries the bulk of the poem's significance, delivering fully on the ecocentric perspective promised earlier. I quote it here in full:

> *A clear, attentive mind*
> *Has no meaning but that*
> *Which sees is truly seen.*
> *No one loves rock, yet we are here.*
> *Night chills, a flick*
> *In the moonlight*
> *Slips into Juniper shadow:*
> *Back there unseen*
> *Cold proud eyes*
> *Of Cougar or Coyote*
> *Watch me rise and go.* (1990b, 8)

Dean is led by the anthropocentric focus of our discipline to conclude that the final image of the poem "weakens the effect" and that "[t]he state of rarefied perception, which seems to have been achieved within the interstice of the stanza break, is problematised, however, by the sense that the subject of perception is no longer the speaker—who becomes instead an object of the gaze of the Other—but is rather the unseen, merely imagined, wild beast" (1991, 167, 168).

From my own experiences with Snyder's poetry and with wild predators in the Sierra Nevada, however, I would argue that the opposite is true. The final lines of the poem fully develop Snyder's ecocentric perspective and strengthen rather than weaken the poem as a whole. Second, the "beast" is not "merely imagined," as Snyder explicitly acknowledges, seeing "a flick / In the moonlight" that then "Slips into Juniper shadow." From his own vast experience in the wild, Snyder is able to surmise that this "flick" and the "Cold proud eyes" that can still be seen in the shadows are those of either a

cougar or a coyote. This wealth of experiential nonhuman knowledge constitutes a different discipline or tradition than the textual and culturally
based discipline of literary criticism.

For Dean, working within the textual confines of traditional literary criticism, the poem appears to be about the romantic sublime and thus is weakened by shifting the perspective away from the human—the only perspective that acknowledges the sublime—and toward the nonhuman. For Snyder,
however, who openly admits that his perspective "came out of some very
intense personal experiences that I had as a young man in direct relation to
nature. Face-to-face experience of something else happening from a connection to mountains, forests, and animals. Hair raising experiences, in some
cases," the poem is about shifting the perspective away from the human
(1980, 154). Rather than representing a weakness, this represents the poem's
greatest strength. Dean, for example, claims, "The transcendent moment
dissolves, however, when the subject becomes aware of itself as object of
another's watchful gaze" (1991, 170). For Snyder, this moment of awareness of
the self as "an object of the gaze of the Other" *is* the moment of transcendence. It is at this moment that he is able to transcend the anthropocentric
perspective and accept both the predator and the inhuman landscape on
their own terms.

In order to set up this moment of transcendence, Snyder opens the stanza
by stating:

> *A clear, attentive mind*
> *Has no meaning but that*
> *Which sees is truly seen.*

There are two possible interpretations for how this passage functions in the
stanza; both develop the ecocentric perspective and, I believe, are intended
to operate simultaneously. On the one hand, the "clear, attentive mind" is
Snyder's, and he has succeeded in transcending the problematic anthropocentric perspective that started the first stanza by trying to find something
of human scale in the vast wilderness. He is now able to "see" the natural
world for what it is—a living system with its own subjectivity apart from
human values, uses, or desires—and thus is "seen" by a member of that nonhuman community as he, Snyder, rises and goes. From this perspective,
Snyder is no longer trying to make something human out of the natural

landscape. He has transcended those anthropocentric concerns and is rewarded by coming to a more immediate understanding of the natural world and his place within it.

Simultaneously, one might read those same lines as indicating that the "clear, attentive mind" is the predator's, who is also "that / Which sees" and is now "truly seen" by Snyder. The predator is "truly seen" because Snyder no longer views it from his own anthropocentric, subjective perspective, but rather sees it from an ecocentric perspective, from which he is able to "see" himself as the "other."

In both cases, the purpose of the poem seems to be to dislodge the reader's anthropocentric perceptions by moving him or her from viewing the landscape with Snyder's eyes to viewing Snyder with the predator's eyes. The textual emphasis of traditional literary criticism, however, confines the critic's attention to cultural artifacts and impedes a full understanding of Snyder's poetry.

PARTING ADVICE

Noting such discrepancies between critical interpretations of Snyder's work and the natural world to which he refers is important because it demonstrates the ever present danger ecocritics face when they allow themselves to be restricted by the textual confines of traditional literary criticism. In addition, it also emphasizes the manner in which field studies can be used to augment and support traditional textual analysis. Such an observation does little to question the authority and insightfulness of Molesworth's, Murphy's, and Dean's work or that of other traditional literary scholars. In fact, I believe it demonstrates the need to be completely versed in all the components of Snyder's world—his poetry, the scholarship surrounding it, and the physical world giving rise to it—if we are to fully understand his work.

In an interview with John P. O'Grady, Snyder laments the fact that most critics have failed to recognize some of the most important dimensions of his work, implying that it is because literary critics are not grounded, because they do not "practice" what is preached in his poetry, that they often miss the point of his work: "[M]ost political, educated, intellectual type people don't quite get it yet. That belongs to the next generation, I think" (1998, 288). One might ask what Snyder thinks the "next generation" might have that this one does not. I believe that he has already given it to them, and to us, if we choose to listen. In "For the Children," he offers a guiding principle for our practice:

> *one word to you, to*
> *you and your children:*
>
> stay together
> learn the flowers
> go light. (1992, 259; emphasis in original)

CHAPTER EIGHT

Putting Snyder's Reinhabitory Principles into Practice

I am foremost a person of the Yuba River country in the Sierra Nevada of northern
California. The San Juan Ridge and the many people there with whom I share
work, rituals and ideas are at the core of this exercise.

GARY SNYDER,
The Practice of the Wild

The Boy Scouts lie huddled in their sleeping bags for warmth, heads erect
and eyes attentive, as my students stand, reading Gary Snyder's poetry and
sharing their own thoughts on what it means. We are camped at an elevation of eighty-three hundred feet, on the shores of Gilmore Lake, deep in the
heart of the Desolation Wilderness Area. We have been participating in a
weeklong field-study course in environmental literature, focusing on Gary
Snyder's work and the natural history of the Pacific Crest Trail. The boys in
the Scout troop are on their own sort of field-study expedition, and at the
request of their Scout leaders, my students and I are giving an impromptu
poetry reading and class on environmental literature. One by one these
undergraduate and graduate students, some from Korea, Japan, and China,
others from various parts of the United States, share the poetry and ideas we
have been wrestling with, and carrying in our packs, for the past few days on
the trail. As I watch them talk to the young boys, the Scout leaders busy in
camp preparing gear for the next day, I cannot help but think of Snyder's

famous poem "Axe Handles." In it he describes the process of using a working axe to make a new axe handle out of a stave of wood:

"In making the handle
Of an axe
By cutting wood with an axe
The model is indeed near at hand." (1992, 266)

In the poem, Snyder is working alongside his son Kai and remembering this
phrase as it first came to him in the writings of Ezra Pound, and later when
he rediscovered it in Lu Ji's *Wen Fu*, and finally as he was reminded of its
simple wisdom again by his teacher Shih-hsiang Chen. Snyder writes:

And I see: Pound was an axe,
Chen was an axe, I am an axe
And my son a handle, soon
To be shaping again, model
And tool, craft of culture,
How we go on. (266)

I watch my students and the young Scouts interact, hoping that in some
small way we might be useful models—good axes—for the next generation
that takes to these trails. I believe that both, the older axes (the students) and
the unshaped staves of wood (the Boy Scouts), will be affected by this unique
educational experience, this fortuitous meeting in the California wilderness.
From reading my students' journals and participating in their discussions, I
am convinced that participating in this process of cultural transmission and
reflecting on its significance have given them a deeper understanding of
Snyder's message in "Axe Handles" than any literary interpretation, historical
information, or explication I have provided.

We leave the Boy Scouts with a final bit of sage hiking advice, taken
straight from the pages of our classroom texts:

stay together
learn the flowers
go light. (259; emphasis in original)

These words have been with us all week as we have navigated the rugged terrain of the Desolation Wilderness. With a group of ten students, some with a

great deal of hiking experience, others who have never slept outside of a man-made building in their lives, it has been a challenge at times to stay together, both physically and intellectually. But the diversity of the group has brought us together in many unexpected ways. The first few days on the trail, I was constantly stopping to identify flowers, shrubs, and trees, showing the students how to use a field guide to key out species, but by now they are doing it on their own, dropping beside the trail to sketch or photograph some new subalpine beauty or hauling out the field guides during a water break to read about its medicinal or edible uses. By the standards of a PCT thru-hiker we are not "going light," our packs weighted down with books and journals; however, we make good time and carry everything we need on our backs: simple shelters, simple food, and a lot of communal sharing of supplies. In many ways, I think it will be these aspects of "lived experience" in the wilderness that will bring these students to a better understanding of Snyder's poetry and perspective than any of our literary discussions. In one short week, they have begun to amass a series of experiences and memories that are akin to Snyder's own background, living, studying, working, and exploring in the Sierra Nevada.

REINHABITATION

The daily practices required by such a field-study expedition—simplicity, self-sufficiency, physical work, communal sharing, interdependence, environmental awareness, and wilderness experience—become occasions for exploring Snyder's work both physically and intellectually. Coupled with Snyder's persuasive discussions of environmental issues, in both his prose and his poetry, field experiences enable and encourage students to alter their own attitudes and actions toward the natural world. Such a process aids students in developing what Snyder has termed *reinhabitory practice*. Reinhabitation, according to Snyder,

> refers to the tiny number of persons who come out of the industrial societies (having collected or squandered the fruits of eight thousand years of civilization) and then start to turn back to the land, back to place. This comes for some with the rational and scientific realization of interconnectedness and planetary limits. But the actual demands of

a life committed to a place, and living somewhat by the sunshine green-plant energy that is concentrating in that spot, are so physically and intellectually intense that it is a moral and spiritual choice as well. (1995, 191)

As Snyder notes, the science of ecology holds significant ethical and spiritual ramifications for humankind. As we come to recognize our dependence on naturally functioning ecosystems, and our ability to degrade them and our own lives in the process, we also come to realize our responsibility toward those life-support systems and all who rely upon them. Fulfilling our ecological obligations, or expressing this spiritual dimension of ecological insight, entails, according to Snyder, "feeling gratitude to it all; taking responsibility for your own acts; keeping contact with the sources of the energy that flow into your own life (namely dirt, water, flesh)" (188).

These reinhabitory, or ecologically responsible, practices are required for living and traveling in the backcountry. After a ten-mile-day on the trail, lugging a forty-pound pack and learning about the subsistence-living techniques of local indigenous cultures, students come to appreciate the simple fare of camp cooking more than many a gourmet meal, just as they find that they are more conscious of, and grateful for, the warmth and comfort provided by their simple tents and sleeping bags than they have ever been for their heated, air-conditioned, carpeted, and electrically lit homes. Pumping and hauling one's own water, washing up after meals, setting up and breaking down camp, and following Leave-No-Trace principles for disposing of waste all aid students in understanding viscerally what it means to be responsible for oneself. And living exposed to the elements, gathering fuel and water from the natural environment, and learning the names and habits of wild plants and animals increase students' awareness of their own interconnectedness with the natural world. In short, field-study experiences offer students the opportunity to put Snyder's reinhabitory principles into practice in their own lives.

Reinhabitation represents much more than a mere environmental philosophy for Snyder; in fact, it is the guiding principle directing his own personal actions and lifeways. As Katsunori Yamazato observes, "Snyder, by beginning to live in the back country, in an abandoned rural area in California, chose to explore how to live in a place, to become 'placed' or 're-placed,' an act that would lead him to a new, alternative culture, and eventually to a new sense of 'what it means to be human'" (1993, 51). Snyder perceives and practices reinhabitation not merely as a philosophy, but also as an exercise, a daily performance of physical, intellectual, and spiritual actions that define oneself and one's relationship to the world. He explained the action-oriented nature of reinhabitory practices in a 1977 interview: "The problem is, where do you put your feet down, where do you raise your children, what do you do with your hands" (1980, 55). Reinhabitory practice, then, according to Snyder, is better understood as a process, a consciously developed lifeway embodied in one's daily actions, rather than an environmental philosophy.

This process, however, is not new for Snyder. In *A Place in Space,* for example, he relates that even at a young age on his parents' farm he found that his relationship to the natural world in which he lived was of paramount importance to him. He writes, "I defined myself by relation to the place" (1995, 184). Not surprisingly, many years later, Snyder is again involved in defining himself by his relationship to place, in both his life and his work. Place and our relationship to it are the central features of reinhabitory practice. As Snyder notes, "Our place is part of what we are" physically, intellectually, culturally, and spiritually (1990a, 27). Of course, our place is literally a part of us in the air we breathe, the water we drink, and the food we eat, as well as the plants, rocks, and dirt we use to build the homes in which we live. Place also affects who we are in less tangible but no less important ways. It influences how we think, speak, and make a living, what we value, fear, and find beautiful. Snyder asserts, "Thus, knowing who we are and knowing where we are are intimately linked" (1995, 189). Engaging in reinhabitory practices, then, promises to teach us about ourselves, our culture, and the places in which we live.

In addition to helping us come to a deeper understanding of, and appreciation for, who we are and where we live, reinhabitation is focused on protecting our local communities and lands while ensuring a sustainable future for our children and grandchildren. Snyder explains that reinhabitation "means, for most of us, find your place on the planet, dig in, and take responsibility from there" (43). As a pragmatic practice, reinhabitation is concerned with maintaining healthy natural ecosystems and sustainable communities capable of passing on to future human and nonhuman generations the same resources, processes, skills, and values that have made life possible throughout the earth's evolutionary history. Snyder emphasizes the forward-looking nature of reinhabitation as well as its focus on personal action, asserting, "Doing things right means living as though your grand-children would also be alive, in this land, carrying on the work we're doing right now, with deepening delight" (190).

Because of its emphasis on place and action, reinhabitory philosophy cannot adequately be taught, learned, or practiced in the classroom. It demo-cratically resists and subverts the elite and disembodied nature of the higher educational system by asserting that the most important knowledge, skills, and technologies for developing a sustainable future are to be found in the relationship between ordinary people and places. Although ecological prin-ciples can be learned in a classroom, one cannot learn how to grow food, identify native species, build a sustainable home, or meet one's neighbors there. As Snyder notes, "Our relation to the natural world takes place in a *place,* and it must be grounded in information and experience" (1990a, 39). Traditional classroom-based instruction, libraries, and the Internet can all offer useful information for reinhabitory people, but they cannot replace the experience, the practice, of consciously and purposefully inhabiting a place or participating in a community. We must do this work for ourselves, in our own bioregions, neighborhoods, and homes, and with our own hands, feet, bodies, and minds.

Field-based environmental education offers students just such an oppor-tunity. It requires them to engage in practices, to interact physically with the natural environment, in a self-conscious and purposeful manner. These interactions can be directed and given an intellectual context and theoretical basis by coupling them with Snyder's reinhabitory philosophy. By synthesiz-ing the persuasive power and intellectual insight offered in Snyder's prose and poetry with students' actions in the field, we can effectively guide them through the beginnings of the reinhabitory process. After engaging in rein-habitory practices themselves, it is much more likely that our students will carry them into their personal lives.

For the purposes of teaching students and guiding them through the reinhabitory process, I find it useful to divide reinhabitation into three cate-gories: bioregional literacy, bioregional restoration, and bioregional respon-sibility. The first category, bioregional literacy, entails learning about your bioregion, its natural history, processes, native inhabitants, and the subsis-tence practices of indigenous cultures who lived, or still live, in the area. The second type of reinhabitory practice, bioregional restoration, involves participating in the political process—local, state, and federal—by which naturally functioning ecosystems and native species are protected and engaging in the long, slow process of restoring degraded landscapes and damaged ecosystems to a healthy, self-regulating, and sustainable state. Finally, bioregional responsibility means accepting responsibility for your own actions by reducing your own ecological impacts and passing on reinhabitory insights, values, and practices to those in your community.

Bioregional Literacy

Bioregional literacy entails learning about the natural features, processes, history, weather patterns, and native species of your own region, as well as the cultural history and subsistence lifeways of past and present indigenous peoples. A bioregion is defined, in this sense, as a region sharing common biological features, species, and processes. It often contains multiple watersheds, shares similar weather patterns, and can be distinguished from neighboring bioregions by clearly distinguishable shifts in vegetation types, topographic features, and native wildlife. Bioregional awareness is meant to bring us into a closer relationship with the natural world in which we live. We are asked to identify our home region by its natural biogeophysical features rather than by arbitrary political designations that exist solely on maps and have no basis in the physical reality of the area. Reinhabitory practices focus on the bioregion because, as Snyder notes, "these are exercises toward breaking our minds out of the molds of political boundaries or any kind of habituated or received notions of regional distinctions" (1980, 54). From this perspective, I can better understand my place in the world by noting that I live in the Truckee River watershed, in an ecotone between the Great Basin and eastern Sierra bioregions, than if I solely identify my home place with the political designation Reno, Nevada, USA. Likewise, Snyder defines his "place" as the San Juan Ridge, in the Yuba watershed, on the Pacific slope of the Sierra, Turtle Island (1990a, ix).

Bioregionalism asks us to be more aware of the natural systems in which we live and upon which we depend. It helps us understand the relationship among ourselves, our local area, and the larger natural region in which it is located and by which it is affected. Snyder argues, "One's sense of place expands as one learns the *region*" (27). We not only learn how our local area fits into this larger region, but also become more comfortable there as we come to know its processes, features, history, and inhabitants. As Bill Devall and George Sessions contend in *Deep Ecology*, because we are starting close to home, "[o]ur bioregion is the best place to begin cultivating an ecological consciousness" (1985, 21). As we learn more about the natural region in which we live and come to identify with its native species, weather patterns, and topographical features, we will be encouraged to value and protect it. In addition, we will be much more likely to develop ecologically appropriate ways of living in that region if we understand its characteristics and limitations.

I divide bioregional literacy into two components. The first facet of bioregional literacy entails learning the natural history of one's region, whereas the second is concerned with understanding the cultural history that has affected the area.

Using Snyder as a model for our practice, I begin by guiding students through their field studies in the natural history of our region. According to Snyder, "You should really know what the complete natural world of your region is and know what all its interactions are and how you are interacting with it yourself. This is just part of the work of becoming who you are, where you are" (1980, 16). I introduce students to this process by having them study the native plants of our region because plants are easier to find and observe than animals, display more striking distinguishing characteristics than rocks and soils, and form a major part of the native biota. In addition, because most students are not even aware that they do not know the native plants of their home bioregions, such exercises aid them in recognizing the degree of ecological alienation and ignorance that has been pressed upon them by modern industrial culture.

We study these local species directly, using field observations and textual research, and return to Snyder for direction and inspiration. In "Foxtail Pine" Snyder demonstrates that close observation and poetry are not mutually exclusive:

> *foxtail pine with a*
> *clipped curve-back cluster of tight*
> > *five-needle bunches*
> > *the rough red bark scale*
> *and jigsaw pieces sloughed off*
> > > *scattered on the ground.* (1992, 96)

We practice describing our plants as accurately as Snyder and try to memorize their distinguishing characteristics. The process aids us in becoming more aware of our region and the various habitats and microclimates inside it. Students learn to identify a wide variety of species and come to recognize common plant associations.

During this phase of our field studies, I introduce students to David Orr's concept of "ecological literacy," the idea that the natural world can be read much like a text. Just as we must be versed in the system of signs, and their interrelationships, in a given language in order to be able to interpret it, we must learn what particular plants signify and how they are related to each other and the larger ecosystem in which they are found. Snyder makes a similar comparison, expanding it to include other features of the natural environment: "A text is information stored through time. The stratigraphy of rocks, layers of pollen in a swamp, the outward expanding circles in the trunk of a tree, can be seen as texts. The calligraphy of rivers winding back and forth over the land leaving layer upon layer of traces of previous riverbeds is a text" (1990a, 66).

Although Snyder is careful, later in the same piece, to explain the anthropocentric dangers of speaking about the natural world as a text, he recognizes the usefulness of the metaphor. If we learn enough about the natural processes and features of our home bioregion, we will be able to read the movements of animals through a particular landscape, for example, or its history of fires and floods, or even the quality of the coming berry or pine nut harvest. As Snyder notes in the opening stanza of "What You Should Know to Be a Poet,"

all you can about animals as persons.
the names of trees and flowers and weeds.
names of stars, and the movements of the planets
and the moon. (1992, 184)

This type of knowledge, however, cannot be gained from books alone. Snyder argues that "it relates to knowing the land directly, not just intellectually, with one's body, commitment, time, labor, walking. Maps, charts, botanic lists, histories, are all just the menu. You'd starve on that" (1980, 23). Intimate relationships are built through contact, through interpenetration, over time, and with effort, Snyder asserts. Reinhabitory knowledge must be gained with the body as well as the mind, with the feet as much as the eyes, and with the heart in addition to the head.

After learning about the natural features of their home bioregion, students begin studying the ways in which human cultures have interacted with the area in the past. One of the most beneficial methods of engaging in such studies is to learn about the lifeways of local indigenous cultures in one's own region. As Snyder points out, throughout the human species' fifteen million–year evolution, "[c]ountless local ecosystem habitation styles emerged. People developed specific ways to *be* in each of those niches" (1995, 185). By studying the subsistence techniques and cultural practices of native peoples, we can learn more about our own bioregion and the types of cultural practices that are most appropriate for it. Snyder argues, "There is something to be learned from the Native American people about where we all are. It can't be learned from anybody else" (156).

Indigenous cultures offer us a variety of insights and ethics, as well as practices, which evolved organically from their long-standing sustainable relationships with the bioregions in which they live. Simply learning about the subsistence techniques used in one's own region deepens one's understanding of that area. In one of my classes, for example, we studied how the Paiutes in our area gathered and prepared pinyon nuts, *Pinus monophylla,* a major food staple for Great Basin tribes. We learned from a Paiute elder that various bands would meet each year in the same vast pinyon and juniper forests. Each band would arrive within days of the other by using the bright-yellow flowers of the rabbitbrush as a type of seasonal clock. When the flowers reached a particularly bright yellow color in the fall, each group knew that the pinyon nuts were ripe and it was time to travel to the forests and begin their harvest. We enjoyed practicing their techniques for harvesting, roasting, and preparing the nuts; ate them ourselves; and sent them to friends and family as gifts. Such a process gave the students a much greater appreciation for the native peoples of their area and brought them into a closer relationship with their home bioregion. Although we did not gather a large enough amount of nuts to alter our primary modes of subsistence, the experience increased our awareness of, and appreciation for, native species and native peoples. Learning such subsistence techniques is still valuable because, as Snyder says, "even though you might never have to use them in any economic sense, it is a great extension of one's awareness of place" (1980, 16).

Without such experiences it becomes difficult for students to gain an anthropological or historical perspective of their own time and place in history. Contemporary Americans often seem to think that the whole world is industrialized and that it always has been. Our alienation from the natural world and inundation by consumer culture make it difficult to see our own culture, lifestyle, and behavior within its larger evolutionary context. Snyder often uses his poetry quite effectively to broaden our perspectives and shift us out of this technocentric mind-set. The short poem "Civilization" stands as a good example of this technique:

Those are the people who do complicated things.

> *they'll grab us by the thousands*
> *and put us to work.*
World's going to hell, with all these
> *villages and trails.*
Wild duck flocks aren't
> *what they used to be.*
Aurochs grow rare.

Fetch me my feathers and amber. (1992, 200)

Snyder emphasizes the anthropological perspective by describing our modern world of megacities and superhighways as "all these / villages and trails" and describes the resulting loss of biodiversity. He ends by turning toward the primitive as a means of showing where his allegiances lie.

The final point that such studies and experiences drive home is that the "world" most Americans live in today—the urbanized, mechanized, human-constructed, indoor world—is an anomaly in our evolution. It is a place largely foreign to our bodies, minds, and spirits as they have evolved over millennia. The "howling" wilderness—complete with voracious predators, stinging insects, and other hazards—that most industrialized people fear or want to exploit is in fact our evolutionary home. It is much more suited to us, and we are much more suited to it, than the cities and suburbs in which most of us live. Snyder reminds us, "There has been no wilderness without some kind of human presence for several hundred thousand years. Nature is not a place to visit, it is *home*" (1990a, 7; emphasis in original).

Bioregional Restoration

The second type of reinhabitory practice—bioregional restoration—involves restoring the natural processes sustaining one's own bioregion through protecting ecosystems that still function in a self-regulating manner and restoring degraded habitats so that they can be returned to a healthy and sustainable state. From such a perspective, wilderness advocacy, endangered species protection, reforestation, ecological restoration, and urban revitalization all go hand in hand because they seek to protect and re-create sustainable cultural and ecological systems.

Americans, and especially westerners, are fortunate in that our democratic system of government and our large holdings of public lands enable us to affect how vast areas of natural habitat are managed. As Snyder observes, "In North America there is a lot that is in public domain, which has its problems, but at least they are problems we are enfranchised to work on" (1990a, 29). Engaging students in environmental advocacy efforts can be an extremely effective pedagogical tool, in addition to the fact that it may help protect imperiled ecosystems and species. Students learn a variety of research, analysis, and critical-thinking skills as they review land-use decisions and attempt to understand the various sides of land-management controversies. They also learn powerful lessons about how our democracy works and the vital role played by informed and active citizens in directing a representative government.

One of the most effective strategies I have found for engaging students in environmental advocacy efforts, and the easiest to incorporate into course curricula, is to guide them through the various strategies used by grassroots environmental activists. After each of our field courses, we study the wilderness and national scenic trails acts, read sample letters to the editor and letters to land managers and political representatives, and then compose our own letters and send them to appropriate members of the press and government. Students gain experience with the various strategies used in each genre, learn more about the issue and place they are writing about, and feel a sense of empowerment by seeing their words in print and participating in the public process.

As Snyder makes clear in "Tomorrow's Song," the stability of both the natural world that supports and sustains us and the democracy that protects and empowers us are threatened. Our political marginalization of the rights of nonhuman entities and our cultural marginalization of the power of the individual citizen to direct democratic governments are causing the slow but inevitable collapse of the natural and political systems upon which we rely. Snyder writes:

> The USA slowly lost its mandate
> in the middle and later twentieth century
> it never gave the mountains and rivers,
>> trees and animals,
>> a vote.
> all the people turned away from it. (1992, 250)

The only way we can develop, or maintain, functioning sociopolitical and natural systems is if we train those who will have the power to protect or destroy those systems in the methods needed to sustain them.

A second useful method for teaching students the benefits of and methods for preserving and restoring their bioregion entails engaging them in a hands-on environmental restoration project. Using the Hindu concept of ahimsa, or nonharming, Snyder explains, "[T]he precept against taking life, against causing harm, doesn't stop in the negative. It is urging us to *give* life, to *undo* harm" (1990a, 182). Thus, for students living and studying in the Sierra Nevada, 95 percent of which was clear-cut during the Comstock era, participating in some aspect of reforestation or forest-health enhancement is morally obligatory. As Snyder notes, reinhabitation means "moving back into a terrain that has been abused and half-forgotten—and then replanting trees, dechannelizing streambeds, breaking up asphalt" (178).

Depending upon the needs of one's bioregion, students can be directed to engage in a variety of restoration projects, from building and maintaining hiking trails to planting trees, thinning forest fuel loads, picking up trash, stenciling storm drains, removing invasive species, restoring stream banks and -beds, and decommissioning illegal off-road-vehicle routes.

In the past, my students and I have participated in all of these projects. On one particular project, which involved planting trees and thinning fuel loads in a second-growth forest in the Tahoe Basin, my students were treated to a hands-on lesson in Sierra Nevada fire ecology and the natural and cultural history of the region. From ecologists and historians we learned about the effects of Comstock-era clear-cutting and the years of subsequent fire suppression. Like Snyder, we "were struck by the tremendous buildup of fuel. The well-intentioned but ecologically ignorant fire-exclusion policies of the government agencies over the last century have made the forests of California an incredible tinderbox" (1995, 260). We built burn piles of dead and downed timber, removed dangerous ladder fuels (saplings that ground fires can climb up to crown in the mature trees), and planted preferred tree species to alter forest composition and improve wildlife habitat.

During a lunch break, I read Snyder's poem "Control Burn" to the students, and we used the occasion to discuss how the landscape itself had changed due to human interactions with it. Snyder opens the poem by describing Native American practices of using fire to manage the Sierra Nevada landscape. He explains that they were

> *keeping the oak and the pine stands*
> *tall and clear*
> *with grasses*
> *and kitkitdizze under them,*
> *never enough fuel there*
> *that a fire could crown.*

In addition to reducing the threat of catastrophic crown fires, such frequent thinning by low-intensity ground fires increased the availability of grasses and legumes, improving wildlife habitat and foraging grounds.

A few lines later, Snyder explains his plans for helping to restore the natural fire regime and original health to the forests in which he lives, stating that he would like

> *to help my land*
> *with a burn. a hot clean*
> *burn.* (1992, 219)

We then discussed the procedures for, benefits of, and dangers inherent in the use of prescribed fire to manage mountain forests. The students learned theoretically and practically how such fuel-reduction projects mimic the role of natural ground fires and prepare the forest for the reintroduction of fire after its century-long absence.

Regardless of the project, such activities offer a variety of pedagogical benefits. First, they can often be incorporated into the course curriculum quite easily, a particular project taking up a single day or even several days. Second, they can be coupled with either scientific or humanities-based course material to increase students' engagement and deepen their understanding of the subject. Finally, by engaging students in practical actions that benefit their own region, we are more likely to have a lasting effect on them than through classroom-based instruction alone. Many of my former students, I have found, return to sites where we have planted trees or built trails, often bringing friends and family members with them to share their work. This generates a ripple effect throughout the student's life and community, where the lessons learned in a particular course do not stop at the end of the semester but continue to reverberate across space and time.

Bioregional Responsibility

The final aspect of reinhabitory practice involves taking responsibility within one's own life and community for the health and stability of the bioregion in which one lives. Bioregional responsibility means first, and foremost, taking responsibility for our own ecological impacts and reducing them wherever possible. Second, bioregional responsibility entails passing on our ecologically informed insights, values, and actions to others—sharing with our neighbors, students, friends, and families why they should, and how they could, begin living a less destructive life.

Like all forms of responsibility, ecological responsibility begins with the self, with our own actions and in our own homes. Snyder uses the Hindu precept of ahimsa—"to cause no unnecessary harm"—as an injunction against the environmentally and socially destructive levels of consumption that characterize the American lifestyle. Snyder confronts consumer capitalism in poems like "The Trade," for example, arguing that in addition to the social and ecological costs of such high levels of consumption, we also pay a heavy psychological price. He describes twentieth-century consumers shopping in a mall—"a massive concrete shell / lit by glass tubes, with air pumped in"—critically observing that they "Were trading all their precious time / for things" (1992, 191). Snyder argues that contrary to media-driven opinion—the average American views more than two thousand advertisements each day—"The actual 'real wealth' is knowing how to get along 'without'" (1980, 51). Because a single American uses between 30 and 150 times the natural resources of a single person living in a Third World nation, Snyder's criticism of consumer capitalism is both ecologically and culturally appropriate.

By directing our students to take a critical look at their own rates of consumption and then asking them to attempt to reduce these consumptive activities, if only for the short duration of a class project, we may be able to affect their long-term behavior. I often introduce students to these subjects using the "Five-R Mantra" described by Julia "Butterfly" Hill in her book *One Makes the Difference:* respect, rethink, reduce, reuse, and recycle (2002, 12).

Whereas the other reinhabitory practices described above aid students in respecting the natural world and its limits, bioregional responsibility encourages them to rethink their buying patterns, teaching them to vote with their dollars. Similarly, students can be encouraged to try reducing their consumption for a period of time, walking and riding bikes instead of using cars, saving water and electricity, and abstaining from purchasing things they do not need. Students can also be shown the benefits, both ecological and economic, of reusing items that are often discarded and recycling "trash" that is often unprofitably thrown away.

Regardless of the specific activity, students can be encouraged to practice reducing their ecological impacts. With enough encouragement and practice, they may eventually come to exclaim along with Snyder and Han Shan:

> *Thin grass does for a mattress,*
> *The blue sky makes a good quilt.*
> *Happy with a stone underhead*
> *Let heaven and earth go about their changes.* (1992, 24)

: : :

After students have begun learning about their bioregion, started working to protect and restore it, and accepted responsibility for their own impacts upon it, they should be encouraged to pass these insights on to others within their community. One of the best ways to reinforce such values and practices is to put students in the position of teachers, asking them to find persuasive and informative manners for encouraging others to follow their example. As Snyder puts it in "Ethnobotany," "Taste all, and hand the knowledge down"

(239). On one of our tree-planting projects, for example, I invited a science classroom from a local middle school to join the university students for the day. Each college student was paired with a small group of middle schoolers to help them with the planting, share what he or she had learned about the project, and act as an adult mentor or model. The younger students bene-fited from and enjoyed the attention and knowledge of the adults, while the older students' commitment to the project deepened from the experience of sharing it with others. Such a cascading mentorship model holds tremen-dous social and educational benefits for participants on both ends of the spectrum and deepens their experience and sense of community. Snyder observes, "One's culture is in the family and the community, and it lights up when you start to do some real work together, or play, tell stories, act up" (1990a, 179).

In "Painting the North San Juan School," Snyder describes the commu-nal experience of working together, a common experience a few generations ago but one that most of our students have never known. He describes the adults who are painting the school, "White paint splotches on blue head bandanas," and their children who are also participating in the work in their own way, "Little kids came with us are on teeter-totters / tilting under shade of oak" (1992, 272).

The multigenerational experience of working together as a family, as a community, has been all but lost to most Americans, unless they live on a farm or ranch. I still fondly recall hauling hay with my family in the unbear-able heat and humidity of Kansas's late summer. When I was too little to throw the forty- to seventy-pound bales, I drove the tractor. When I was a little older, I threw and stacked the bales, working alongside the men.

As children, this is where we have traditionally learned to work, how to discipline ourselves to accomplish a task, and what a "work ethic" is. However, without such experiences our youth are growing up devoid not only of the sense of the dignity and purposefulness of work, but also of the experience of spending time with adults, with their parents, neighbors, and relatives. Although we cannot completely counter the trajectory of modern history, we can aid our students in developing a more cohesive sense of com-munity and encourage them to experience the benefits of participating in their own campus and neighborhood communities.

Working and sharing alongside our students, we become an axe and they a handle. But as Snyder notes, they will soon

> . . . *be shaping again, model*
> *And tool, craft of culture,*
> *How we go on.* (266)

RESURRECTION THROUGH REINHABITATION

The late morning sunlight warms us as we sit in a circle just outside of our camp, discussing Snyder's poetry. The Boy Scouts have broken camp and hit the trail early to cross Dick's Pass, which rises a thousand feet above us. A dusky grouse, *Dendragapus obscurus,* and several chicks pass within fifteen feet of us as we sit quietly talking. Her dark-gray, mottled coat blends perfectly with the dappled shadows of sun and shade below the pines, a fitting demonstration of her scientific name, *obscurus.* Suddenly, a chorus of yips and howls erupts from somewhere above us. They seem to be coming from a stand of pine and fir, higher up the mountain, near Dick's Pass. Although it seems quite unlikely that coyotes would be howling at this time of day, it is possible that a pack has caught a grouse or marmot and is simply celebrating. I recall following a similar chorus of yips, barks, and howls when I was a child, only to find a pack of coyotes noisily dismembering a large wild turkey.

Later that day, as we crest Dick's Pass, we meet a PCT thru-hiker who says she also heard the howls but thought they belonged to the troop of Boy Scouts, celebrating their successful ascent of the steep pass. As we hike on, I wonder whether it was really a pack of coyotes, *Canis latrans,* or a group of coyote-like boys howling in the wilderness. After debating the matter for some time, I decide that maybe it was both. In "Call of the Wild," Snyder writes,

> *I would like to say*
> *Coyote is forever*
> *Inside you.* (1992, 222)

Perhaps their sojourn in the wilderness has infused the Boy Scouts with some semblance of coyote spirit, what Snyder calls in the poem "Long Hair" "takeover from the inside" (197).

As I hike with my own students and imagine the coyote-boys howling from the mountaintops around us, I am reminded of Terry Tempest Williams's short prose poem "Redemption," in which she writes, "We can try and kill all that is native, string it up by its hind legs for all to see, but spirit howls and wilderness endures. Anticipate resurrection" (1994, 144). It is my hope that through interdisciplinary field-based education we can resurrect the wilderness around us as well as the wild inside us.

....
In the Footsteps of Literary Activists

Can literature help protect a place? Can some reciprocity exist between the real, fixed anchor of a wild place, and the intangible values—chief among them, the art—produced from that source? Can art give back to the land?

RICK BASS,
Brown Dog of the Yaak: Essays on Art and Activism

One of the major preoccupations of contemporary nature writers is to attempt, through their work, to stave off the destruction of imperiled natural landscapes, endangered species, and local communities. Rick Bass notes this concern and asks, "Can literature help protect a place?" (1999, 86). Although such a rhetorical question is difficult to answer quantitatively, or in a precise and direct manner, it does point out a significant tradition that can be seen running throughout the long tradition of American environmental literature. Much of our current concern for protecting natural places is a result of our growing awareness of ecological limits, carrying capacity, and the very real and present danger of environmental catastrophe. Although in the past decades we have enjoyed tremendous developments in the field of ecology, American nature writers have recognized for centuries that the abundance of life on the North American continent and the peaceful solitude and inspiring beauty of open landscapes are in danger of being lost forever.

Each of the three iconic Californian authors I have been studying attempted through their work to counteract this history of environmental degradation. Though their efforts have primarily been to write lovingly and lyrically about the natural world and what they find of value there, Austin, Muir, and Snyder have also used their work to fulfill specifically activist agendas, to create cultural, political, and on-the-ground change. Bass critiques nature writers for not recognizing and responding to the need for activism, stating: "I understand, I think, the impulse, if that is what it can be called, to write about the natural world, as a means of preserving it and paying respect to its shadow, its memory. But I understand also how tiny that act is, compared with, say, protecting a mountain, or two mountains, or a string of mountains, like vertebrae, or sentences" (38).

A careful exploration of Austin's, Muir's, and Snyder's professional and personal lives reveals that they have attempted, and often succeeded, in answering the challenge Bass poses for us today. Although they have written beautifully about the natural world, their writing has less often been directed at preserving the memory of places and has more often been focused on protecting the places themselves. Through both their literary and activist-oriented work, they have often succeeded in protecting the actual mountains, rivers, deserts, and people they write about from real-world exploitation and degradation. All three authors have demonstrated the effectiveness of uniting environmental art and activism in an enterprise that can create permanent environmental protection.

Whereas our most common, and in the short-term most effective, activist strategies involve a much more simplified, propagandistic approach than those used by these environmental authors, their aesthetically refined, linguistically sophisticated, and intellectually complex explorations of environmental issues have proved effective in their own way. They have often succeeded in achieving short-term conservation goals, but they have been even more effective in creating social and political change over a longer period of time. As Jay Kardan observes in "Activism, Taste, and Conscience," our political experience tells us that in the short term, "[s]logans, sound-bites, and arguments based on threats to human health—especially the health of children—are effective. Complexity, ambiguity, elaboration, irony, polysyllabism, appeals to biological and wilderness values are not" (2002, 15).

Responding to such a recognition does not, however, necessarily mean that we have to oversimplify complex ecological issues and accept the standard economic and anthropocentric terms of the debate in order to be effective activists. Although we may do all of these things in a particular situation, or to craft a specific message, we also benefit from acknowledging the complexity of environmental issues and attempting to transform both the terms and the values by which such debates are framed. Depending upon our audience, our objectives, and the time frame involved, different approaches offer different advantages.

Kardan argues persuasively that the subtler, more complex, and more artistic approaches adopted by Austin, Muir, and Snyder have their place as well.

> Persuading the masses is important, but so is persuading the few who have enough leisure, intelligence, and education to appreciate subtler arguments. Effective leaders are likelier to come from the latter than the former, and conservation groups should recognize the need for communications, and communicators, adapted to their tastes. This is not preaching to the converted, or "talking to ourselves," as my political friend put it. Think of it rather as talking to people who are ready to join us, the incubation of conservationists *in ovo*. (16)

Austin, Muir, and Snyder have demonstrated their work to be extremely effective in this regard. Although their influence on American environmentalists is impossible to quantify precisely, they have been collectively responsible for countless conservationist "conversions," have provided much needed inspiration to weary activists, have helped to improve public perceptions of and attitudes toward wild landscapes, and have directly affected public policy and on-the-ground protection of native species and ecosystems.

Kardan concludes: "Until it can find a mutually satisfying place for activists with what I would call a 'literary conscience,' our movement will be making inadequate use of those who could be some of its strongest advocates" (17). Similarly, I contend that until we recognize the practical efficacy of such environmental authors as Austin, Muir, and Snyder in advancing the environmentalist agenda, we will continue to marginalize some of our most effective tools for instituting the long-term cultural and political change necessary to achieve a sustainable relationship with the natural world. A closer look at these three authors demonstrates that they all sought to use their work in activist manners, took advantage of their professional positions to advance social and environmental agendas, and were—and Snyder still is—committed activists in their own personal lives.

MARY AUSTIN AS ENVIRONMENTAL ACTIVIST

Through her work, Austin attempted to teach her readers to love the arid lands of the West. She demonstrated that no landscape can rightly be considered ugly or useless, but rather that each is beautiful and useful to those who understand such landscapes on their own terms. Austin taught readers to develop ethical relationships with the land, to recognize natural limits, and to respect the West's native inhabitants, both human and nonhuman. Austin believed that it was her responsibility to teach Americans about the value of their western wildlands and, as Carol Dickson and other scholars have observed, saw literature as the appropriate medium for achieving this goal (2000, 226).

One of the most common approaches Austin employed to advance her activist agenda was to subtly argue for the inherent biological and aesthetic values in desert landscapes through writing about them in an ecologically informed, emotionally powerful, and lyrically beautiful manner. She also, however, periodically included explicit observations and criticisms of the despoilation of western lands in order to make her case more direct and forceful. In *Lands of the Sun,* for example, Austin criticizes the grazing practices of shepherds for both their ecological devastation as well as their shortsightedness.

> On the Sierra side the guttered mesas, the hoof-worn foothills advertise the devastation of the wandering flocks. Early in the sixties there appeared little, long-armed French and Basques, with hungry hordes of sheep at their heels, pasturing on the public lands. They ate into the roots of the lush grass and left the quick rains to cut the soil. The wool in the hand was always worth the next season's feed to the sheep herder. (1927, 151)

Austin often wrote affectionately of stockmen, farmers, and pocket hunters— praising their love of solitude, dedication to work, and connection to the land—but she was not shy about criticizing them when their practices promised to ravage those landscapes, endanger native species, and threaten their own chances of survival. Criticizing their practices of "predator control," she writes, "Always there is a war on between horse and cattle men and the wolves" (181). Austin often praises the intelligence, beauty, and ecological importance of predators like wolves and coyotes, arguing that like the desert, there is no such thing as an ugly or useless landscape or species.

Writing just after and during the first decades following the turn of the century, Austin's defense of "inhospitable" landscapes and "dangerous" predators was revolutionary. In fact, such a position remained controversial even into the late 1940s when Aldo Leopold wrote "Thinking Like a Mountain." In this short narrative, the forester and wildlife manager develops a similarly ecocentric perspective, recognizing the inherent value of all nonhuman nature. Leopold tells of shooting a wolf for no reason other than wolves kill deer, and he thought at the time that "because fewer wolves meant more deer, that no wolves would mean hunter's paradise." Once he approached the dying wolf, however, Leopold recognized how wrong he had been. He confesses, "We reached the old wolf in time to watch a fierce green fire dying in her eyes. I realized then, and have known ever since, that there was something new to me in those eyes—something known only to her and to the mountain" (1949, 150). Leopold realized, like Austin, that wild creatures and wild ecosystems have their own lives, identities, and sentience apart from our narrow perceptions of them.

Such an ecocentric perspective allowed Austin to recognize the injustice and danger involved in many of the unquestioned land-management practices of her day. In fact, her criticism of the exploitative and destructive practices of lumbermen, stockmen, and miners was so effective that, as she notes in her autobiography, "After *The Flock* was published, Roosevelt sent a forestry expert to interview her" (1932, 289). However, such events were not out of the ordinary for Austin. As she confesses in a letter to author Sinclair Lewis, "[T]he head of the Department of Irrigation wrote me that though he had been studying irrigation all his life, I had given him new ideas" (1979, 142).

Austin's literary descriptions of the landscapes and land-management practices of the West were authoritative and persuasive enough to catch the eye of presidents, scientists, and land managers, often placing her in a position to directly influence environmental policy at the highest levels. In fact, Austin was personally acquainted with Presidents Theodore Roosevelt and Herbert Hoover, and as she notes in her autobiography, and her correspondence verifies, she often used her position to lobby on behalf of specific environmental and social causes.

This synthesis of art and activism was common for Austin, who often designed her literary projects with a specific social function in mind. In a 1931 letter to Sinclair Lewis, for example, Austin proposes a collaborative project for a series of books to tell the long, sordid history of ecological and cultural devastation that lay in the wake of western land reclamation. She suggests to Lewis "that we might pool our separate knowledges in a work of fiction around the destiny of one of those rivers which have meant so much to the development of the west" (141). She then goes on to describe a series of three books that would be needed to cover the topic. Austin's hope that the book, or books, would advance an activist agenda becomes clear in a later paragraph:

> I know everything that needs to be known: How the Indians learned irrigation and taught it to the Whites; how the cities "framed" the farmers and stole the river for the use of the realtors, all the bitterness and greed; how three lives and fortunes are sacrificed to every title to irrigated lands. . . . I know all about the corruption both commercial and political that goes to that business. I lived through the Owens River theft and know why the Watterson brothers still languish in jail. I know why the San Francisquite Dam went down—I think I know what threatens in Boulder Dam. (142)

That Austin wanted such a book written more for its effectiveness as an activist tool than as a means to advance her authorial career is evidenced by the fact that she even suggests that Lewis may want to complete the project alone. She writes, "I want to see these things told in imperishable form as you can do it, and as I can't alone. If you feel we can't do it together, then buy my knowledge and do the book or books yourself" (142).

Austin's involvement in water reclamation issues stemmed from her experiences beginning in 1903 in the Owens Valley, fighting a losing battle against the City of Los Angeles for water that rightfully belonged to the lakes, streams, aquifers, irrigation ditches, and fields of the region. As Austin explains in her autobiography, delegates from the city presented themselves as representatives of the federal government in the valley and began buying up lands and their associated water rights. "There were lies and misrepresentations," she writes. "No citizen protested, no clergyman, no State official" (1932, 307). Although Austin appears to have realized what was occurring, she explains that most of the valley's residents recognized neither the intent nor the impact of the project until it was too late. In 1904, Austin managed get an interview with William Mulholland, the chief engineer on the project. According to an aide, after the interview the visibly upset Mulholland is said to have remarked, "By God, that woman is the only one who has brains enough to see where this is going" (Reisner 2000, 82).

Knowing the ecological and social devastation that would result in her beloved valley and its local communities from the reclamation project, Austin attempted to resist it as well as she knew how. As she admits in her autobiography, "Mary did what she could and that was too little." She persuaded her husband to file a complaint with the Reclamation Bureau, and in 1905 she wrote Theodore Roosevelt about the issue, but neither gained a satisfactory response. Austin confesses in her autobiography, "She walked in the fields and considered what was to be done. She called upon the voice and the voice answered her—Nothing." And so she moved from the Owens Valley to Carmel, where, as she admits, she became ill, knowing "that the land of Inyo would be desolated, and the cruelty and deception smote her beyond belief" (1932, 308).

Although Austin felt as if she had utterly failed to help the Owens Valley region in any way, the fight over the Inyo's waters continues today. And, in fact, Austin is still involved. As the salinity of the treasured Mono Lake increases and its ecological health and sustainability decrease, a number of organizations have come together to regain some of the region's water. Austin's descriptions of what the region was like in 1903 are currently being used, along with scientific evidence, to document the environmental, aesthetic, and social costs to the region from the loss of its waters. Austin's observation that from anywhere in the Owens Valley one is "within hearing of the lip-lip-lapping of the great tideless lake" is being used as a historical counterpoint to the contemporary alkali flat that now occupies the lake's waterless boundaries, continually generating dust and sandstorms to plague the area (1997, 58). Austin may not have been capable of preventing the waters from being stolen in the first place, but she may be instrumental in having them returned to the region after a century's absence.

Austin's failure to save her beloved valley from the greed and nearsightedness of the Los Angeles developers colored her approach to activism from that point forward. She remained involved in environmental issues, especially those concerning water, but retained a healthy dose of realism, and perhaps an unhealthy dose of cynicism, regarding what such forms of activism could accomplish. In 1927 Austin was appointed to the Seven States Conference on Colorado River Basin Development—a group charged with considering the construction of "Boulder Dam," now known as Hoover Dam, and the development of Lake Mead. Austin strongly opposed the project, arguing for the river's importance to the region as well as to Mexico, but had little effect on the other delegates. As she notes, "I said what I had to say, being profoundly convinced against it: but I discovered there is little one can say against an enterprise that will not come to the proof for perhaps fifty years. . . . None of us will live to see that *debacle*" (1932, 363; emphasis in original). Unfortunately, those of us living in the American Southwest today have seen the debacle Austin prophesied. Probably as a result of her past experience with such reclamation projects, Austin "withdrew from the Conference, although not from foresight and opposition" (363). I imagine that although the dam was constructed, Austin would be happy to know that a variety of organizations are working today to dismantle the dam and have the flooded canyons restored to their original state.

Austin was also dedicated to supporting issues of social justice. She was a staunch defender of Native American land rights and religious freedoms, women's rights, the suffrage movement, and the concerns of the poor. She was friends with, and supported the work of, such notable activists as Walter Lippmann, Bill Haywood, Emma Goldman, Lincoln Steffens, Max Eastman, Elizabeth Gurely Flynn, Margaret Sanger, and Mabel Dodge Luhan.

In addition to working on labor and feminist concerns, Austin always had time and energy to defend her Native American friends. She defended Native American religious freedoms when their dances were banned by Commissioner of Indian Affairs Charles H. Burke and rallied enough support to defeat the Bursum Bill, which would have taken vast tracts of Pueblo land from native ownership. Austin was so well known as an advocate of Native American cultures that in 1930 the Mexican government appointed her as a consultant to help in the restoration of their own indigenous populations and cultures.

As with her environmental advocacy, Austin's involvement in issues of social justice seems to stem from her own experience with injustice. In *Earth Horizon* she describes a brutal instance of rape that initiated her advocacy efforts on behalf of Native Americans. Austin notes, "What set me off on that trail was dreadful enough, a flagrant instance of a local pastime, known as *mahala* chasing." As she explains it, this fairly common practice for white men was to waylay Indian women on their way back to the "campoodies" after working in town. In this particular instance, two young girls were waylaid by a gang of youths and an older man and brutally raped for the greater part of the night. Austin notes that after their release the two young girls committed suicide "by eating wild parsnip root—the convulsions induced by that bane being mercifully shorter than the sufferings they had already endured" (267).

Austin explains her defense of Native Americans: "I took the defense of Indians because they were the most conspicuously defeated and offended against group at hand" (266). Far from adopting a position of cultural superiority, Austin chose to represent those who seemed to be the least represented in the power structures of her time. Similarly, Austin's defense of the desert's unique beauty and complexity and the rights of its inhabitants to have water, space, and protection arose from her desire to speak for those people and places who were given the least voice in U.S. society. Like many environmental, labor, and civil rights activists working today, Austin chose to speak for those whose voices were not being heard in the political process. She attempted, in her literary work and in her professional and personal life, to defend the land she loved and its human and nonhuman inhabitants from those who would exploit them.

JOHN MUIR AS ENVIRONMENTAL ACTIVIST

Like Austin, Muir was a committed environmental activist who used his literary abilities as well as his personal and professional reputation to advance environmental causes. Whereas Austin and many of Muir's contemporaries were involved in issues of social justice, Muir remained steadfastly focused on environmental protection. Partly because of this focus and partly because of his prodigious energy and enthusiasm, Muir is still perceived as one of America's most successful citizen conservationists.

Muir enjoyed a number of significant successes, but it was his greatest failure that taught him the most about activist strategies and the realities of American politics. Like Austin, Muir fought but could not prevent the destruction of a prized valley by the water reclamation programs of the early twentieth century. In Muir's case the valley was Hetch Hetchy, and the city was San Francisco. Unlike Austin, however, Muir never gave up the fight to save his valley. As Michael P. Branch notes in *John Muir's Last Journey,* the seventy-three-year-old activist and adventurer remained involved in the Hetch Hetchy controversy even as he was preparing to embark on an eight-month forty thousand–mile journey to South America and Africa, a journey for which he had waited his whole life and would probably be his last. Branch records that Muir "hoped to use the East coast portion of the trip to lobby representatives in Washington (and prominent men everywhere he could) on the need to preserve the endangered Hetch Hetchy Valley. . . . Muir's correspondence from early 1911 is also replete with concerns about Hetch Hetchy Valley, the fate of which had already been a matter of contention for more than a decade" (2001, 5). Although Hetch Hetchy was part of Yosemite National Park—the 1891 establishment of which was Muir's first great preservationist victory—the fact that it did not remain safe from commercial interests was an important lesson in American politics Muir would never forget.

Muir began his literary defense of his beloved California wilderness very early in his career. In 1876 he sent "God's First Temples: How Shall We Preserve Our Forests?" to the *Sacramento Record Union* in an effort to influence California legislators. In the article, Muir emphasized the utilitarian value of California's forests as watershed protection, acknowledging the practical mind-set of westerners at that time. A short while later he wrote "New Sequoia Forests of California" for *Harper's,* emphasizing the aesthetic and recreational values to be found in California's forests rather than their utilitarian uses.

Muir soon recognized that the kind of protection he sought for western wilderness could be provided only by the federal government, and thus he would also need to develop a large public constituency of wilderness lovers. Muir attempted to build the public support he needed through his literary work, which emphasized divinity in nature and the inherent beauty and value of wilderness areas and wilderness experiences. He also reluctantly became an avid supporter of tourism as he recognized the political necessity of gaining public support for preservationist causes and as he weighed the relatively benign impacts caused by tourists when compared to those of lumbermen, stockmen, and miners.

Muir used his literary publications to advance specific preservationist pro-
posals and to generate in the American public the kind of environmental values, perceptions, and experiences that would evolve into an ecological conscience. Michael P. Cohen explains: "[H]e would attempt to radically re-create
public attitudes and taste, hoping to lay the groundwork for an ecological
conscience in America, a reevaluation of the management of Yosemite, the
desire for new parks, and wise use of agricultural lands and forests" (1984,
206). Muir attempted to create these shifts in public sentiments through arguing for the divinity of the natural world, developing an ecocentric appreciation of nonhuman nature based upon scientific understanding, and modeling
a vigorous outdoor ethic based upon recreation and wilderness experience.

Muir's first strategy, and one of the most salient characteristics of his literary defenses of wild nature, was to place the divine directly in the physical
and natural world. In *The Mountains of California,* for example, he describes
the glorious effects of the sun in his beloved Range of Light, exclaiming,
"This was the alpenglow, to me one of the most impressive of all the terrestrial manifestations of God. At the touch of this divine light, the mountains
seemed to kindle to a rapt, religious consciousness, and stood hushed and
waiting like devout worshipers" (1916b, 66). In this passage Muir claims not
only that God is manifest in wild nature, but that the elements of nature
themselves are religious adherents as well. Muir consistently asserts that the
works of nature are, in fact, the works of God and that to mar them is to
blaspheme the Creator. This view is nowhere so clearly indicated than in his
defense of the ill-fated Hetch Hetchy Valley. Muir closes *The Yosemite,* published in 1912, only two years before his death, with these words:

> These temple destroyers, devotees of ravaging commercialism, seem to
> have a perfect contempt for Nature, and, instead of lifting their eyes to
> the God of the mountains, lift them to the Almighty Dollar.
>
> Dam Hetch Hetchy! As well dam for water-tanks the people's cathe-
> drals and churches, for no holier temple has ever been consecrated by
> the heart of man. (1962, 202)

In addition to attempting to defend the natural world on the basis of its
own divinity, Muir developed preservationist arguments founded upon an
ecocentric and scientifically informed recognition of the inherent complexity and value of nonhuman nature. In *A Thousand-Mile Walk to the Gulf,* for

example, in which he tells the story of his epic botanizing expedition from Indiana to Florida, Muir criticizes the prevalent anthropocentric views of his day: "Now, it never seems to occur to these far-seeing teachers that Nature's object in making animals and plants might possibly be first of all the happiness of each one of them, not the creation of all for the happiness of one. Why should man value himself as more than a small part of the one great unit of creation?" Here Muir exhibits two important facets of his defense of wild nature: first, the infusion of the natural world with the divine, and second, an ecocentric sensibility that values all life equally. Muir's preservationist stance is further displayed when he writes, "The Universe would be incomplete without man; but it would also be incomplete without the smallest transmicroscopic creature that dwells beyond our conceitful eyes and knowledge" (1916a, 137). Such a strong defense of nonhuman life, though more common in contemporary nature writing, was revolutionary in Muir's time. In fact, it still stands as a highly contentious assertion, as suggested by the George W. Bush administration's attempt to gut the Endangered Species Act by arguing that it was intended to apply only to charismatic megafauna and not to such "trivial" animals as fish and insects.

Like contemporary ecologists, Muir recognized that each species plays a vital role in maintaining the balance, health, and sustainability of ecosystems, regardless of our own anthropocentric perceptions of them. In fact, Muir can be credited with making an early recognition that would later become one of the founding principles of the science of ecology. In *My First Summer in the Sierra,* Muir writes, "When we try to pick out anything by itself, we find it hitched to everything else in the universe" (1916c, 157). This recognition of the interconnectedness of different species and features of natural ecosystems represents the ideological foundation upon which the ecological sciences are built—sciences that aim to study and understand the *relationships* between organic and inorganic features of natural systems.

Such ecologically informed insights led Muir to adopt an ecocentric ideological position, in opposition to the strong anthropocentrism of his time. In *A Thousand-Mile Walk to the Gulf,* Muir explicitly states, "The world, we are told, was made especially for man—a presumption not supported by all the facts" (1916a, 354). By arguing that nonhuman nature has value apart from the uses to which humans can put it, Muir combats the utilitarianism and anthropocentrism of his time while prophesying the recent recognitions

contemporary ecologists have made regarding how healthy ecosystems function and maintain stability in order to support human and nonhuman life.

Muir's final literary strategy for generating an ecological conscience in his
readers was to develop a persona or subculture of people who participated
in and valued outdoor recreation and wilderness experience. Although Muir
did develop the literary persona of the adventurous mountaineer in order to
offer his readers vicarious wilderness experiences, he was more committed
to encouraging readers to claim those experiences for themselves. Throughout his career, Muir never tired of encouraging others to visit the Sierra
Nevada and experience them directly, claiming, "Every rock, mountain,
stream, plant, lake, lawn, forest, garden, bird, beast, insect seems to call and
invite us to come and learn something of its history and relationship" (1916c,
241). For Muir, convincing people to come visit, and experience directly, the
majesty of the Sierra Nevada wilderness was the best use to which his literature could be put. As he stated in a Sierra Club address, "Few are altogether
deaf to the preaching of pine-trees. Their sermons on the mountains go to
our hearts; and if people in general could be got into the woods, even for
once, to hear the trees speak for themselves, all difficulties in the way of forest preservation would vanish" (qtd. in Cohen 1984, 303). Thus, despite
Muir's disdain for the tourist, much of his writing took the form of promo-
tional literature of the West's natural areas. It also served, for those who
never reached Yosemite and the Sierra Nevada, as a type of vicarious wilderness experience, one they could turn to imaginatively to find value in wild
nature.

When he was not writing, Muir was often either exploring the Sierra
Nevada himself or helping others to experience the California wilderness. He
was a staunch supporter of the Sierra Club's outings program that William
Colby initiated in 1901. This first trip included Muir's *My First Summer* and
Joseph Le Conte's *Rambles* as recommended reading, as well as educational
talks by William Dudley, C. Hart Merriam, and Muir. Colby asserted, "An
excursion of this sort, if properly conducted will do an infinite amount of
good toward awakening the proper kind of interest in the forests and other
natural features of our mountains" (qtd. in Cohen 1984, 311). The promise of
being able to develop an environmental ethic in the public through such outings led Muir to support and participate in the program. In addition to supporting Sierra Club outings, Muir himself consistently served in the capacity

of tour guide and field-studies instructor for a number of important people, ranging from Ralph Waldo Emerson to Theodore Roosevelt.

In fact, Muir camped with Presidents Roosevelt and Taft as well as Secretaries of the Interior Richard Ballinger and John W. Noble, using such opportunities to press his cause for legislative protection and preservation of the West's shrinking wildlands. The success of such camping trips, combined with Muir's other literary and epistolary appeals, is difficult to overstate. In addition to being responsible for the creation of Yosemite National Park, Muir's influence on Roosevelt alone resulted in the establishment of 148 million acres of new national forests, the creation of sixteen new national monuments, including the Grand Canyon (which was later changed to a national park by Congress), while the total number of national parks nationwide doubled (1923, 2:414). In addition, as founding member and first president of the Sierra Club, Muir left us with what has become America's largest, and most widely recognized, environmental advocacy organization.

Muir's entry into the political life was slow, but as the devoted naturalist grew to recognize the severity of the threats facing his beloved wilderness, he also came to realize the necessity of legislative protection. Although he believed, as Michael P. Cohen notes, "his best efforts could be made as a private citizen and independent writer," Muir joined the Forestry Commission in the summer of 1896 as an ex-officio member (1984, 286). However, his primary role would be one of defense rather than creation, as he spent the years following his service on the commission defending both President Harrison's 1891 reservation of 13 million acres of Pacific slope for watershed protection and President Cleveland's 1897 reservation of an additional 22 million acres from harmful extractive industries.

Muir's literary gifts were indispensable to his role as defender of public lands as he worked to rally public and political support for his cause. Early in his career Muir recognized that if the wilderness areas of the West were to survive, they would need both the active support of private citizens and the sympathetic ears of key politicians. In a characteristic letter to President Roosevelt requesting his opposition to the proposed Hetch Hetchy Dam, Muir demonstrates that he has conceded the political necessity of encouraging tourism as a means to generate public support for preservation, as well as his faith in the public for supporting such causes:

I am anxious that the Yosemite National Park may be saved from all sorts of commercialism and marks of man's work other than the roads, hotels, etc., required to make its wonders and blessings available. . . . I pray therefore that the people of California be granted time to be heard before this reservoir question is decided, for I believe that as soon as light is cast upon it, nine tenths or more of even the citizens of San Francisco would be opposed to it. (1923, 2:419)

Muir remained a committed and effective environmental activist through-out his career, never losing faith in the American public's willingness to defend that which they had come to know and love and the federal govern-ment's ability to enforce those wishes. Though many contemporary environ-mental activists would rightly question Muir's faith in the federal government and the American public, we still owe many of our specific strategies, a num-ber of our national parks and protected public lands, and much of our tradi-tion of seeking environmental protection through legislation to Muir's work at the turn of the twentieth century.

He concludes *Our National Parks* with characteristic optimism, in an attempt to generate public support and propose federal protection for the remaining Sierran forests: "Through all the wonderful, eventful centuries since Christ's time—and long before that—God has cared for these trees, saved them from drought, disease, avalanches, and a thousand straining, lev-eling tempests and floods; but he cannot save them from fools,—only Uncle Sam can do that" (1916d, 393).

GARY SNYDER AS ENVIRONMENTAL ACTIVIST

Like Austin and Muir, Gary Snyder has demonstrated an unwavering com-mitment to environmental activism in both his personal and his profes-sional life. Though Snyder, like Austin, has also been integrally involved in the social justice movement—supporting the rights of laborers, the poor, and indigenous cultures around the world—for the purposes of this study, I will focus on aspects of his career that have been specifically directed toward issues of environmental protection and sustainability. Despite the breadth of Snyder's activist interests and work, this focus is warranted given that he defines himself as an environmental activist. As he states in *The Real Work,* "My political position is to be a spokesman for wild nature. I take that as a primary constituency." Snyder elaborates this self-definition, explaining that through his prose and poetry he is able to speak for or represent the interests of nonhuman nature within the human sociopolitical realm. He explains, "It's a position of simple advocacy, taking the role of being an advocate for a realm for which few men will stand up" (1980, 49). Just as we have advocates to represent the interests of such exploited or underrepresented classes as the poor, children, minorities, and women, Snyder sees himself as representing the "'classes' which have so far been overlooked—the animals, rivers, rocks, and grasses—now entering history" (1990a, 41).

In a 1968 interview for the *Berkeley Barb,* Snyder playfully discusses his activist intentions, stating, "I want to get out there and agitate them trees and grasses into revolting against the exploiting class . . . (*laughing*) . . . stir up a few earthquakes and volcanic eruptions" (1980, 14). Although Snyder is having fun here, and he has not initiated any known earthquakes or volcanic eruptions yet, he has successfully shaken up the literary world, agitated a large number of authors and activists into writing about and resisting the destruction of the natural world, and caused an eruption or two in the political arena as well.

Snyder views the function of poetry—his primary activist tool—from an anthropological perspective, arguing that literature carries on important cultural work and can both reflect and direct our attitudes, values, and actions. In fact, Snyder graduated from Reed College in 1951 with a bachelor's degree in anthropology and literature. He argues:

> For at least a century and half, the socially engaged writers of the developed world have taken their role to be one of resistance and subversion. Poetry can disclose the misuse of language by holders of power, it can attack dangerous archetypes employed to oppress, and it can expose the flimsiness of shabby made-up mythologies. It can savagely ridicule pomp and pretension, and it can offer—in ways both obvious and subtle—more elegant, tastier, lovelier, deeper, more ecstatic, and far more intelligent words and images. (1995, 93)

Although Snyder admits that poetry "has indirect effects, not direct effects if you want to talk about 'masses,'" he believes, with good reason, that these "indirect" effects can be quite powerful and enduring (1980, 73). According to Snyder, the images, metaphors, and ideas contained within socially active poetry can evolve over time into common ideology and political policy. This evolutionary process from poetic metaphor to public policy may be understood by exploring the implications of Snyder's frequent personification of trees. In "Two Logging Songs," for example, he writes:

Forestry. "How
Many people
Were harvested
In Viet-Nam?"

Clear-cut. "Some
Were children,
Some were over-ripe." (1992, 257)

In this stanza, Snyder equates the indiscriminate "harvesting" of trees with the indiscriminate murder that necessarily comes with war. Humans and trees are metaphorically conflated, linking the emotional power and tragedy of war with the destruction of our native forests. Such a technique has been adopted by environmental activists and scientists alike who have begun referring to our current biodiversity losses as the "biological holocaust." For those of us living in the twentieth and twenty-first centuries, the word *holocaust* carries powerful connotative meanings these activists would like us to associate with the wholesale eradication of species that we are now witnessing.

Snyder anthropomorphizes trees in a number of other poems as well, attempting to link them to both our common humanity and to the exploited classes of humans who are also being victimized by modern industrial culture. In "Front Lines," he vividly describes a developer's bulldozer grinding over

The skinned-up bodies of still-live bushes
In the pay of a man
From town. (218)

In another poem he explicitly states:

"From the masses to the masses" the most
Revolutionary consciousness is to be found

> Among the most ruthlessly exploited classes:
> Animals, trees, water, air, grasses. (183)

These poetic metaphors, which imaginatively link human sentience and morality with the lives and rights of nonhuman nature (in this case trees), enter our cultural consciousness, germinate, and grow, until they flower into full-fledged ideology and policy. As Snyder explains it:

> Thus, you proceed from an animistic idea that you can hear voices from trees. And a few decades later a lawyer like Christopher Stone writes a *legalistic* argument—"Should Trees Have Standing?"—arguing that trees should be involved in the democratic process. . . . And you push it forward a generation or two in the future you can actually feel on a gut level that nonhuman nature has rights. And that will be the work of the poet, to set that direction. (1980, 72; emphasis in original)

Snyder often deploys his poetry for expressly political purposes. In *A Place in Space,* he explains why he wrote and how he used the famous "Smokey the Bear Sūtra." He had just returned from Japan and read about the Sierra Club Wilderness Conference of 1969, which was to be held the next day. He wrote and printed the sutra overnight and the next morning was in the lobby of the conference hotel handing the poem out, saying,

> "Smokey the B__r literature, Sir." Bureau of Land Management and Forest Service officials politely took them. Forest beatniks and conservation fanatics read them with mad glints and giggles. The Underground News Service took it up, and it went to the *Berkeley Barb* and then all over the country. *The New Yorker* queried me about it, and when I told them it was both free and anonymous, they said they couldn't publish it. It soon had a life of its own, as intended. (1995, 31)

As Snyder's story illustrates, he often writes poems with an activist goal in mind, and in such cases the purpose of the poem supersedes any professional gain he might accrue from it. "Four Changes with a Postscript" is another excellent example of Snyder's activist-oriented poetry. In this prose poem, Snyder details four major problems facing the earth and the cultural and personal changes required to solve those problems. Like "Smokey the Bear Sutra," "Four Changes" "was widely distributed in several free editions" (45).

This synthesis between Snyder's professional career as an author and his personal practice as an activist is also illustrated in a story Jim Dodge, a fellow environmental activist and bioregionalist, relates about the poet. Dodge explains that after witnessing Snyder quietly slip a portion of his reading fee to an organizer to donate to a local charity, he "later confirmed, Gary often donated part of his fee to the local community defense fund." Like his predecessors Mary Austin and John Muir, Gary Snyder often uses his professional position, reputation, and income to directly support environmental causes. As Dodge observes, "Since Gary was talking the talk—revolution begins at home, less is more, enough is plenty, mutual aid, give something back—I was glad to see he walked the walk. Showed class" (1991, 144).

It should come as no surprise that in his personal life Snyder remains a committed and effective environmental activist. To reduce his and his family's ecological impact, Snyder built, with the help of friends, a bioregional home (a house built sustainably out of local materials) on the San Juan Ridge of the Yuba watershed on the Pacific slope of the Sierra Nevada. He continues to engage in biological surveys, clear brush to prevent wildfire, and plant trees to restore damaged landscapes, all in an effort to develop a reciprocal relationship with the land upon which he lives, a lifeway that gives as much to the land as is taken from it.

Snyder has often served on boards and as an active member of nonprofit organizations. As Ryo Imamura, a fellow activist and Buddhist, notes, when Snyder was treasurer of the Buddhist Peace Fellowship Board, he gave a poetry reading and donated all the proceeds to get the books back into the black. He also served on the California Arts Commission at the request of Governor Jerry Brown and acted in an informal capacity as an adviser to the governor on a variety of matters. All of these things suggest that Snyder consistently practices the philosophy he preaches in his writing.

In a 1979 interview, Snyder detailed his long-term vision for environmental and social activists everywhere to defend the planet and direct us toward a sustainable future, but he could just as accurately have been describing the way in which he has chosen to live his own personal life.

The fact is that the dynamics of industrial capitalism are still so enormous that until it slows down of its own glut there isn't much we can do except holding actions, and try to keep our heads clear about what can be and should be. . . . And as it does so we would be well advised to have in mind what kinds of skills we really need and what it means to be self-governing, and to increasingly take responsibility for our own lives, our own neighborhoods, and our own communities. (1980, 143)

As Snyder's professional work and personal life attest, a powerful synthesis can be achieved between activist-oriented works of environmental literature and the daily practices of activists themselves. Snyder should be seen as working within the same tradition as Mary Austin and John Muir, a tradition that pays tribute to endangered species and imperiled wildlands through art and literature as well as through protection and preservation.

PLEDGING ALLEGIANCE TO THE LAND

Without the work of such activist-authors as Mary Austin, John Muir, and Gary Snyder, we would be much poorer as Americans, losing some of the finest works in our literary tradition and some of the most valuable parts of our natural heritage. Each of these authors has demonstrated his or her commitment to "king and country," or in this case "land and community," by expressing through both their words and their deeds an allegiance to the places in which they live.

Snyder's poem "For All" contains a revised pledge of allegiance that honors our reliance on and responsibility to the land upon which we live, a recognition clearly shared by both Austin and Muir. In the poem, Snyder replaces *the United States of America* with the bioregional and indigenous term *Turtle Island,* which he has explained is "the old/new name for the continent, based on many creation myths of the people who have been living here for millennia, and reapplied by some of them to 'North America' in recent years" (1974, 1). He also replaces *the flag,* the object to which one pledges his or her allegiance in the original version, with *the soil,* the bedrock of our existence. Snyder encourages us to rethink what patriotism means, returning to the original roots of the word—*terra patria*—the love of the land of one's birth. However, the allusion to the United States as a political entity contained in the poem's title and form—the "pledge of allegiance"— also reminds us that we must be politically and socially active. One can almost imagine Mary Austin and John Muir reciting, along with Gary Snyder,

> *I pledge allegiance to the soil*
> *of Turtle Island,*
> *and to the beings who thereon dwell*
> *one ecosystem*
> *in diversity*
> *under the sun*
> *With joyful interpenetration for all.* (1992, 308)

CHAPTER TEN

··

Education for Cultural Transformation

It goes on one at a time
it starts when you care
to act. It starts when you do
it again after they said No,
it starts when you say *We*
and know who you mean, and each
day you mean one more.

MARGE PIERCY, The Moon Is Always Female

I am marching with a group of students, faculty, and community members across our university campus. Some carry placards and signs displaying anti-war slogans, and others lead chants, rhythmically shouting, "This is what democracy looks like!" While I push our two-and-a-half-year-old son in a stroller, my wife walks beside me carrying a sign that reads, "Why are some so threatened by peace?" It is the early spring of 2003, and we are part of an international student strike and peace rally held in opposition to the Bush administration's proposed invasion of Iraq. All day long we have been holding teach-ins on the university lawn about U.S. foreign policy, veterans' affairs, Gulf War syndrome, democracy, and student activism. The majority of students passing by look up from cell phone conversations with bored and listless eyes, others point and laugh, and still others shout fascist slogans like "Love it or leave it!" Suddenly, as we are marching across the campus quad, a man bursts through the center of the protesters, rips the cloth banner out of the hands of a woman leading the march, and strikes her force-fully. A few steps later, he slams his shoulder and forearm into a second woman's chest. I watch as she is thrust backward, saved from falling to the concrete by those walking directly behind her. Letting go of the stroller, I start toward my wife in an attempt to intercept the attacker, but I am too late. Before I can reach her, he has jumped up, struck her in the face, and knocked her sign to the ground. I watch as her head snaps backward and her plea for peace falls to the pavement unheard.

Fortunately, I am able to physically subdue the man after a short scuffle, and no other marchers are hurt. We proceed with our march, and the rest of the day's speeches, activities, and workshops are completed without further incident, except for the intermittent jeers and verbal assaults of passing students. I cannot help feeling frustrated and dismayed that, regardless of their own political positions, so many of these students demonstrate no under-standing of how their democracy functions and are incapable of respecting their fellow citizens' freedom of speech and assembly rights.

I also feel a deep sense of frustration as so many of my friends and colleagues—all of whom have voiced strong opposition to the war, support of democratic principles, and dismay at the apathy of their students—sit in their offices and classrooms while we march, teach, and defend ourselves from physical and verbal assaults outside. Though, as instructors, we surely need to be careful about imposing our political opinions on stu-dents, participating in, witnessing, questioning, and even peaceably oppos-ing such an event could be extremely effective educational experiences for them. More important, such participation would do much to resist the institutional bias within the educational system against active learning, student engagement, and civic involvement.

The curriculum of a wide variety of college courses ties so directly into such events that it is difficult to understand why university faculty and graduate students did not take greater advantage of the opportunity to engage their students actively and educationally in the democratic process. One would expect political science, U.S. history, journalism, and sociology classes to benefit from the type of engagement, discussion, and critical reflection that attending the event would have generated. However, these obvious choices for pedagogical participation were conspicuously absent. I met only two instructors—one from the English Department, the other from Journalism—who asked their students to attend, witness, and reflect on the day's events.

Almost without exception, university faculty chose to ignore and thereby marginalize the democratic scene outside their windows. And in so doing, they taught their students more effectively than any curriculum they could have designed that our democratic rights and responsibilities are not important and do not need to be respected, protected, or used. By failing to recognize the event as significant and refusing to use it for its important educational possibilities, they also failed to uphold the stance of political neutrality that was a major concern of those foregoing participation. If there had been three hundred marching instead of thirty, we probably would not have been attacked. If there had been a thousand instead of a hundred students attending the teach-ins, the passing students might not have been so quick to scoff at and dismiss the participants as "unpatriotic," "freaks," and "outcasts." If as instructors we had the courage and conviction to tell our classes that regardless of what they thought politically, what was happening outside was significant intellectually and democratically, students might have learned to respect rather than criticize democracy when they were faced with it in action. Instead, many instructors chose to privilege concerns for "political neutrality," "attendance," and "curriculum," without recognizing that their inaction, their marginalization of the democratic process, was far from neutral and that regardless of what "curriculum" they taught that day, the real lesson their students learned was one of apathy and intolerance. From a transformative learning viewpoint, they failed as educators to take advantage of one of the most engaging, experiential, intellectually stimulating, and emotionally powerful educational opportunities to occur on our campus in years.

In all fairness, however, it should be noted that many of these graduate students and faculty members are extremely active in their personal lives, participate in the public process, and support environmental and social causes in which they believe. However, when afforded the opportunity to engage in these same democratic actions professionally—to model these practices for their students—they were extremely reluctant. The major reason for their reluctance, I believe, is because we have come to think of the process and purpose of education as a politically neutral, values-free enterprise. The point of noting student and faculty inaction is not to condemn or criticize individual faculty members or students; rather, it is to critique the way in which we teach students, the educational system itself, and how we think of education generally.

Unfortunately, we have come to think of higher education as a type of vocational training in this country, one that should impart professional and intellectual skills while avoiding ethical, moral, political, or values-based issues and ideas. Many faculty chose not to participate in the day's events because they rightly recognized that any form of participation would be construed as "forcing" their own political opinions on students and would carry with it some element of personal and professional (and, as we unfortunately discovered, physical) risk. Teachers are encouraged not to take such risks by the educational environment itself, which exhibits a very strong institutional bias against incorporating values-based and action-oriented education into the curriculum. Because we view education as the passive acquisition of objective knowledge and intellectual skills, instead of the active production of knowledge and utilization of civic abilities, participating in such events carries too great a risk for educators. Because we view education as a passive, intellectual, and amoral exercise, anything that does not fit into these categories is deemed uneducational.

We will continue to run significant professional risks when we attempt to incorporate such activities into the classroom unless we begin to change how we think, talk, and write about, as well as enact, education at all levels. Until we recognize that our current educational system actually marginalizes and represses most of the intellectual and social skills required by democracies to function, we will fail to prepare our students adequately for citizenship in this country and the world.

This institutional bias toward passivity is evidenced by the fact that only a week before the student-led demonstration, faculty members and graduate and undergraduate students packed one of the English Department's classrooms—standing-room only—to hear Rebecca Solnit talk about the connections between her art and activism. They all smiled and nodded appropriately as she discussed a series of international peace rallies held earlier that same month:

> For me the eleven to thirty million people who marched last weekend
> were already celebrating victory marches—not because we had definitively

defeated the war Bush wants in Iraq, but because we had temporarily overcome the isolation and disembodiment and lack of public life and lifelessness of public space that is part of the accelerated and technologically driven present. Just to be there, particularly for us Americans, was to inhabit a metaphysical space called democracy and participation that is also being clearcut by John Ashcroft and neglected by most of the rest of us. (2003, 9)

However, when those same faculty members and students were given the opportunity to actively participate in, rather than passively pontificate about, such issues, they were extremely reluctant. Many of the students were, in fact, required to attend the lecture in the classroom but were not similarly required, or even encouraged, to attend the "event" outside. Although both the "event" and the "lecture" supported precisely the same political position, the lecture was deemed educationally worthy and the event was not, betraying the institutionalized bias of the contemporary educational system.

To require students to listen to a one-sided politically oriented lecture, without a forum in which to respond with agreement or opposition, has come to be viewed as somehow less authoritarian and more educational than requiring students to attend a politically oriented event in order to hear the positions of other citizens and voice their own opinions. There was, for example, an open microphone at the event with which all students, pro- and antiwar alike, were encouraged to express their opinions.

Though both the lecture and the event have educational benefits, guiding students through the participatory process offers opportunities for critical thinking, self-reflection, logical argumentation, rhetorical persuasion, and a host of other intellectual skills that the lecture alone does not. In addition, such participation promises to empower students with the knowledge, skills, and inclination to become civically involved and effective—a rudimentary requirement for them to function as citizens in a democracy.

As Marshall McLuhan so famously remarked, "The medium is the message." And the message of our current educational system is, especially when we marginalize such events, that theory is more important than application, posture is as good as practice, and verbalization is paramount to action. As participants in, or victims of, the traditional educational system, the students and faculty members who chose not to take educational advantage of the democratic scene outside were merely conforming to the lessons they had been taught through twelve to twenty years of training.

In order to adequately prepare our students for the world they will face following graduation, we must, as David Orr concludes, "rethink the substance and process of education at all levels" (1992, 90). We must recognize that in addition to preparing our students to work in the professional world, we are also responsible for preparing them to participate in their own democracy while living within the finite limits of the natural environment. Such preparation will involve doing much more than suspending class for a day to participate in the political process. It will entail reinventing our entire approach to the pedagogical process, including a wide variety of participatory teaching strategies, and emphasizing the types of skills required by academic, civic, and ecological competence. If as individual educators we incorporate action-oriented education into our curriculum in a comprehensive manner, it will become much easier to participate in such events, avoid professional and personal risk while doing so, and ensure that our students acquire the targeted skills and knowledge while maintaining their own freedom of opinion.

Noting the manner in which our educational system suppresses individual and social change, and our dire need to reform that system, brings to the fore a central theme that has been implicitly underlying this exploration of Austin's, Muir's, and Snyder's work: the utilization of the democratic process to induce personal and social transformation. In this chapter, I would like to explore the pedagogical issues relating to individual and social change. Each of these authors has encouraged sociopolitical change through direct participation in the democratic process. In addition, they have tried to engender individual change within their readers while at the same time encouraging those readers to work toward cultural and political change themselves, through participation in the democratic process.

As David Orr observes in *Ecological Literacy,* "The environmental movement is almost without exception one in which citizens forced governments and large economic interests to do something they were otherwise not inclined to do. It is quite literally a democratic movement, but it will not necessarily remain such without an unwavering commitment by educational institutions to foster widespread civic competence" (84). Civic competence, however, cannot be taught in isolation from civil society. It cannot be taught without active participation in the democratic process. In addition, whatever incipient civic competence students might already have gained is effectively eroded when educators and educational institutions encourage inaction, demonstrate apathy, and marginalize democratic practices on their own campuses.

In "Transformative Learning and Transformative Politics: The Pedagogical Dimension of Participatory Democracy and Social Action," Daniel Schugurensky records the abysmal participation in the democratic process evidenced by contemporary Americans and links it to our failure to educate students in the foundations, principles, and practices of their own democratic government. Referring to the highly esteemed early American educator John Dewey, Schugurensky notes, "The guiding principle we can extract from Dewey, even a century later, is that the best and most effective way to learn democracy is simply by doing democracy" (2001, 69). Unfortunately, however, by the time they have left the university, most college graduates have never voted in a local, state, or federal election and have never lobbied their political representatives through direct appeal, participated in a political campaign, attended a public hearing, volunteered for or donated to a nonprofit community service organization, or used their freedom of speech and assembly rights. This is why, in the past two presidential elections, only 47 percent of those who were eligible to vote actually voted, and the numbers drop drastically from there as we begin looking at participation in local and state elections. Thus, on a good day, when the elections are run without deceit, approximately 27 percent or less of the voting population elects the representatives who will govern the other 73 percent of American citizens. Voting, of course, is not the culmination of democratic practice, the end all and be all of our democratic rights and responsibilities, but merely the beginning, the foundation upon which the rest of our practice is built. If we cannot get Americans to participate even on such a foundational level, how do we expect them to participate in the more meaningful, more difficult, more effective, and more time-consuming methods of the democratic process? By failing to incorporate these essential practices into the curriculum, and especially by marginalizing them when they organically evolve on our own campuses, we are effectively teaching our students that they do not matter.

Teaching—in fact, showing—our students how to participate in the democratic process, however, is perhaps the single most important curriculum we have for developing sustainable relationships with our fellow citizens, other nations, and the environment in which we live. As Gregory Smith and Dilafruz Williams assert in *Ecological Education in Action,* "The creation of viable community and regional governments, responsive to the needs and viewpoints of all citizens, will necessitate inducting the young, and re-educating their elders, into the give and take of political life" (1999, 11). Unless we teach students how to participate in the democratic process, how to instigate social and political change, whatever "environmental awareness" we are capable of imparting will be ineffectual and insignificant.

Smith and Williams go on to observe that within the past twenty years we have seen a dramatic shift in educational values and approaches. They note that in the past, "Individuals were not educated for themselves alone but for what their education would mean to the welfare of the whole" (16). With the recent rise of pluralist and relativist philosophies, contemporary educators have come to increasingly emphasize political and moral neutrality in an attempt to create a "values-free" educational environment. However, in so doing they have neglected the fact that education always already takes some moral point of view. In attempting to remain "politically neutral," educators are in fact upholding the status quo, marginalizing the need for critical thought and active participation in the public process, reinforcing student apathy toward current political events, and encouraging intolerance of those who participate in an active, democratic, and constitutionally protected manner. Such a curriculum, whether intended or not, is anything but neutral.

Regardless of what course we teach, it is our responsibility as educators to prepare our students for the world they will inhabit after graduation and to ensure that they possess the skills and knowledge required to be competent in that world. As members of a democracy, then, our students will need not only an understanding of how democracies function, but also the skills and conviction to participate in that process in a practical, informed, and active manner. As David Orr contends, "More than any other institutions in modern society, colleges and universities have a moral stake in the health, beauty, and integrity of the world our students will inherit" (1999, 235). Of course, one of the most significant factors affecting the beauty, health, and integrity of our students' future world will be their ability and inclination to participate effectively in solving social and environmental problems through the public process. Unfortunately, however, our current educational system does not teach students or give them practice with these skills, and it actively discourages any inclination they may have to develop them on their own.

Education can, however, be a very effective force in engendering personal and social transformation, especially through teaching students how to participate in the public democratic process. Rosa Parks, for example, participated in a nonviolent civil-disobedience seminar just a few weeks before she refused to sit on the back of a segregated bus. Those of us living in twenty-first-century America, enjoying the freedom, tolerance, and opportunity engendered by the actions of people like Rosa Parks and Dr. Martin Luther King Jr., can surely see that our society is stronger, healthier, more stable, and more just as a result of the education they received and publicly enacted. The only way for us to succeed as educators in producing a cultural transformation toward sustainable and just relationships with each other and the natural world is to actively demonstrate to, teach, and practice with our students the skills and actions required to make such a transformation. Cultural change begins with individual change. And individual change, on the part of the student, begins with personal and pedagogical change on the part of the instructor. The locus of responsibility ultimately lies within each of us.

TEACHING INDIVIDUAL AND CULTURAL TRANSFORMATION

Because most environmental education programs are designed, at least to some extent, to encourage changes in students' knowledge, perceptions, attitudes, and behavior, some understanding of the psychological mechanisms affecting personal transformation is required for developing effective pedagogical strategies. Far too often, environmental educators operate under what Scott Slovic has termed "the assumed power of awareness" (1992, 169). The assumption is that if you make people aware of a particular problem, they will, based upon this new knowledge, alter their behavior accordingly to solve it. Unfortunately, however, the findings of cognitive and behavioral psychologists contradict this unexamined assumption.

One need merely look at smoking to illustrate this point. Smoking-related illnesses currently account for more than 430,000 American deaths each year, representing the leading cause of death in this country. At the same time, the American public, especially the educated American public, is well aware of the health dangers associated with smoking. As Daniel Schugurensky explains, "If awareness was directly correlated to changes in behavior, it would be impossible to explain why, with all the evidence available, many doctors and scientists still smoke." A similar phenomenon occurs with regard to our awareness of environmental problems, democratic processes, and our continued reluctance to change behaviors that exacerbate those problems and marginalize those processes. As the smoking example suggests, if awareness led directly to action, then it would be impossible to explain why the students and faculty who were aware of the march and the issues it supported failed to participate. Schugurensky asserts that we must "make an analytical distinction among transformation of individual consciousness, transformation of individual behavior, and social transformation. The three often are related, but it cannot be assumed that the first necessarily leads to the second and this to the third" (2001, 61).

If we are serious about attempting cultural transformation through educationally induced individual change, then we must incorporate pedagogical practices that are capable of encouraging personal transformation. Simply put, we must be capable of moving students (and ourselves) from awareness to action. Students must be guided through a three-step process that leads them from "I know" to "I care" and finally to "I act." Our current educational system is failing to develop democratic competence in its graduates simply because it refuses to recognize the need for moving beyond the first step in this threefold process of growth and development.

Noted psychologist David Gray tackles this problem in *Ecological Beliefs and Behaviors: Assessment and Change,* observing that in order for education to induce social transformation "[p]eople need to know that they are expected to change individually; they need help in attaining new skills and realistic individual goals. They may also be trained in how to influence the larger corporate and collective sectors" (1985, 204). Thus, an educational program designed to encourage individual and social change will need to incorporate the following elements. First, students will need to be guided through critical self-reflection of their preexisting beliefs, values, attitudes, and behaviors. Second, they will need to be given real-world experience, which will often include removing them from the familiar and guiding them through subsequent reflection on their new experiences. And third, they must engage in the democratic practices whereby individual change is trans-lated into social transformation. Without engaging in such an approach, there is little chance that the larger individual, cultural, and environmental objectives of environmental education will be realized.

Though critical self-reflection is not sufficient, by itself, to predictably induce individual transformation, it is a necessary first step in the process. Most environmental education programs, especially those grounded heavily in the sciences, have a tendency to ignore values-based exploration and criti-cal reflection as pedagogical tools. Most of these programs begin by provid-ing students with information on ecology, environmental problems, and their potential solutions. However, as David Gray observes, "There is an apparent gap between that logic and the psychology of how people change. If you want to change the person, begin with the person and some of his or her most central ties with his or her own subjective reality; do not begin with the science of ecology" (206). Environmental educators, then, must guide stu-dents through a critical examination of many of their unconsciously held assumptions and beliefs, such as their anthropocentrism, belief in continual progress, faith in technological fixes to ecological problems, and lack of per-sonal responsibility for current social and environmental problems. By doing so, one may first expose, confront, question, and explore students' unexam-ined assumptions about the world and their place in it and then offer alter-native information, ideologies, and ethics to replace those that have begun to appear untenable. Unless we first make a space for ecological awareness and environmental ethics within our students' belief system, we will find it difficult, if not impossible, to help these new ideas take hold.

A second important facet of transformative education is to afford stu-dents the opportunity to gain direct experience with their subject matter. Scientific, historical, and other discipline-based forms of information can have some effect on students' belief systems and behaviors, but direct expe-rience has proved to be a more significant factor in influencing how we think, feel, and act. David Gray observes, "One is not likely to deny immedi-ate concrete experience; thus, the more abstract old negative beliefs will be changed in order to reduce the dissonance and restore harmony and consis-tency in the belief system" (238).

After the students have examined and questioned their preexisting belief structures, gaining some form of direct experience upon which to build new attitudes and beliefs is extremely effective. This experiential basis of personal growth is emphasized by psychologist Donald G. Tritt, who asserts that "learning and growth are facilitated by an integrative process that begins with here-and-now experience and proceeds to observations and reflections about that experience" (1991, 595). By providing our students with both new experiences and guidance in reflecting upon their significance, we have a much better chance of replacing their preexisting belief structures with ones that are compatible with living in a democratic society and within naturally functioning ecosystems.

In order to be effective, such experiences should be purposively designed and contain some element of the unfamiliar. Adult educator D. Heath asserts, "[I]f you wish to provoke a person to become more aware, learn how to reflect, think freshly, then disrupt his usual patterns by forcing him into situations that create contrasts, confrontations, and challenges" (qtd. in Tritt 1991, 597). We cannot easily offer students new experiences worthy of critical self-reflection by staying in the university classroom and remaining within the traditional paradigm of the educational system. Both are experiences that have become so familiar to our students that they have, for the most part, ceased to mean anything significant and continue to reinforce the dominant self-destructive hegemony. Dennis Sumara and Terrance R. Carson agree, arguing that "relearning how to perceive is not merely a matter of changing one's mind about matters. It may mean, in fact, a matter of changing one's circumstances or changing one's habits" (1997, xvii).

By changing the circumstances, the places and practices, by which students are educated, we can more effectively alter their perceptions and actions. We can, in other words, more effectively inculcate an environmental consciousness and enact a sense of civic and environmental responsibility by engaging students in educational practices that take place outside of the classroom and the traditional educational paradigm. This entails dropping the myth of political neutrality or values-free education, resisting our traditional reliance on passive acquisition of textually based knowledge, and engaging our students in physical, intellectual, and emotional practices in the real world.

In addition to the transformative learning potential of experiential education and practice-oriented pedagogy, such forms of instruction have proved much more effective than classical top-down and text-based pedagogical approaches. Students succeed in retaining key concepts and skills much more readily in courses that involve such active forms of learning than in the more passive—primarily verbal and textual—forms of learning currently privileged by the educational system. As Edgar Dale's cone of learning experience demonstrates, students tend to retain only 10 percent to 20 percent of the information provided through reading and listening to lectures. On the other hand, students who are required to give a speech, simulate a real experience, or engage in actual practice retain anywhere from 70 percent to 90 percent of the instructional content (1969, 108–35). Although individuals favor some particular learning styles over others, students generally tend to learn most effectively through the coordinated use of all the senses—seeing, hearing, and doing. To be effective as instructors, then, we must incorporate experiential activities into our curricula and find ways to engage our students actively in the learning process, rather than relying on the primarily passive methods traditionally used in most courses.

Though an active, practice-oriented pedagogy is the most effective way to transmit course content and discipline-specific skills, it has also proved to be the most successful way to modify student values and behaviors. The third facet of transformative learning arises from this recognition—that passive acquisition of knowledge has no direct correlation to changes in beliefs and behaviors—and asserts that for transformative learning to occur, students must engage in the practices we want them to learn about or adopt as their own. David Gray summarizes recent research in the field, concluding, "Educational approaches dealing with deeply internalized beliefs and values are considered to be of utmost importance, but activity-oriented and behavioral strategies are viewed as being critical and complementary to the cognitive-affective approaches" (1985, 19). By engaging students in the actual practices we want them to learn about or adopt or both—such as environmental advocacy, conservation, or restoration—several things happen. First, and most important, they learn that it is not enough to simply talk, read, or write about social and environmental problems but that one must, at some point, take the information available, make an informed decision, and act upon that decision. In fact, a number of experts have contended "that if the social action dimension is missing, critical reflection can easily become an irrelevant and egocentric exercise" (Schugurensky 2001, 63). Second, students learn firsthand how to engage in such efforts in the real world and are able to develop the skills necessary to participate in them on their own. As

David Gray observes, "[I]n addition to providing knowledge about an issue, information must also be made available regarding both the type of action implied by that knowledge and specific guidance as to how to carry out that type of action" (1985, 75). A good education will not only impart new knowledge to students but also teach them what to do with it. By engaging our students in these practices ourselves, we can provide them with just the sort of guidance they require. Finally, as recent work in behavioral psychology has demonstrated, our attitudes are significantly influenced by past behaviors; thus, engaging in these practices provides a strong influence on future attitudes and their resultant behaviors. Students who engage in such practices have a statistically higher probability of undergoing identity and attitudinal transformation and thereby have a greater likelihood of continuing to engage in individual actions based upon these altered identities and attitudes after the course is completed.

Far from being an authoritarian imposition of the instructor's personal values or political opinions, transformative education promises to liberate students from the chains of apathy and ineffectualism with which our current educational practices bind them. Students who proceed through a process of critical self-reflection, direct experience, and committed action may choose to hold on to or alter their preexisting beliefs and attitudes. Regardless of their decision, they will at least be empowered with the tools, skills, and understanding to support those beliefs and transform them into effective individual and social action. Donald G. Tritt asserts:

> Such persons are more likely to be lifelong, self-educating individuals because they have learned the skills of active involvement in concrete experience, reflection upon such experience, formulation of generalizations and conceptual models, and the testing of these conceptualizations through new experience. In so doing, they have gained control of their own growth. (1991, 597)

ENVIRONMENTAL EDUCATION: PRACTICES FOR PERSONAL AND SOCIAL TRANSFORMATION

As I noted earlier, the solutions to our current environmental problems lie, for the most part, in changing individual and collective human behavior.

Environmental education, therefore, offers one of our most effective and lasting, albeit slow, strategies for developing sustainable relationships with the natural world that supports us. In order to create collective or cultural change, however, we must first engender personal transformation. David Gray explains: "National values undoubtedly do not spring like magic from nowhere, but rather are nurtured by influential leaders and vocal minorities, and even eventually by moderately supportive majorities. Whether our change strategies be collective or individualistic, individual change must occur—changes in beliefs, attitudes, values, ethics, and behavior" (1985, 18). In order to effectively engender personal transformation, environmental education programs must work on both objective and subjective levels. Thus, they need to be comprehensive and interdisciplinary, utilizing approaches from both the humanities and the sciences to direct values-based reflection and relay cognitive information. Likewise, students in such programs will benefit from having strong role models who display conviction and commitment, who are willing to work alongside and guide students through practices that lead to and result from an ecological consciousness. The end goal of environmental education, unlike an ecology course, is, as Gray contends, "that the individual will have begun to internalize, in his or her own manner, an environmental ethic" (202). Additionally, the ultimate goal of environmental education should be that students begin acting upon this ethic in an effective manner.

In order to accomplish this objective, we need to distinguish between environmental education as a transformative learning practice and most of our traditional discipline-based pedagogical approaches. The pedagogical approach traditionally adopted in our current educational system has been to merely teach students *about* a particular subject, such as the environment. However, as Joy A. Palmer asserts, for environmental education to be effective, for transformative learning to occur, "[t]asks should be planned that educate *about* the environment, *for* the environment, and are accomplished *in* the environment. Within this framework, three elements are crucial: personal *experience* in the environment, the development of personal *concern* for the environment, and the taking of personal *action* on behalf of the environment" (1997, 7; emphasis in original).

With these three elements in mind, I would like to detail four pedagogical practices that promise to engender the personal transformation sought by

environmental education programs and that are required by our current ecological crisis. First, students should be led through critical reflection of their
previously unexamined environmental beliefs, attitudes, and actions, reflection illuminated by the insights and research of ecologists, environmental
authors, philosophers, scientists, historians, and artists. This represents education *about* the environment and one's relationship to it. Second, environmental education programs should incorporate field experiences for students
so that they may be educated *about* the environment while living and studying *in* that environment. Third, classes should engage in some form of direct
conservation or restoration in the region in which they are studying. By
doing so, students not only learn *about* the environment while working *in* it,
but also learn *for* the environment, that is, how to act on its behalf. Finally,
students should practice several of the various democratic strategies utilized
by environmental advocates and activists to alter public perception and policy. This represents an opportunity to learn *about* natural resource policy
while acting *for* the natural environment and working *in* the sociopolitical
arena. By adopting such a comprehensive interdisciplinary and practice-
oriented approach, we will be able to more effectively empower our students
with the knowledge, skill, and conviction required to solve the current ecological crisis and develop a sustainable relationship with the earth.

Values–Based Reflection

As I noted, one of the best ways to begin teaching students about the natural
environment and their relationship to it is by helping them to examine their
preexisting environmental attitudes, beliefs, and values. Because most contemporary Americans live estranged from the natural world surrounding
them, such a process, though at times painful, is absolutely necessary to provide a context in which to talk and think about human relationships with
the environment. Our dominant social paradigm has been one of conven-
ience, consumption, anthropocentrism, and an unfailing confidence in
progress and technology, while it has ignored ecological limits, carrying
capacity, and the rights of other species. These more primitive and fundamental beliefs must be challenged and questioned before one can progress to
explore and examine derived beliefs relating to conservation, pollution,
preservation, and other contemporary environmental issues.

One successful pedagogical strategy I have found for directing students through the self-reflective process is to assign a series of short position papers covering the environmental attitudes and beliefs I want to focus on, coupled with reading and discussion of scientific and literary treatments of the same issues. I ask students to write, for example, a position paper on the relationship of the human species to nonhuman nature. I encourage them to consider such questions as: Are we above, under, or with the rest of the natural world? Are we separate from animals? Without trying to influence what they write, I direct them to write a persuasive argument supporting their position, to relate why they maintain that position, and to describe where their beliefs first originated. We then use these position papers in class discussions and debates and use selected readings to offset, both scientifically or objectively and artistically or emotionally, ecologically inaccurate or logically fallacious arguments. I often use selections from Muir's *Thousand-Mile Walk to the Gulf*, in which he cogently refutes the anthropocentric assumptions of his time, or Snyder's "Song of the Taste," in which he demonstrates our interconnections with nonhuman species. We compare how the different versions of evolution represented in Christian and Native American myth and evolutionary theory have directed various individuals and cultures to perceive, conceive, and act differently toward nonhuman nature. After we have read, discussed, debated, and re-formed our various notions of the topic, I direct the students to write a second position paper describing if and why their attitudes and beliefs have changed.

By guiding students through a critical examination of their fundamental environmental beliefs and augmenting those beliefs with accurate scientific knowledge and differing perspectives, we can more effectively encourage them to willingly adopt an environmental ethic based upon their own explorations and conclusions. Until students critically examine their preexisting environmental beliefs and compare them with reality and the beliefs of others, they cannot make the psychospiritual space required for adopting a new paradigm. Thomas Kuhn argues, in *The Structure of Scientific Revolutions*, "The decision to reject one paradigm is always simultaneously the decision to accept another, and the judgment leading to that decision involves comparison of both paradigms with nature *and* each other" (1962, 77).

Critical self-reflection aids students in examining their preexisting assumptions about the environment and their place in it—a necessary practice, as many of these assumptions are based upon inaccurate suppositions about the natural world and have been assimilated while being completely estranged from nature. Once these previously unexamined assumptions have been brought to light, it becomes much easier to replace them with ecologically informed ideas, values, and ethics. David Gray encourages environmental educators to utilize just such a technique: "After a person is fully aware of his or her primitive ecological beliefs and how profoundly they affect behavior, then begin building the countervailing beliefs of the land and environmental ethic" (1985, 206).

Such a process has proved extremely effective in altering the environmental attitudes of students, but it still maintains a respect for, and allows them the freedom to retain, any environmental belief they choose. Students are merely asked to examine, compare, analyze, and evaluate their beliefs and those of others and then to decide which seems most appropriate, logical, ethical, and beneficial to them and their community. However, once the students have examined their own beliefs and their often hidden origins and have compared them with scientific evidence, the views of their peers, and assigned environmental authors, they often come to the conclusion, on their own, that some reformulation of their original position is both necessary and beneficial.

Additionally, it should be noted that values-based reflection is useful not only at the beginning of a course. It can be used at any point during the educational process and is usually most effective if completed both before and after the students have a significant environmental or educational experience. For example, I often assign several values-based reflections at the beginning of the course and then wait until after we have engaged in field experiences and restoration or advocacy efforts to ask the students to reflect upon how their values have changed. Regardless of the particular approach, we must recognize that environmental issues are value laden and that individual behavior arises from often unexamined belief systems. By bringing these things to the fore, we can make our students aware of how their beliefs and values direct their behavior and impact others and the natural world that supports and surrounds them.

Field-Based Experiences

A second necessary component for environmental education to be effective concerns the setting in which pedagogical practices are performed and educational experiences attained. The traditional assumption of our educational system has been that there is no correlation or competition between the subject and the setting, that we can teach students *about* the natural world and their relationships to it *in* an artificial setting that completely divorces them from that environment. However, as David Orr observes, "academic architecture is a type of crystallized pedagogy and . . . buildings have their own hidden curriculum that teaches as effectively as any course taught in them" (1996, 16). If we are serious in our desire to teach students effectively *about* the natural world and their place in it, then we must teach them *in* that natural environment. To do any less will undermine whatever curriculum we devise.

I have experimented with a wide variety of field-trip formats, ranging from taking students on weeklong backpacking trips into rugged wilderness areas to visiting a local park for a single day, to engaging in a single hour of nature study on campus or even observing and studying "nature" in heavily trafficked, built-up or run-down urban areas. Most studies indicate that weeklong camping trips consistently demonstrate measurable changes in the environmental attitudes and social relations of participating students, but the participants themselves must be adequately prepared for the experience for it to be effective. Studies in behavioral psychology indicate that a "classical conditioning approach" is the most effective for persons without positive feelings toward nature or who have very little direct experience of the natural world. David Gray asserts, "The early associations should be good, warm, and friendly" and "brief" in most cases (1985, 162). Such an approach conditions participants to be more aware and appreciative of the natural world while preparing them for the rigors of longer, more engaged experiences.

Gray lists seven key conditions that must be met to adequately prepare participants for a long field-study experience. The first, "Readiness," is met through values-based reflection and classroom or textually based cognitive and affective knowledge. Students who have already begun to think about their relationship to the natural world and have learned something of the native plants and processes of the region they will be entering tend to benefit more from the experience than those who have not. The second condition, "Duration and Pace," relates to the fact that longer experiences and slower-paced trips that include time to study, wander, and rest tend to produce greater results. The third and fourth conditions, "Varied Exposure" and

"Pleasant Associations," refer to the participants' need to develop a variety of positive, interesting, and pleasant memories upon which later ecological attitudes and values can be built. The fifth and sixth conditions, "Proper Gear" and "Physical Conditioning," are similarly related to whether the field experience is enjoyable for participants or proves to be a rigorous and painful exercise. The seventh and final condition Gray proposes is to have an "Interpreter and Model," someone, preferably the instructor, who can teach students about the region and model appropriate and attractive forms of behavior in that region (236). Interpreters and models can also be found, however, in environmental authors like Mary Austin, John Muir, and Gary Snyder. In fact, Gray also agrees that "the role of vicarious conditioning," such as that provided by reading the work of environmental authors, "should not be overlooked" (162).

There are a variety of ways to incorporate field experiences into environmental education curricula, but a few specific examples may be helpful to provide models and generate ideas for meeting a particular instructor's or class's needs. The easiest approach for including field experiences into traditional classroom-based courses is to incorporate short nature-study activities near the campus or school into class activities. Students can be directed to observe, study, and journal about particular plants, insects, or animals living in their urban or suburban environment.

The variety and intensity of "wildness" existing within many of our urban environments can be quite surprising once we begin to pay attention to it. During one such campus-based exercise, I was fortunate enough to witness a red-tailed hawk hunting pigeons. The hawk struck a pigeon in midair, punctuating its rapid dive with an explosion of feathers and a long, laborious ascent back up to the top of the chemistry building. The pigeon appeared to be at least as large as the hawk, and before the small raptor could bring its quarry back to the top of the building the weight must have become too much for it. Released from the hawk's piercing talons, the pigeon tumbled toward the ground, regained its bearings on the way down, sped off as fast as it could toward safety, and crashed with a resounding thud into one of the clear glass windows of a three-story-high catwalk between buildings. I traced the now unconscious pigeon's path to the ground with my eyes and walked over to see if it would regain consciousness and fly off again. To my surprise, there below the glass catwalk lay three pigeons with broken necks and puncture wounds that all appeared to come from the hawk's talons. At this point the story of the young hawk's aborted hunting attempts became easy to read. Though most of our on-campus nature study sessions do not produce such dramatic results, they do offer students many of the same opportunities of longer backcountry experiences and also begin to make students more aware of the natural world surrounding them.

Urban environments also afford students the opportunity to study a variety of things that they often take for granted. I have had some luck with engaging students in such observation and analysis exercises as Dumpster diving, architectural and landscape studies, and explorations of urban planning and automobile and pedestrian traffic. Regardless of the subject of focus, the urban environment outside of our classrooms offers countless opportunities to study the natural world, the human environment, and our relationship to both.

A second strategy that I have used to include field experiences in campus-based courses is to offer a field-study component as a required or optional lab, or even as an additional credit. These generally take the form of a single day's excursion to a nearby park or natural area or even a single overnight camping trip. On such occasions I have taken students to nearby parks and arboretums and have even driven a few hours to more distant and wild destinations. As with the campus-based activities, these short field excursions can be prepared for during regularly scheduled on-campus classes and incorporated into classroom activities following the trip. Though day trips are significantly easier to prepare for and manage, overnight excursions tend to produce greater results in changes in both environmental attitudes and group relations.

A final method for offering students field-based experiences—the one that I used for my studies of Austin, Muir, Snyder, and the Pacific Crest Trail—is to take students on an extended backcountry camping trip. I have had success with both taking students on week- to ten-day-long trips and spreading the camping experiences out over a series of three to five weekends. In either case, students are afforded the opportunity to interact with, study, and live in a wild, natural environment for an extended period of time. The administrative, financial, logistical, and pedagogical challenges, not to mention the safety concerns, of taking students into the field for an extended period should not be taken lightly. However, there is no better way to counteract students' alienation from the natural world, provide them with

exciting and significant environmental memories, and alter their understanding and appreciation of the natural world.

Regardless of how we choose to incorporate them into our curricula, field
experiences are essential for the environmental educator who wishes to do
more than merely teach his or her students about the natural world. From
such experiences students gain, often for the first time in their lives, some
direct experience with, and knowledge of, the natural world. And most
important, they gain this new understanding under the direction and guidance of an ecologically informed instructor.

As many outdoor educators have noted, there exists a considerable
difference between appreciative and consumptive outdoor experiences.
Because we are almost constantly estranged from the natural world, it is
often difficult for students to leave behind their learned consumptive attitudes and behaviors; thus, the presence of a model or guide becomes exceedingly beneficial. Consumptive outdoor experiences would include such
activities as skiing at a resort, waterskiing or riding Jet Skis, driving off-road
vehicles, and sport hunting or -fishing. Appreciative outdoor activities might
include hiking, backcountry skiing, nature study or photography, and some
forms of hunting and plant gathering.

The distinction between the type of experience rests upon what its primary goal is. Although consumptive outdoor experiences take place in outdoor environments, the environment itself is merely a backdrop or a setting;
it is not the focus of the activity or the experience. During appreciative outdoor experiences, on the other hand, the goal is the direct study and appreciation of the natural world itself. Modeling this behavior, distinguishing it
from other activities, and demonstrating the need for, and benefit of, following Leave-No-Trace principles and outdoor ethics are vital components of
any field-based experience. By affording students the opportunity to gain
pleasurable and edifying experiences in the natural world, with the proper
guidance for recreating responsibly in it, we can aid them in the development of their own environmental consciousness and hold some hope that
they will continue to nurture it throughout their lives.

Conservation and Restoration Practices

To ensure that our educational field experiences are more than just another
form of extractive industry, we must find ways to give back to the places in

which they are set. Using the principles and practices developed in the field of Service-Learning, field-studies instructors can design projects that provide students the opportunity to offer direct service to the public lands in their home bioregion. Depending upon the instructor's goals, one can develop project-based field courses that are centered almost completely around a particular restoration project or conservation practice. Or one can utilize a smaller restoration or conservation component at the end of a longer field-study excursion. Regardless of how the conservation or restoration activities are incorporated into the students' field-based experiences, engaging in such projects helps the places in which our field studies are set and aids students in developing important skills, environmental ethics, and a personal identity that is committed to environmental protection.

For some courses it is appropriate to engage students in conservation research or practice. I have worked alongside students to band birds, study the impacts of invasives on native species, collect data for breeding-bird atlases, and monitor water quality in and around grazing allotments. In some instances, we have even had college students act as environmental educators, leading younger students through their own field-study experiences. At times I have led these projects myself, and in other instances I have invited a local expert who could set up and guide us through the project while using the data we produced in a practical manner.

For other classes, especially those not focused on the sciences, participating in some form of ecological restoration may be more appropriate. I have had good experiences working with students to plant trees, build and maintain backcountry trails, install soil erosion–control measures, remove invasive species, and restore streams. Often local land managers are happy to accommodate such volunteer projects, especially if they are designed in collaboration to meet both the park's and the students' needs.

Regardless of the type of conservation or restoration activity, it is imperative to guide students through some form of reciprocal activity toward the places in which they have been studying. Such a process not only gives students the skills and knowledge to engage in similar projects on their own, but is also tremendously effective in developing an environmental consciousness and sense of responsibility in students. In a study of recycling behavior, for example, David Gray notes, "Voluntary recycling behavior was significantly established among persons who had no such history by asking for very small steps at first, followed by more substantial ones later" (1985, 179). By leading students through the process first and engaging them in the practices we want them to later adopt, there is an increased likelihood that they will continue those same practices in the future and voluntarily participate in park and neighborhood cleanup projects, trail-work days, and community-based restoration events.

In addition, by providing the opportunity for students to give back to their home bioregions, we are able to help develop their sense of participation in and identification with the local community. In my experience, students are generally grateful for the opportunity and often express surprise that they are "allowed" to engage in such activities on public lands. Such projects not only teach students about their natural environment and the techniques needed to care for it, but also teach students *in* and *for* that environment, developing their own commitment to act on its behalf. In fact, one's sense of identity, or personal commitment, which strongly influences the actions one will take, is usually created or altered through action and personal experience. Mitchell Thomashow terms these identity-forming actions "practices of commitment" (1995, 97). Students who engage in practices of commitment have a statistically higher probability of undergoing identity and attitudinal transformation and thereby have a higher likelihood of continuing to engage in individual actions based upon these altered identities and attitudes.

Engaging students directly in the practices needed to care for our natural environment empowers them with the knowledge and the skills that will be required to solve the contemporary ecological crisis. In addition to teaching students how to act, it encourages them to act, an element sorely missing from the bulk of our traditional educational system. One often finds student commitments to such projects are quite strong. On a number of occasions I have heard of students returning to restored sites or trails that they built with one of our classes and bringing friends or family members along to view and discuss their work. On such occasions, they have transcended their role as students and adopted their emerging role as environmental educators and activists, committed to sharing their work and vision with others.

Advocacy and Activist Practices

A final method through which students can be taught and encouraged to protect their natural environment is to engage them in the practices used by environmental advocates and activists. Although these activities do not have to take place *in* the natural environment, they do take place *in* the public sociopolitical arena—the social environment in which students will have to work in order to solve the problems we now face. In addition, such activities teach students much *about* the natural world and the current threats to it, as well as about the public process and environmental policy, and they educate students *for* the environment, teaching them how to act on its behalf.

Though engaging in some form of environmental advocacy can easily be incorporated into a campus-based class, I have found it more effective if the students have had some form of field experience first. In order to gain the commitment and engagement of students, it is necessary to afford them the opportunity to gain some direct experience with the place or species they will be trying to protect so that they can form a cognitive and affective attachment to it. Once this condition has been met, the students can begin working on its behalf from their own home, classroom, college campus, and local community.

One of the easiest forms of environmental advocacy to incorporate into a course curriculum is to have students write their local political representatives, public land managers, and newspapers about the specific issue with which they have been involved. Whether the focus of the course is environmental policy, journalism, rhetoric, or science, such projects require students to review recent research concerning their issue, craft logical and persuasive arguments on its behalf, and gain some experience using the appropriate democratic channels for changing public policy.

I have also had success with student-organized poetry readings and environmental celebrations designed to increase public awareness and support of a particular local issue. Attending city council and county commissioner meetings, as well as public land-management hearings, with students and guiding them through the presentation process can also be extremely effective and powerful educational experiences. Regardless of the specific activity, it is essential to teach students how to engage in the public process and make others aware of their concerns in an effective way.

At the end of each field-studies course, I direct students to write letters to the editor of their local paper and to contact their political representatives in order to share some aspect of their experience, what they found of value in it, and what needs to be done in order to preserve that opportunity, place, or species for others. For one creative writing course, we secured outside grant funding and published a multimedia magazine of the students' own photography and creative writing. We had been studying in the Silver Peak Wilderness Study Area, an area proposed for protection through wilderness designation, and we used the journal to lobby on its behalf. After it was published, we sent it to key land managers, political representatives, and supportive environmental organizations to encourage support for the cause. The students were grateful for the opportunity and extremely committed to the effort of trying to preserve Silver Peak for the benefit of future generations as well as for the species of plants and animals that call it home.

In addition to raising public and political awareness of environmental issues and helping to save endangered species and places, such projects teach students vital skills for participating in their own democracy. The vast majority of college students have never written or lobbied their political representatives or their local press, nor do they understand the political efficacy of participating in the public process in such a manner. Unless students are trained how to participate, and given experience participating, in the democratic process, they are not likely to do so as adults.

Regardless of the curriculum we teach, empowering students to be informed and active citizens, to know how to participate and be committed to participating in their own democracy, is one of the greatest responsibilities we have as educators. Regardless of a particular student's political inclinations, understanding how our government works and gaining the skills necessary to participate in it are extremely liberating and empowering experiences.

Engaging in such forms of environmental advocacy, much like conservation and restoration practices, also encourages students to continue similar forms of behavior in the future. As David Gray notes, in a recent study "persons who had signed a petition supporting clean streets in New York City subsequently littered by about 50 percent less than persons not asked to sign the petition" (1985, 176). According to self-perception theory, the act of signing the antilitter petition aided the individual in perceiving him- or herself as more antilitter oriented, and thus he or she behaved accordingly. The same effect has been observed in students who have participated in environmental advocacy efforts. Their participation, even if gained within the confines of a college class, becomes at least a small part of their overall self-identity, making them more likely to engage in or support such activities in the future.

Such activities do much more than the immediate work of helping to save a particular place or species. They inculcate an environmental consciousness in students while also training them in the practices required for acting upon their own environmental commitments. As citizens of a nation that has been severely degraded both democratically and environmentally, empowering our students to participate in the public process and encouraging them to do so on behalf of their own imperiled environments are powerful and necessary steps toward achieving a sustainable political and ecological future.

"WE" MEANS WORKING TOGETHER

I am sitting atop a rock in the middle of the Marble Mountain Wilderness, not far from the Pacific Crest Trail as it winds its way northward to the California border. I have been meditating in the morning sun, but now I just sit and silently watch the shadows slip back from the edges of the meadows to hide under Douglas fir and lodgepole pine. We found some fresh sign of bear the preceding day, and I am hopeful that I will be fortunate enough to see one. Almost immediately after thinking this, just up the hillside about fifty yards from where I sit, a black bear sow and a cub about half her size emerge from the thick forest. A large swath of trees has been cleared by a recent avalanche, and I am afforded a clear view as they amble across the open area and up the canyon. The large hulking shape of the mother takes the lead, moving steadily through the lush meadow grass and stopping only occasionally to graze on some choice plant or root in the rich soil. In a few minutes they are gone, hidden in the shadows of the thick trees, and I am left watching the wind billow through the grass and the shadows shift with time.

I decide to sit still and see if the early morning will bring any more visitors into the large open meadow cut through the trees. Within ten or fifteen minutes a flitting shape of brown alerts me to the presence of a mule deer, a young spike buck, in the trees. He proceeds through the clearing in a much more leisurely fashion than the bears, stopping often to nibble and forage, and drops down toward the stream where I am sitting. I remain as motionless as possible, noting that the wind is blowing down the canyon toward me, as he passes within thirty feet of where I sit. I watch him calmly dip his head to drink from the stream's clear and cold running waters before moving off into the trees.

"What wild animal will appear next?" I cannot help but wonder. And in about ten minutes I am given the answer. Appearing to follow the same trail taken by the bears and deer, I see my wife enter the clearing, on her way back from an early morning scramble up the nearby ridge.

A few days later we are mailing letters written on the trail about our experience in the Marble Mountain Wilderness, and why we find it of so much value, to California's congressional representatives. I think about the bear and the deer, my wife, myself, and my students, and Marge Piercy's words come back to me:

> *it starts when you say* We
> *and know who you mean, and each*
> *day you mean one more.* (1996, 317)

From our experiences together in that high and rugged country, bear and deer and human are linked in a common cause and a common destiny. Mary Austin, John Muir, and Gary Snyder understood this and sought through their personal and professional lives to share it with others. As instructors we are responsible for educating future generations of Americans and developing in them the skills and inclinations to work together in order to solve environmental and social problems. Educators and students alike must learn that "We" means working together and that "We" are responsible for maintaining the beauty, health, and stability of both our cultural and our natural environments. And each day someone discovers Austin's, Muir's, or Snyder's work for the first time, each day someone takes to the trail to hike the California crest, each day we teach others to love and protect this miraculous planet, "We" can only hope that it means one more.

WORKS CITED

Abramovitz, Janet. 1998. *Taking a Stand: Cultivating New Relationships with the World's Forests*. WorldWatch Paper 140. Danvers, Mass: WorldWatch.

Armitage, Shelley. 1990. "Mary Austin: Writing Nature." In *Winds Trail: The Early Life of Mary Austin*, ed. Peggy Pond Church and Shelley Armitage, 3–31. Santa Fe: Museum of New Mexico Press.

Austin, Mary. 1927. *Lands of the Sun*. Boston: Houghton Mifflin.

———. 1932. *Earth Horizon*. Boston: Houghton Mifflin.

———. 1979. *Literary America, 1903–1934: The Mary Austin Letters*. Ed. T. M. Pearce. Westport, Conn.: Greenwood Press.

———. 1987. "Lost Borders." In *Western Trails: A Collection of Short Stories by Mary Austin*, ed. Melody Graulich, 39–99. Reno: University of Nevada Press.

———. 1990. "The Friend in the Wood." In *Winds Trail: The Early Life of Mary Austin*, ed. Peggy Pond Church and Shelley Armitage, 183–98. Santa Fe: Museum of New Mexico Press.

———. 1996a. "One Hundred Miles on Horseback." In *Beyond Borders: The Selected Essays of Mary Austin*, ed. Reuben J. Ellis, 24–30. Carbondale: Southern Illinois University Press.

———. 1996b. "Regionalism in American Fiction." In *Beyond Borders: The Selected Essays of Mary Austin*, ed. Reuben J. Ellis, 129–40. Carbondale: Southern Illinois University Press.

———. 1997. *The Land of Little Rain*. 1903. Reprint, Albuquerque: University of New Mexico Press.

Bass, Rick. 1999. *Brown Dog of the Yaak: Essays on Art and Activism*. Minneapolis: Milkweed Editions.

Bergman, Charles. 2002. "Academic Animals: Making Nonhuman Creatures Matter in Universities." *Interdisciplinary Studies in Literature and Environment* 9, no. 1 (winter): 141–47.

Bowers, C. A. 1999. "Changing the Dominant Cultural Perspective in Education." In *Ecological Education in Action,* ed. Gregory Smith and Dilafruz Williams, 161–78. Albany: SUNY Press.

Brady, Emily. 1998. "Imagination and the Aesthetic Appreciation of Nature." *Journal of Aesthetics and Art Criticism* 56, no. 2 (spring): 139–47.

Branch, Michael P. 1994. "Ecocriticism: The Nature of Nature in Literary Theory and Practice." *Weber Studies* 11, no. 1 (winter): 41–55.

———, ed. 2001. *John Muir's Last Journey: South to the Amazon and East to Africa.* Washington, D.C.: Island Press.

Branch, Michael P., Rochelle Johnson, Daniel Patterson, and Scott Slovic, eds. 1998. Introduction to *Reading the Earth: New Directions in the Study of Literature and the Environment.* Moscow: University of Idaho Press.

Buell, Lawrence. 1995. *The Environmental Imagination: Thoreau, Nature Writing, and the Formation of American Culture.* Cambridge: Harvard University Press.

———. 1999. "The Ecocritical Insurgency." *New Literary History: A Journal of Theory and Interpretation* 30, no. 3 (summer): 699–713.

Carew-Miller, Anna. 1998. "Mary Austin's Nature: Refiguring the Voice of Tradition Through the Voices of Identity." In *Reading the Earth: New Directions in the Study of Literature and the Environment,* ed. Michael P. Branch, Rochelle Johnson, Daniel Patterson, and Scott Slovic, 79–95. Moscow: University of Idaho Press.

Caswell, Kurt. 1998. "A Place to Begin: Community and Sense of Self in the Interdisciplinary Classroom." In *Stories in the Land: A Place-Based Environmental Education Anthology,* ed. John Elder, 26–32. Great Barrington, Mass.: Orion Society.

Cohen, Michael P. 1975. "John Muir's Public Voice." *Western American Literature* 10: 177–87.

———. 1984. *The Pathless Way: John Muir and American Wilderness.* Madison: University of Wisconsin Press, 1984.

Cracraft, Joel, and Francesca T. Grifo, eds. 1999. Introduction to *The Living Planet in Crisis: Biodiversity, Science, and Policy.* New York: Columbia University Press.

Cronon, William. 1995. *Uncommon Ground: Toward Reinventing Nature.* New York: Norton.

Dale, Edgar. 1969. *Audiovisual Methods in Teaching.* 3d ed. New York: Dryden Press.

Dean, Tim. 1991. *Gary Snyder and the American Unconscious.* New York: St. Martin's.

Devall, Bill, and George Sessions. 1985. *Deep Ecology.* Salt Lake City: Gibbs M. Smith.

Dickson, Carol E. 2000. "Sense, Nonsense, and Sensibility: Teaching the Truth of Nature in John Burroughs and Mary Austin." In *Sharp Eyes: John Burroughs and*

American Nature Writing, ed. Charlotte Zoe Walker, 220–31. Syracuse: Syracuse University Press.

Dodge, Jim. 1991. "Ten Snyder Stories." In *Gary Snyder: Dimensions of a Life,* ed. Jon Halper, 143–56. San Francisco: Sierra Club Books.

Donnelley, Strachan. 1999. "Perspective: Scientists' Public Responsibilities." In *The Living Planet in Crisis: Biodiversity, Science, and Policy,* ed. Joel Cracraft and Francesca T. Grifo, 298–300. New York: Columbia University Press.

"Driving Up CO2." 1997. *WorldWatch* 10, no. 6 (November-December): 39.

Eaton, Marcia Muelder. 1998. "Fact and Fiction in the Aesthetic Appreciation of Nature." *Journal of Aesthetics and Art Criticism* 56, no. 2 (spring): 149–56.

Ehrenfeld, David. 1996. Foreword to *Greening the College Curriculum: A Guide to Environmental Teaching in the Liberal Arts,* ed. Jonathan Collett and Stephen Karakashian, ix–xi. Washington, D.C.: Island Press.

Elder, John. 1981. "John Muir and the Literature of Wilderness." *Massachusetts Review* 22, no. 2 (summer): 375–86.

———. 1985. *Imagining the Earth: Poetry and the Vision of Nature.* Urbana: University of Illinois Press.

———, ed. 1998. *Stories in the Land: A Place-Based Environmental Education Anthology.* Great Barrington, Mass.: Orion Society.

Ellis, Reuben J. 1996. *Beyond Borders: The Selected Essays of Mary Austin.* Carbondale: Southern Illinois University Press, 1996.

"Fire, Flood, and Drought." 1998. *WorldWatch* 11, no. 6 (November-December): 37.

Fischer, Norman. 1996. "From Aesthetic Education to Environmental Aesthetics." *Clio: A Journal of Literature, History, and the Philosophy of History* 25, no. 4 (summer): 365–91.

Flavin, Christopher. 1998. "Last Tango in Buenos Aires." *WorldWatch* 11, no. 6 (November-December): 10–18.

Fleischner, Thomas Lowe. 1999. *Singing Stone: A Natural History of the Escalante Canyons.* Salt Lake City: University of Utah Press.

Ford, Thomas W. 1970. "*The American Rhythm:* Mary Austin's Poetic Principle." *Western American Literature* 5, no. 1 (spring): 3–14.

Foster, Cheryl. 1998. "The Narrative and the Ambient in Environmental Aesthetics." *Journal of Aesthetics and Art Criticism* 56, no. 2 (spring): 127–37.

Gare, Arran E. 1995. *Postmodernism and the Environmental Crisis.* New York: Routledge.

Glotfelty, Cheryll. 1996. "Introduction: Literary Studies in an Age of Environmental Crisis." In *The Ecocriticism Reader,* ed. Cheryll Glotfelty and Harold Fromm, xv–xxxvii. Athens: University of Georgia Press.

Godlovitch, Stan. 1998a. "Evaluating Nature Aesthetically." *Journal of Aesthetics and Art Criticism* 56, no. 2 (spring): 113–25.

———. 1998b. "Valuing Nature and the Autonomy of Natural Aesthetics." *British Journal of Aesthetics* 38, no. 2 (April): 180–97.

Goldstein, Laurence. 1977. "Wordsworth and Snyder: The Primitivist and His Problem of Self-Definition." *Centennial Review* 21: 75–86.

Graulich, Melody. 1987. *Western Trails: A Collection of Short Stories by Mary Austin.* Reno: University of Nevada Press.

Gray, David. 1985. *Ecological Beliefs and Behaviors: Assessment and Change.* Westport, Conn.: Greenwood Press.

Grumbling, Vernon Owen. 1996. "Literature." In *Greening the College Curriculum: A Guide to Environmental Teaching in the Liberal Arts,* ed. Jonathan Collett and Stephen Karakashian, 151–73. Washington, D.C.: Island Press.

Hays, Samuel P. 1998. *Explorations in Environmental History.* Pittsburgh: University of Pittsburgh Press.

Hill, Julia "Butterfly." 2002. *One Makes the Difference.* San Francisco: HarperSanFrancisco.

Holmes, Steven J. 1998. "Place Making, Sacred and Erotic: John Muir's Mountain Meadow." *Soundings* 81, no. 3-4 (fall-winter): 397–412.

———. 1999. *The Young John Muir.* Madison: University of Wisconsin Press.

Kardan, Jay. 2002. "Activism, Taste, and Conscience: Literary Intellectuals and Their Role in Conservation." *Wild Earth* 12, no. 3 (fall): 14–17.

Karrell, Linda K. 1997. "The Immanent Pattern: Recovering the Self in Mary Austin's *Earth Horizon.*" *Auto/Biography Studies* 12, no. 2 (fall): 261–75.

Kaza, Stephanie. 1999. "Liberation and Compassion in Environmental Studies." In *Ecological Education in Action,* ed. Gregory Smith and Dilafruz Williams, 143–60. Albany: SUNY Press.

Kennedy, Paul. 1993. *Preparing for the Twenty-first Century.* New York: Random House.

Kern, Robert. 2002. "Mountains and Rivers Are Us: Gary Snyder and the Nature of the Nature of Nature." In *The Beat Generation: Critical Essays,* ed. Kostas Myrsiades, 235–57. New York: Peter Lang.

Kerridge, Richard. 1998. Introduction to *Writing the Environment: Ecocriticism and Literature.* New York and London: Zed Books.

Kuhn, Thomas. 1962. *The Structure of Scientific Revolutions.* Chicago: University of Chicago Press.

Lawrence, Claire. 1998. "Getting the Desert into a Book: Nature Writing and the Problem of Representation in a Postmodern World." In *Coyote in the Maze: Tracking Edward Abbey in a World of Words,* ed. Peter Quigley, 150–67. Salt Lake City: University of Utah Press.

Leopold, Aldo. 1949. *A Sand County Almanac.* New York: Oxford University Press.

Limbaugh, Ronald H. 1992. "John Muir and Modern Environmental Education." *California History* 71, no. 2 (summer): 171–77.

Lyon, Thomas J. 1991. "The Ecological Vision of Gary Snyder." In *Critical Essays on Gary Snyder,* ed. Patrick D. Murphy, 35–44. Boston: G. K. Hall.

Marshall, Ian. 1998. *Story Line: Exploring the Literature of the Appalachian Trail.* Charlottesville: University Press of Virginia.

Martin, Julia. 1992. "Practicing Emptiness: Gary Snyder's Playful Ecological Work." *Western American Literature* 27, no. 1 (spring): 3–19.

McClintock, Robert. 1994. *Nature's Kindred Spirits: Aldo Leopold, Joseph Wood Krutch, Edward Abbey, Annie Dillard, and Gary Snyder.* Madison: University of Wisconsin Press.

McIntosh, Robert. 1977. "Ecology Since 1900." In *History of American Ecology,* ed. Frank N. Egerton III, 353–72. Salem, Mass.: Ayer.

Molesworth, Charles, ed. 1991. "The Political and Poetic Vision of *Turtle Island.*" In *Critical Essays on Gary Snyder,* ed. Patrick D. Murphy, 144–56. Boston: G. K. Hall.

Muir, John. 1916a. *A Thousand-Mile Walk to the Gulf.* Ed. William F. Bade. Boston: Houghton Mifflin.

———. 1916b. *The Mountains of California.* 1894. Reprint, Boston: Houghton Mifflin.

———. 1916c. *My First Summer in the Sierra.* 1911. Reprint, Boston: Houghton Mifflin.

———. 1916d. *Our National Parks.* 1901. Reprint, Boston: Houghton Mifflin.

———. 1923. *The Life and Letters of John Muir.* Ed. William F. Bade. 2 vols. Boston: Houghton Mifflin.

———. 1962. *The Yosemite.* 1912. Reprint, Garden City, N.Y.: Doubleday.

———. 1986. *The John Muir Papers.* Microfilm. Stockton, Calif.: University of the Pacific.

Murphy, Patrick D. 2000. *A Place for Wayfaring: The Poetry and Prose of Gary Snyder.* Corvallis: Oregon State University Press.

Nash, Roderick. 1967. *Wilderness and the American Mind.* New Haven: Yale University Press.

O'Grady, John P. 1993. *Pilgrims to the Wild: Everett Ruess, Henry David Thoreau, John Muir, Clarence King, Mary Austin.* Salt Lake City: University of Utah Press.

———. 1998. "Living Landscape: An Interview with Gary Snyder." *Western American Literature* 33, no. 3 (fall): 275–91.

Olscamp, Paul J. 1965. "Some Remarks About the Nature of Aesthetic Perception and Appreciation." *American Society for Aesthetics* 34, no. 2 (winter): 251–58.

Oravec, Christine. 1981. "John Muir, Yosemite, and the Sublime Response: A Study in the Rhetoric of Preservationism." *Quarterly Journal of Speech* 67, no. 3 (August): 245–58.

Orr, David. 1992. *Ecological Literacy: Education and the Transition to a Postmodern World.* Albany: SUNY Press.

———. 1996. "Reinventing Higher Education." In *Greening the College Curriculum: A Guide to Environmental Teaching in the Liberal Arts,* ed. Jonathan Collett and Stephen Karakashian, 8–23. Washington, D.C.: Island Press.

———. 1999. "Reassembling the Pieces: Ecological Design and the Liberal Arts." In *Ecological Education in Action,* ed. Gregory Smith and Dilafruz Williams, 229–36. New York: SUNY Press.

Palmer, Joy A. 1997. "Beyond Science: Global Imperatives for Environmental Education in the 21st Century." In *Environmental Education for the 21st Century,* ed. Patricia J. Thompson, 3–11. New York: Peter Lang.

Paul, Sherman. 1986. *In Search of the Primitive: Rereading David Antin, Jerome Rothenberg, and Gary Snyder.* Baton Rouge: Louisiana State University Press.

Phillips, Dana. 1999. "Ecocriticism, Literary Theory, and the Truth of Ecology." *New Literary History* 30, no. 3 (summer): 577–602.

Phillips, Rod. 2000. *Forest Beatniks and Urban Thoreaus.* New York: Peter Lang.

Piercy, Marge. 1996. *The Moon Is Always Female.* New York: Knopf.

Pryse, Marjorie. 1987. Introduction to *Stories from the Country of Lost Borders,* by Mary Austin. New Brunswick: Rutgers University Press.

Reisner, Marc. 2000. *Cadillac Desert: The American West and Its Disappearing Water.* New York: Viking.

"Road Rage." 2000. *WorldWatch* 13, no. 5 (September-October): 11.

Rose, Mary Carman. 1976. "Nature As Aesthetic Object: An Essay in Meta-Aesthetics." *British Journal of Aesthetics* 16, no. 1 (winter): 3–10.

Ruppert, James. 1983. "Mary Austin's Landscape Line in Native American Literature." *Southwest Review* 68, no. 4 (autumn): 376–90.

Saito, Yuriko. 1998. "The Aesthetics of Unscenic Nature." *Journal of Aesthetics and Art Criticism* 56, no. 2 (spring): 101–11.

Schaffer, Jeffrey P., et al. 2000. *The Pacific Crest Trail.* Vol. 1, *California.* 1973. Reprint, Berkeley: Wilderness Press.

Scheick, William. 1992. "Mary Austin's Disfigurement of the Southwest in *The Land of Little Rain.*" *Western American Literature* 27, no. 1 (spring): 37–46.

Schugurensky, Daniel. 2001. "Transformative Learning and Transformative Politics: The Pedagogical Dimension of Participatory Democracy and Social Action." In *Expanding the Boundaries of Transformative Learning,* ed. Edmund O'Sullivan, Amish Morrell, and Mary Ann O'Connor, 59–76. New York: Palgrave.

Scigaj, Leonard. 1999. *Sustainable Poetry: Four American Ecopoets.* Lexington: University Press of Kentucky.

Slovic, Scott. 1992. *Seeking Awareness in American Nature Writing: Henry David*

Thoreau, Annie Dillard, Edward Abbey, Wendell Berry, Barry Lopez. Salt Lake City: University of Utah Press.

Smith, Gregory, and Dilafruz Williams, eds. 1999. *Ecological Education in Action.* Albany: SUNY Press.

Snyder, Gary. 1974. *Turtle Island.* New York: New Directions.

———. 1980. *The Real Work: Interviews and Talks.* Ed. William Scott Mclean. New York: New Directions.

———. 1990a. *The Practice of the Wild.* New York: North Point.

———. 1990b. *Riprap & Cold Mountain Poems.* 1958. Reprint, San Francisco: North Point.

———. 1992. *No Nature.* New York: Pantheon.

———. 1995. *A Place in Space: Ethics, Aesthetics, and Watersheds: New and Selected Prose.* Washington, D.C.: Counterpoint.

Solnit, Rebecca. 2000. *Wanderlust: A History of Walking.* New York: Penguin Books.

———. 2003. "How to Fold a Map into a Drinking Cup." University of Nevada, Reno. February 24.

Sumara, Dennis, and Terrance R. Carson. 1997. "Reconceptualizing Action Research As a Living Practice." In *Action Research As Living Practice,* xiii–xxxv. New York: Peter Lang.

Tallmadge, John. 1997. *Meeting the Tree of Life: A Teacher's Path.* Salt Lake City: University of Utah Press.

———. 2000. "Toward a Natural History of Reading." *Interdisciplinary Studies in Literature and Environment* 7, no. 1: 33–47.

Thomashow, Mitchell. 1995. *Ecological Identity: Becoming a Reflective Environmentalist.* Cambridge: MIT Press.

Tritt, Donald G. 1991. "Cognitions of Self As Learner: A Necessary Objective in Experiential Education." *Psychological Reports* 69, no. 2 (October): 591–98.

Trocco, Frank. 1985. "The National Audubon Society Expedition Institute: Environmental Reeducation." In *Teaching Environmental Literature: Materials, Methods, Resources,* ed. Frederick O. Waage, 137–42. New York: MLA.

Tuan, Yi-Fu. 1974. *Topophilia.* Englewood Cliffs, N.J.: Prentice-Hall.

Ulman, H. Lewis. 1998. "Seeing, Believing, and Acting: Ethics and Self-Representation in Ecocriticism and Nature Writing." In *Reading the Earth: New Directions in the Study of Literature and Environment,* ed. Michael P. Branch, Rochelle Johnson, Daniel Patterson, and Scott Slovic, 225–33. Moscow: University of Idaho Press.

Waage, Frederick, ed. 1985. *Teaching Environmental Literature: Materials, Methods, Resources.* New York: MLA.

Williams, Terry Tempest. 1994. *An Unspoken Hunger.* New York: Vintage.

Wilson, E. O. 1984. *Biophilia.* Cambridge: Harvard University Press.

Worster, Donald. 1977. *Nature's Economy: A History of Ecological Ideas.* New York: Cambridge University Press.

Yamazato, Katsunori. 1993. "Kitkitdizze, Zendo, and Place: Gary Snyder As Reinhabitory Poet." *Interdisciplinary Studies of Literature and Environment* 1, no. 1 (spring): 51–63.

Zwinger, Ann. 1994. Introduction to *Writing the Western Landscape.* Boston: Beacon Press.

INDEX

Graulich, Melody, 56
Gray, David, 209–10, 212–14, 217–19, 222, 225
Great Basin Desert, 21–22, 44, 47–48, 88, 166, 169
Grifo, Francesca, 18
Grumbling, Vernon Owen, 41

Hays, Samuel, 17–18
Heath, D., 211
Hetch Hetchy Valley, 4, 9, 188, 189
Hill, Julia "Butterfly," 175
Holmes, Steven J., 99, 103–4, 121
humanities. *See* environmental humanities

Indians. *See* Native Americans
indigenous, 22, 134, 138, 141, 147, 163, 165–66, 169, 193, 198
interdisciplinary: in ecocriticism and environmental literature, 14–15, 31, 42, 45, 83, 116, 137, 142, 144–45, 150–51, 153, 178; in ecology and environmental studies, 28, 30–31, 38, 41–42, 45, 120, 214–15
Isidro (Austin), 7

journals: in the field, 93, 116–17, 120–25, 127–28, 130–32, 140, 161–62, 219; John Muir's, 94–96, 98, 102–5, 108–12, 114, 119–20

Kardan, Jay, 180–81
Karrell, Linda, 65
Kaza, Stephanie, 40
Kennedy, Paul, 28
Kern, Robert, 141
Kerouac, Jack, 148
Kerridge, Richard, 14

Kitkitdizze, 10, 144, 173
Kitkitdizze (Snyder's home place), 143, 144, 151, 152–53
Klamath Mountains, 9
Kuhn, Thomas, 216
"Kusioqqobi" (Snyder), 146–147

Lake Tahoe, 9, 72, 134, 172
Land of Little Rain, The (Austin), 7, 47–48, 53, 55, 57–60, 64–65, 69, 71, 78–79
Lands of the Sun (Austin), 54, 84, 182
Leave-No-Trace Principles, 221
Leopold, Aldo, 45, 129, 183
Limbaugh, Ronald, 94–95, 100, 106
literary representation, 52–54, 56–57, 62–64, 95–96, 101, 108, 122, 130
"Logging" (Snyder), 150–51, 153
"Long Hair" (Snyder), 177
Lopez, Barry, 45
Lost Borders (Austin), 7, 48–49, 55, 63, 76
Lyon, Thomas J., 146–48

"Manzanita" (Snyder), 144–45
Marshall, Ian, 14, 34
McClintock, Robert, 16–17, 139–40, 142
"Mid-August at Sourdough Mountain Lookout" (Snyder), 137
Mojave Desert, 6, 22, 44, 47, 88
Molesworth, Charles, 137, 144–45, 153–54, 158
Mono Lake, 185
Mountains and Rivers Without End (Snyder), 10
Mountains of California, The (Muir), 9, 43, 109–10, 112, 114–15, 121–22, 189
Muir, John: activism, 180–81, 187–93, 197–99, 205, 216, 219–20, 227;